# OFF THE GROUND

# OFF THE GROUND

## PAUL McCARTNEY IN THE 1990s

JR MOORES

REAKTION BOOKS

*Dedicated to the memories of Jean 'Bubbles' Cobb (1926–2024) and Owen David Pegg (1982–2021)*

*Published by*
Reaktion Books Ltd
Unit 32, Waterside
44–48 Wharf Road
London N1 7UX, UK
www.reaktionbooks.co.uk

First published 2024


Printed and bound in Great Britain by TJ Books Ltd, Padstow, Cornwall

A catalogue record for this book is available from the British Library

ISBN 978 1 78914 942 5

# CONTENTS

Paul McCartney, accompanied by his wife Linda, letting his hair down before a Hamburg press conference, 1991.

# Introduction: Looking for Changes

> The trouble is that we have a bad habit, encouraged by pedants and sophisticates, of considering happiness as something rather stupid. Only pain is intellectual, only evil interesting. This is the treason of the artist: a refusal to admit the banality of evil and the terrible boredom of pain. If you can't lick 'em, join 'em. If it hurts, repeat it. But to praise despair is to condemn delight, to embrace violence is to lose hold of everything else. We have almost lost hold; we can no longer describe a happy man, nor make any celebration of joy.
>
> URSULA K. LE GUIN,
> 'The Ones Who Walk Away from Omelas' (1973)

On the second track of his 1993 studio album *Off the Ground*, Paul McCartney did something unprecedented. He sang a naughty word. The decision to include a 'bastard' in the lyrics to 'Looking for Changes' had not been taken lightly. Another song recorded during the same sessions, one that would find its use as a B-side, took the expletives one step further. On 'Big Boys Bickering', McCartney went as far as to drop a few F-bombs.

On the surface, 'Rock Musician Swears in His Lyrics' is not the most eyebrow-raising headline of all time, especially in the early 1990s. The dust had long settled since the members of Sex

Pistols and their punk rock entourage shocked Middle England by calling Bill Grundy a 'fucking rotter', among other rude names, on live television. By the time *Off the Ground* came out, five years had passed since N.W.A released their incendiary track 'Fuck tha Police'. It had been nearly a decade since the American Parents Music Resource Center (PMRC) formed, with their futile aim to curb the perceived unsavoury content of popular music. In late February 1993, Rage Against the Machine's 'Killing in the Name' began three weeks in the UK Top 40, with its seventeen counts of the F-word. Given this is Paul McCartney we are talking about, however, closer inspection is warranted towards the sudden introduction of the phrase 'fucking it up' and a line about some 'bastard' laughing his head off. These acts of verbal horseplay were only minor and infrequent occurrences, yet they had greater implications, not to mention important ramifications for the latest phase on which McCartney was embarking.

As we shall see, Paul McCartney's 1990s were an era like no other. It could even be argued that this was the most significant decade of his entire career after the 1960s. Sure, the ten years following that objectively crucial time had seen him shake off the weight of The Beatles when establishing himself as an artist in his own right, broadly speaking, with his next band, Wings. Of equal importance on a personal level, McCartney put his bachelor days and the Swinging London scene firmly behind him after his marriage to Linda (née Eastman) and their raising of a family together on a remote Scottish farm. The 1970s were creatively prolific for the ex-Beatle too, beginning with the lo-fi triumph *McCartney* (unfairly disparaged on its release in 1970) and encompassing massive commercial and critical hits such as Wings' chart-topping classic *Band on the Run* (1973), as well as certain less robust offerings. There was also the odd controversy. There were public and institutional objections to 'Give Ireland Back to the Irish' (1972).

For rather different reasons, others couldn't stomach 1977's Christmas number one, 'Mull of Kintyre'.

Those achievements pale in comparison to both the magnitude and sheer breadth of McCartney's activities in the 1990s. Following a quieter and less certain 1980s, this decade would see McCartney re-emerge with such energy, momentum and reinforced self-belief that, when viewed from either the macro or micro perspective, it's hard to believe these were really the actions and ideas of a quinquagenarian rock star who had long earned the right to complacency and laziness if he preferred. It is no exaggeration to say that this output would rival, and in some ways even surpass, the achievements McCartney had made as a young man in his twenties. This canon included impressive studio and live albums, colossal tours, unexpected side projects and imaginative collaborations, the foray into classical composition, a wealth of fantastic music in a myriad of styles, some new Beatles numbers and a whole lot more. Various shifts and events in the broader culture, alongside some much-needed updates and revisions regarding the Fab Four's historiography, also impacted McCartney's reputation so that he was, generally speaking, perceived by the public in more generous terms than the past couple of decades had allowed. Whether you are a fan of this period of his career or not – as good, bad, ugly, mild, bonkers or baffling as you may find the work (or some aspects of it) – one thing becomes clear when it is assessed more thoroughly than in previous biographies: this is the decade in which McCartney's output and activities reveal more about the person behind them than any other. How did that happen?

## Back to the Eff

Jerry Seinfeld was in his mid-teens when The Beatles announced they had called it a day. The void left this young New Yorker craving more music from his favourite band, just as it did millions of other fans the world over. Nearly three decades on, when Seinfeld chose to end his incredibly successful eponymous sitcom, he did it partly because of the impact The Beatles' split had had on him. 'The Beatles ended too soon for me, and it was also nine years,' the comedian explained in a radio interview.

> It was something about the single digit . . . It seemed a lot less [than ten]. The Beatles did nine years, and that hunger for The Beatles has lasted my whole life. Whenever a Beatles song comes on the radio, I reach for the volume and turn it up, because I still haven't gotten enough of them. That was really how I made the decision.[1]

Unlike the sitcom, Seinfeld's stand-up career has continued unabated, and his routines are noted for their absence of swearing. He has also been critical of fellow comedians who rely heavily on curse words and other coarse material. This is not because Seinfeld is offended by such content. Rather, he sees it as the cheapest method of getting a laugh. Seinfeld had experimented with more colourful language when starting out on the stand-up scene. He soon decided to cut this out altogether, after worrying that the swear words themselves – and the sense of rhythm they provided – were causing his audiences to chuckle, regardless of the actual quality of the jokes. In his own sitcom *Curb Your Enthusiasm*, *Seinfeld* co-creator Larry David has ploughed his own swearier and cruder comedy furrow, one that has earned him a reputation as the edgy John Lennon to Jerry Seinfeld's cuddlier Paul McCartney. As we shall see in our further discussions of Paul, this is a comparison that isn't entirely cogent, even if, as one writer put it when reviewing Seinfeld at the Hammersmith Apollo, 'This man can do comic timing like Paul McCartney does melody.'[2]

One award-winning British comedian who operates broadly in the Jerry Seinfeld tradition of observational comedy is the

Kettering-born James Acaster. Before trying his hand at joke-telling, he had been the drummer in various unsuccessful local bands. One of Acaster's early shows sought to absolve Yoko Ono of the long-standing and widely accepted accusation that she had been responsible for the disbandment of The Beatles. All Ono really did, in Acaster's words, was to 'eat a few too many of their biscuits and maybe sit on a couple of amps. Is that enough to split a band up?'[3] In 2018–19 Acaster would receive his most positive reviews to date, for *Cold Lasagne Hate Myself 1999*, a show that opened with an ironic yet expletive-laden renunciation of his own Seinfeld-like, self-imposed ban on swearing. While this was not, in my opinion, Acaster's most purely or consistently hilarious show, it was the one that revealed the most detail about his personal life. Already long prone to praising comedy shows about dead relatives or other morbid experiences on account of the fact that it seems more important than sillier or absurdist comedic techniques, the critics commended Acaster for his openness, especially after they had informed us all that Hannah Gadsby's *Nanette* (which debuted the previous year) was a watershed moment in live comedy. Even in this branch of entertainment, seriousness, openness and the idea of the 'tortured artist' are perceived as supplying extra gravitas and poignancy to the value of any given stand-up set. The press and the public really do lap up the idea of the sad clown, just as they are drawn to the mystique of the troubled musician. As Paul Du Noyer has written, 'McCartney spurns the Tortured Artist routine, perhaps at the cost of some charisma. He lacks that manic, dark otherworldliness that people have read into stars like David Bowie, Jim Morrison, or Kurt Cobain.'[4] On the page, Du Noyer left out of this list the name of McCartney's old musical partner. Lennon, as ever, lurked in the subtext.

The premise of the BBC's *Room 101* is that celebrity guests have to argue the case for their various pet hates to be banished into George Orwell's fictional torture room. When he appeared on the show in 2018, Acaster's friend and fellow comedian Josh Widdicombe proposed that 'People Being Rude about Paul McCartney' should be expelled to Room 101. 'I feel quite strongly about this,' Widdicombe explained, 'that being half of the greatest songwriting partnership of all time, changing the face of popular music, [and] changing the face of *society*, doesn't deem respect if you're a bit of a square 74-year-old.'[5]

As one of the most famous musicians on the planet, Paul McCartney has fans in all walks and sub-walks of life. That being said, it is no coincidence that his work has struck a chord with comedians who work in the Seinfeldian, observational vein. Their critical and commercial success notwithstanding, when Jerry, James or Josh do receive criticism, it tends to be for the 'safe' or 'square' nature of their material. This comes either in explicit or implicit comparison to 'edgier' comedians on the scene. The more negative or lukewarm reviews of these comics are routinely peppered with the words 'whimsy', 'cosy', 'trivial' and similar derogatory terms, suggesting a broadness of appeal but an absence of emotional heft and intellectual depth. This is exactly the kind of vocabulary for which McCartney's detractors are always so quick to reach, even though such disrespect has not been legally permitted since Widdicombe was successful in his bid to have all People Being Rude about Paul McCartney condemned to *Nineteen Eighty-Four*'s torture chamber.[6]

For those who were unimpressed with 1993's *Off the Ground*, the record was a 'heart-sinkingly ordinary' collection that contained 'as much bite as an old woolly jumper'.[7] Representing 'yet another tarnish-mark on the legend', its 'dreary' tunes were said to receive only 'polite applause' when performed live, squeezed as they were between older numbers, especially those Beatles classics that could still induce hysterics.[8] Those who have written about *Off the Ground* in more generous terms note its 'honesty' and 'veracity'.[9] Like Acaster's *Cold Lasagne Hate Myself 1999*, the album was interpreted as a little more soul-baring than other recent efforts. It wasn't just the material itself that encouraged this analysis; the impression of emotional openness was enhanced by the production. Given that he missed his chance to ever make a record with raw-production engineer Steve Albini, who died in May 2024, McCartney is never going to sound as gloriously ragged as Neil Young and Crazy Horse or as fuzzy and fragile as lo-fi anxiety rockers Sebadoh.[10] Yet compared to 1989's glossier *Flowers in the Dirt*, *Off the Ground* did sound somewhat stripped-back and rawer, having been recorded live in the studio (with some overdubs) by McCartney with his touring band. While that method of laying down tracks doesn't necessarily make the music any more truthful or sincere than a composition that has been assembled bit by bit by a nerd on a laptop, such recording processes are often interpreted as such by fans and critics alike. In his review for the *Chicago Tribune*, Greg Kot praised *Off the Ground*'s 'uncluttered production'. He considered this an after-effect of McCartney and his backing musicians' 'energizing' set for *MTV Unplugged* two years prior. Kot was also charmed by the 'unexpected toughness' of tracks like 'Looking for Changes': he singled out that song as 'one of McCartney's angriest and most convincing performances in recent years'. He continued, 'McCartney has made a career out of making everything seem easy, sometimes too easy, but his cutie-pie propensities are now balanced by emotional grit.'[11]

Prior to 'Looking for Changes' and 'Big Boys Bickering', McCartney's naughtier side tended to be cloaked in metaphor, ambiguity and innuendo. If we look back, as tradition dictates we always must, to McCartney's Beatles days, then the lyrically minimal 'Why Don't We Do It in the Road?' leaves rather a lot to the audience's imagination in regard to what 'it' might actually be. 'It' could mean any activity that one can conceive being carried out in the road: an impromptu game of badminton, perhaps, or a placard-waving group protest in objection to the pedestrianization of Norwich city centre. (For clarity, though, the song was inspired by the sight of two monkeys copulating in the middle of a street in Rishikesh.) Into 'Penny Lane', McCartney threw some rude slang. Like the rest of the verses, this harked back to his Liverpudlian salad days. The meaning of the phrase 'finger pies' would have been lost on most listeners who didn't grow up in the north of England. Someone says, 'fucking hell' in the middle of 'Hey Jude'. It was left low in the final mix: you have to know it's there, and listen very closely, to actually pick it out. Some parties credit this outburst to McCartney, suggesting he'd yelled it after hitting a wrong note on the piano. Others have attributed it to Lennon. When he was overdubbing his vocal harmonies, John is said to have cursed because the volume had been blasted too loudly through his headphones.

Lennon was the member of the musical partnership who was more openly and frequently explicit in his lyrics. It is Lennon who takes Christ's name in vain on 'The Ballad of John and Yoko'. A single recorded by John and Paul in absence of the other Beatles, its mildly blasphemous lyric had roots in Lennon's infamous 1966 comments about the band being more popular than Jesus. It is Lennon, too, who curses Walter 'stupid get' Raleigh on 'I'm So Tired'. There's a 'stupid bloody Tuesday' in 'I Am the Walrus', alongside a 'pornographic priestess' and somebody with lowered knickers. Into 'I've Got a Feeling', a song that splices two separate McCartney and Lennon half-compositions, the latter felt compelled to throw in an unnecessary 'wet dream', thereby blemishing the otherwise wholesome nature of the piece. This trend continued and intensified in Lennon's solo work, helping to exacerbate his reputation as the 'edgy' one. The supposed edginess was often misinterpreted as a superiority in comparison to Paul's conservative material.

'I don't usually use swear words in a song because it can sometimes seem a bit gratuitous, like you're just trying to shock,'

McCartney explained when promoting *Off the Ground*, surely with some of Lennon's profaner material in mind.[12] Paul had always been proud of the poetic nature of The Beatles' lyrics. Their compositions had broadened the possibilities of what could be achieved within the restrictive form of the popular song, and not just in musical terms. 'I got English Literature, mate. I got "A" level. That's my one big swotty claim to fame,' McCartney once boasted to *Smash Hits* scribe Tom Hibbert.[13] He credited his old sixth-form teacher, Alan Durband, for igniting his love of language and poetry. (Durband died at the age of 66, in the same year as *Off the Ground*'s release.) This mentor had engaged Paul and his schoolmates via the salacious gateway of literature's ruder passages. As Paul recalled:

> What was great about him was he had all these 16 and 17 year old boys on his hands and he was trying to teach us about Chaucer. We were all into rock, man, how was he going to interest us in *that*? So he told us all the dirty bits and once we'd read those, we were hooked . . . I couldn't believe that someone hundreds of years ago was writing something as dirty as that. So I got behind the teacher and I even passed the exam. God knows how. I couldn't even pass a bus, ha ha. Anyway, that got me into literature and John and I, when we were writing songs, we were a little bit swotty and poetic and we liked the fact that we weren't doing mundane lyrics. Some of the stuff, like 'Norwegian Wood' and 'Lady Madonna', was quite poetical and they've started doing it in schools. Imagine that! You can do a GCE in Beatles, I've heard, and in America you can do university courses in Beatleology or something. That really is stretching it a bit.[14]

So why, in 1993, did McCartney suddenly become more gratuitous? For one thing, 'Looking for Changes' was written about a subject close to his heart, as well as that of his wife and band-mate, Linda. The couple had long campaigned for animal rights. Beginning in the 1970s, they had embraced vegetarianism together. Fast-forward a few years and Paul had been flicking through copies of *The Animal's Voice* and *Animal Agenda*. These were 'pretty heavy magazines', as McCartney described them, unflinching in the graphic images they reproduced of vivisection experiments.[15] The first verse of 'Looking for Changes' was inspired by a picture of a cat with some kind of machine implanted into its head. 'They just took off the top of its skull and plugged in a machine to find some data,' said Paul, still sickened by the image.

> I'm not sure what they were expecting to find inside a cat's head. So I started to write the song and came up with the line 'I saw a cat with a machine in his brain' and just made it up from there – how the bloke who fed him didn't feel any pain, so I'd like to see him take out the machine and stick it in his own brain. You know, if you need the information so badly, do it to yourself.[16]

The following verse concerns a rabbit trapped in a laboratory. The third one is where the 'bastard' comes in. This character is amused at the sight of a monkey being taught to smoke cigarettes. Paul confessed to poetic licence on that one, pointing out that beagles were usually used for such purposes: 'but it doesn't matter – it's still some poor defenceless animal with no rights in the world'. 'Looking for Changes' is a protest song, then, on behalf of all vulnerable creatures who are unable to protect themselves. 'I think it's "change or die" time for this planet,' he said of the song's chorus back in 1993.[17] 'I don't normally go for songs about animal experimentation,' McCartney explained when discussing his use of strong language,

> and when you're in that hard area these words start to creep in. I'm certainly not a great user of swear words in front of the kids but occasionally – like in 'Looking for Changes' – it's essential to the plot. The only strange thing is that I haven't done it before. I mean, I played 'Big Boys Bickering', with the F-word, to Paul Simon and he said 'Have you ever used that word before?' and I said no. But that doesn't matter – I think I'm allowed to use it once in every 50 years, don't you? Once in every 50 years I'll use that word. Stick around for the next time.[18]

'Big Boys Bickering' was a protest song for the environmental movement. While petty and macho politicians were busy squabbling among themselves, the state of the planet was in fierce decline. McCartney was particularly irked by those world leaders who had paid lip service to environmental concerns by attending the Earth Summit in Rio de Janeiro in June 1992 and subsequently failed to sign or adhere to the agreements. As McCartney made clear on

A cat with a machine in its brain, 1989, photograph reproduced in the *Off the Ground* CD booklet (1993).

the chorus, these leaders were 'fucking it up for everyone'. The act of Paul McCartney unleashing a few F-bombs hardly competed with the bigger news stories of the day, although it did make for an amusing segment on Fox News after MTV decided to cut the track from McCartney's *Up Close* special. The Fox report included a short interview clip, released by McCartney, offering this explanation: 'If I'm talking about the ozone layer and the big hole in it, a 50-mile-wide hole, I don't think, "Well, that's a flipping hole". I think that's a fucking big hole! And it's gotta be closed, y'know.'[19] (The channel bleeped out the expletive.) *Rolling Stone* writer Alan Light was also interviewed for the segment, noting that Paul had 'always been the cute Beatle, the squeaky clean nice Beatle, and as he gets older he's got to fight his image softening.'[20] Less sympathetic was Pete Fornatale of K-Rock radio, whose station WXRK had announced that it wouldn't be playing the song. Dressed like a laid-back and knowledgeable roadie, but expressing thoughts more in line with the moral outrage of conservative activist Mary Whitehouse, Fornatale argued that 'an artist of Paul McCartney's stature should be remembered for the words that he's written across our hearts and across our minds, not the ones he's scribbled on a subway wall.'[21] McCartney's unshakable reputation as 'the cute Beatle' was so potent that he could never really win when it came to this or other instances of wandering outside the box. His radio-friendly ballads are continually dismissed as safe and saccharine. When he does anything different or riskier, it's seen as trying too hard to attract attention. When the latter occurs, McCartney is always compared to Lennon, whose own efforts to court controversy have been held in higher esteem since his tragic martyrdom than they were when he was still alive. In this particular instance, McCartney even drew the comparison first-hand. In the programme accompanying his 1993 New World Tour, he described 'Big Boys Bickering' as 'Lennonesque to my mind anyway. John wouldn't have thought twice about saying "fuck" in a song.'[22]

## Is Anybody Listening?

Bill Burr grew up near Boston and has developed a more explicit and aggressively exasperated stand-up style than those who operate in the Seinfeldian mode. Burr's comedy is defined by its high-volume rants and provocative comic logic (albeit with a sense of knowing irony that helps to distinguish Burr from some of the clumsier 'edgelord' comics who have become so regrettably prevalent in recent times). Notwithstanding the contrast in form, Burr can still appreciate the cleaner comedians, who, despite putting up a polite front, are often mining deeper sentiments. When he appeared on Jerry Seinfeld's Netflix show *Comedians in Cars Getting Coffee*, Burr said this about his host's stand-up style:

> You've got this ability to make me laugh and to ruin shit, all at the same time. And people for years have said, 'He has an act about nothing.' No it isn't. You're not listening to him! You're not seeing the anger underneath these bits. This guy has contempt for humanity and for 90 per cent of activities. One of my favourite things to see is a comic, especially someone who works clean, to still be able to see that same sort of rage . . . You watch Brian Regan and people think it's goofy. No. This is an angry dude! The way he's telling this story is not the way he reacted when this shit happened to him, I'm telling you right now.[23]

It may be a stretch to suggest that the usually cheerily natured Macca has quite the same level of contempt for humanity as Burr sees in the routines of Jerry Seinfeld and Brian Regan. However, McCartney is clearly maddened by our species' treatment of fellow animals and our collective inability to show our planet the care and respect that it deserves and we require in order to survive. To draw on our musician–comedian parallel once more, beneath the jolly, tuneful and radio-friendly exterior of McCartney's music can be found another 'angry dude'. Just because he didn't always present this fury in the same way that his ex-bandmate John Lennon so often did, with coarser language and 'bare-bones' production, it doesn't mean the emotions contained in McCartney's songs are any less sincere.

Furthermore, sometimes the contrast between presentation and sentiment makes the meaning behind the song all the more powerful. Listen to the lullaby-like 'Blackbird', a metaphor for the civil rights movement and the ongoing state of race relations in the USA. In June 2020, during the worldwide Black Lives Matter protests that erupted after George Floyd was killed by a white police officer in Minneapolis, McCartney issued a short statement calling for people to 'work together to overcome racism in any form'. From 1964, he reminded readers, The Beatles refused to play in front of segregated audiences, and they had this stipulation drawn permanently into their contracts. Paul wrote: 'I feel sick and angry that here we are almost 60 years later and the world is in shock at the horrific scenes of the senseless murder of George Floyd at the hands of police racism, along with countless others that came before.' He called for justice for Floyd's family, and 'for all those who have died and suffered. Saying nothing is not an option.'[24]

A similar sense of anger towards intolerance lay behind The Beatles' 'Ob-La-Di, Ob-La-Da', a tune often written off as a light-hearted piece of cod-reggae fluff. The characters in its lyrics are immigrants who have arrived in Britain from the West Indies. With determination and dignity, the family described in the song have set themselves up in the face of innumerable obstacles, much like McCartney's Irish relatives had done beforehand in Liverpool, a city speckled with physical reminders of the slave trade and British Empire. 'Ob-La-Di, Ob-La-Da' was released in 1968, the same year that Enoch Powell had delivered his 'Rivers of Blood' speech.[25] Fourteen years later, McCartney explored a similar subject-matter on his duet with Stevie Wonder. Again, 'Ebony and Ivory' is considered by many to be the epitome of McCartney's syrupy side. But he wouldn't have written it if he wasn't still incensed and disheartened that people of different skin tones couldn't seem to get along together, after all this time and in light of the lessons of the 1960s, in perfect harmony. The song may be a cheesy one; that is undeniable. Its metaphors are clumsy and its sentiment oversimplified. Yet beneath its shiny veneer is a quiet, burning and bewildered rage. Under the apartheid regime, the duet was banned in South Africa.

Those are just two race-related examples of McCartney's more politically outspoken numbers, of which there are more we could highlight. By 1993, he was tired and frustrated with still being viewed as 'the cute one' and never 'the angry one' or 'the progressive one'. Tracks like 'Big Boys Bickering' or the earlier 'Give Ireland Back to the Irish' (a tune also banned from the airwaves, although it contained no swearing) may stand out from the rest of the McCartney repertoire for their open and uncensored anger. That doesn't mean other songs in his back catalogue were not fuelled by the same or similar emotions. Talking about the business of songwriting in general, a subject on which he has never been one to dwell too long and seems reluctant to overanalyse for fear of diminishing its precious alchemy, McCartney had this to say: 'When I was a kid and you'd get into an argument with somebody, and feel a bit down, you go away and get your guitar. It's like a dummy, or a release, it's like a crutch. It still makes me feel good to write songs. The whole thing about it, it's magic.'[26] Even his 'silly love songs', as he calls them himself after reclaiming this insult, have often had their origins in unhappier incidents. Before its racial theme was applied, the earliest inspiration for 'Ebony and Ivory' had been literally closer to home. It was written, as Paul has explained, 'after a little marital tiff with Linda, it was like "why can't we get it together – our piano can". You just grab any old idea to get yourself out of it.'[27]

McCartney did not share Lennon's habit of blurting out, in lyrics and interviews alike, whatever happened to be on his mind, no matter how frank, unfiltered or imprudent. McCartney has the reputation of being a more guarded individual who likes to hold things back. It's not just the press that has characterized him in this way but also some of those who have known him reasonably well. Different writers have applied varying, often pseudo-psychological explanations for Macca's famous reserve. Some have dated it back to his upbringing, whereas others have used it to chastise his supposed bourgeois aspirations, or to brand him as a savvy, even unscrupulous, manipulator of those around him. A more sympathetic interpretation could date it back to the death of McCartney's mother when he was just fourteen years old. This is how McCartney recalled that earth-shattering loss in the *Beatles Anthology* book (2000):

> My mother's death broke my dad up. That was the worst thing for me, hearing my dad cry. I'd never heard him cry before. It was a terrible blow to the family. You grow up real quick, because you never expect to hear your parents crying. You expect to see women crying, or kids in the playground, or even yourself crying – and you can explain all that. But when it's your dad, then you know something's *really* wrong and it shakes your faith in everything. But I was determined not to let it affect me. I carried on. I learned to put a shell around me at that age. There was none of this sitting at home crying – that would be recommended now, but not then.[28]

It is no coincidence that two of McCartney's greatest 1990s works – the excellent studio album *Flaming Pie* (1997) and the second

Fireman album *Rushes* (1998) – were created as Linda underwent treatment for a cancer that would turn out to be terminal. It was the same illness that had killed Paul's mother.

His lessening eagerness to repress anger is just one of the many fascinating things about Paul McCartney in the 1990s. It is almost as if this era becomes a case of 'Schrödinger's Macca'. Erwin Schrödinger's thought-experiment posited that, if you placed a cat and a radioactive atom that could kill that same cat into a box and then sealed it, you wouldn't know whether the cat was alive or dead until the box was opened. Until that moment, the cat was both dead and alive. The real Paul McCartney is notoriously difficult to unveil, as many of his interviewers and biographers have noted. In that respect, he is a bit like Queen Elizabeth II, about whom he once wrote one of his cheekier songs. Before her death in 2022, we were all familiar with the Queen, and yet we never really knew her in any proper sense. At the same time, everybody had their own idea of the person behind her public veneer, often a vivid one, no matter how unsubstantiated, just as they do with McCartney. These can range from benign national treasure, through Machiavellian public relations mastermind, to reptilian Illuminati insider. A major difference between the two figures is that Elizabeth II's wealth and adulation came as no surprise. As their producer George Martin put it when defending The Beatles' mixed feelings towards fame, fortune and fan worship, 'Royalty are trained from birth to cope with that sort of thing; The Beatles were not. They can hardly be blamed for wanting to put up a barrier against the world.'[29]

What was really going on inside the incomparably famous and yet still difficult-to-disentangle personality that is Paul McCartney, back in the 1990s? As I have tried to explain through the example of his new-found penchant for swearing and the related matters mentioned above, and will continue to reveal hereafter, it was as if McCartney either didn't give a fuck anymore, or he perhaps gave more of a fuck than ever. Or was it a more complicated combination of both attitudes? How many fucks did McCartney give, on a scale of zero fucks to many, many fucks? He threw us a couple of fucks during 'Big Boys Bickering', and a bonus 'bastard' in 'Looking for Changes'. In that same decade, he would start a collaborative techno side project, begin sidelining as a classical composer, open his first exhibition of abstract paintings, help launch his wife's game-changing range of vegetarian foods, accept a knighthood, become hipper again thanks to trends such as Britpop (while also having the wisdom to keep that movement at arm's length), regularly kick against his reputation as the safer and less experimental Beatle and, among other controversies, record some fresh Beatles numbers for the *Anthology* project (1995–2000). Was this Paul McCartney giving more of a fuck, or not giving a fuck any more? Let's try to open the box.

# 1
# The Backstory: McCartney before the 1990s

Paul McCartney transcends the status of national treasure. If anything, he is an international one. He could even be intergalactically so, if the aliens are tuned in, considering NASA's habit of beaming Beatles hits into space.[1] He has been a 'Sir' since accepting a knighthood in 1997, although he prefers to answer to 'Paul', insisting that he is 'just some guy' despite all evidence to the contrary.[2] He has worked with everybody from Johnny Cash to Kanye West. He has gone viral, on a fairly routine basis, thanks to appearances on broadcasts such as 'Carpool Karaoke', in which McCartney was filmed visiting one of the houses where he was raised (now maintained by the National Trust), reminiscing about rehearsing in its toilet (best acoustics in the building), popping into the barber's shop on Penny Lane and performing a set with his touring band in one of the small rooms of the Philharmonic pub, to the astonishment of its afternoon drinkers.[3] In 2021 a short clip from Peter Jackson's *The Beatles: Get Back* documentary was shared an incalculable number of times across social media. In the company of George Harrison and Ringo Starr, McCartney is filmed mucking about on his guitar, casually seeking some kind of hook, and then – BOOM – in the space of about two minutes, before our very eyes, he's written The Beatles' 1969 hit after which Jackson would name his three-part movie.[4] Also spread widely across cyberspace was Ian Leslie's listicle '64 Reasons to Celebrate Paul McCartney' (2020). It argued, convincingly, that McCartney's 'achievement is immense, historic, and will be remembered for centuries if anything will'.[5]

Paul McCartney's unprecedented success, as one-quarter of The Beatles, barely needs reiterating. Only the fool, a naïf or an attention-craving contrarian would deny that these four northerners of humble origins successfully – accidentally, even – changed the face of popular music on a global scale. Their early radicalism included opening songs with fade-ins and feedback. This innate and unimpeded adventurousness led to later achievements such as cooking up postmodern album concepts, devising and popularizing brand-new recording techniques (with George Martin's vital assistance), composing pop music that sounded like nothing before it, and growing startling moustaches. Their influence extended into fashion, film, television, theatre, literature, politics, religion, academia: almost every area of modern life.

The principal focus of his book being 1960s psychedelia, Rob Chapman's words on The Beatles apply well beyond that decade: 'everything that came after is a reaction to them. Groups either copied them directly or deliberately set themselves against everything they supposed The Beatles represented. Either way, it was still about The Beatles. Even when you think it isn't about them, it probably is.'[6] In Bob Stanley's equally door-stopping tome on the history of pop, the following prediction is made, even if it is concealed in one of the many sly footnotes: 'When he's gone, Paul McCartney will be everyone's favourite Beatle.'[7]

These days, McCartney's reputation is not quite so stringently about The Beatles, even if the two entities can never truly be separated. McCartney's later work has been cited as an influence on a huge number and exceptionally broad range of musicians. Songs originally recorded by Wings have been covered by acts as varied as Guns N' Roses, Dr John, Duane Eddy, Foo Fighters, Melvins, Shonen Knife and Neil Hamburger.[8] McCartney's music has been sampled by Dr Dre, De La Soul and Dead Prez (and that's just a few of the 'D's from the hip-hop canon). Solo albums once written off as half-baked and unfulfilling have been reassessed as some of McCartney's most forward-thinking projects. Two notable examples are 1970's *McCartney* and 1980's *McCartney II*. That first solo effort has been heralded as a pioneering experiment, anticipating the later popularity of the 'lo-fi' genre as well as precursing the new millennium's 'bedroom pop' movement. Even Gene Simmons of the brash, arena-filling hard-rock band Kiss has praised *McCartney* as 'a real tour de force'.[9] When first released, especially after the glossy sophistication of *Abbey Road* a year earlier, it left many listeners underwhelmed, including Paul's former bandmates. *McCartney* and its follow-up, 1971's *Ram*, made Ringo Starr 'feel sad . . . He seems to be going a bit strange,' adding for good measure: 'It's like he's not admitting that he can write great tunes.'[10]

Criticized on its release as 'another exercise in pop insignificance . . . with most songs coming across as cute throwaways', *McCartney II* has enjoyed a new lease of life since its discovery by a later generation of listeners (and ravers).[11] Writer and editor Luke Turner used to frequent the London nightclub Trash in the early 2000s. When he heard a beguiling 'dit dit dit dit' song pumping out of the sound system, he assumed it had been made by an exciting new synth act known to few others besides resident DJs Erol Alkan and Rory Phillips. Turns out it was the eternally startling 'Temporary Secretary' from *McCartney II*.[12] The gradual change in acceptance of both those solo albums contributed to the far warmer immediate response that would greet the similarly conceived *McCartney III* in December 2020. Perceptions had also shifted in regard to the person behind this music.

Given McCartney's current standing as a living legend, it's easy to forget how much his reputation suffered in the decade after The Beatles' split, as well as the depths to which it sank in the 1980s. Even now, as Ian Leslie notes, 'there are people, at least here in Britain, who talk about Paul McCartney the way they might a light entertainment celebrity who once hosted a game show.' McCartney is 'still underrated', as Leslie insists.[13] How can that be?

## Cute but Ruthless

Although the Fab Four would soon outgrow and renounce their portrayal in 1964's *A Hard Day's Night*, the film cemented a firm image of the group in the eyes of the public. This included each individual musician's role in the band and their supposed personality type. 'For many Britons and particularly Americans, the film offered the first opportunity to distinguish between the members of the group, who previously had been viewed by many fans as interchangeable personalities underneath bafflingly long hair,' writes historian Erin Torkelson Weber.[14] In defining each Beatle using a couple of simple character traits per person, screenwriter Alun Owen created reductive images of John, Paul, George and Ringo. While it would have been a tall order to create a serviceable script in any other way, Owen's stereotypes had seismic impact on how the four men were perceived for the rest of their Beatles days and beyond. In that debut movie and the following year's *Help!*, in which the stereotypes were distilled even further, Harrison was the quiet and spiky Beatle. Ringo was the clownish outsider. Teased, alienated and undervalued, the drummer was prone to wandering off alone until enticed back by the rest of the boys. With those big doe eyes of his, McCartney was the cute and happy-go-lucky Beatle.[15] He was the pretty thing and, as such, the most androgynous or effeminate member of a gang who had, together, already blurred traditional gender lines.[16] In many minds, McCartney continued to be viewed in such terms, usually by way of comparison to John Lennon, who was thought to be more volatile, manly,

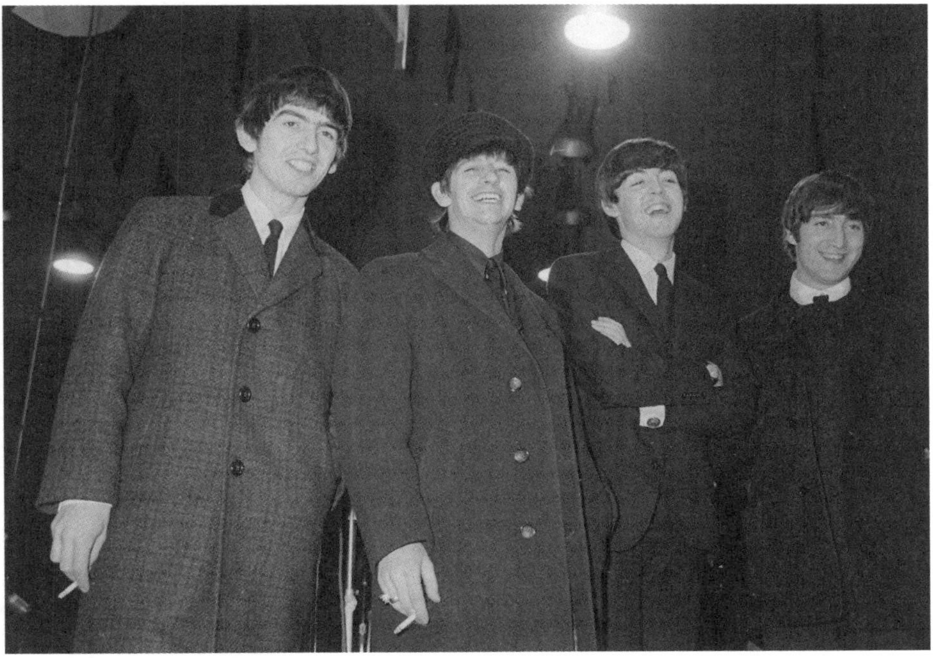

The Beatles gather for a U.S. press conference ,1964.

commanding and intellectual (he wore glasses).[17] It was an equally crude oversimplification, disputed by Lennon himself. Talking to *Melody Maker* about his reputation for acidity and its benefits in striking fear into 'slimy little reporter types', Lennon said he'd never had to 'work for the title of the vicious Beatle, the biting Beatle, the one with the rapier wit. It's a load of crap.' The people who fell for that public image, he observed, often made a beeline for McCartney. 'Paul can be very cynical and much more biting than me when he's driven to it. 'Course, he's got more patience. But he can carve people up in no time at all, when he's pushed. He hits the nail right on the head and doesn't beat about the bush, does Paul.'[18]

Long after The Beatles had ceased recording together, those who didn't blame Yoko Ono for the fallout tended to hold McCartney as most responsible for the Fab Four's seemingly abrupt termination. It was he who publicly announced the end of the group in a press release for the *McCartney* solo album in April 1970. Only later did it emerge that Lennon had declared his intention to leave the group, officially, in a private meeting of September 1969.[19] At first, Lennon made little effort to rectify misconceptions. He was happy to have McCartney branded as public enemy number one. Rather that than he and Yoko, who received enough flak as it was. It hardly helped McCartney's cause that on New Year's Eve 1970, newspapers reported that he was suing the other three Beatles. The band's legal disputes would drag on for decades, long after Lennon's death, keeping fresh in the public's imagination this bitter side to the beloved band's story. McCartney's motivations became clearer over time. Splitting The Beatles' financial affairs in a legal sense was the only way to escape the contract with Allen Klein. In 1969 Klein had been appointed to manage the band and rescue their Apple corporation from financial catastrophe. While Klein succeeded in the latter task and proved useful in other respects, since Lennon had called time on the band their contract with Klein made less sense. Klein's percentage fee was significantly higher than that of The Beatles' former manager, the late Brian Epstein. Furthermore, The Beatles were bound by an agreement that stipulated that the profits from all their activities, bar songwriting but including solo record sales, would be split four ways between each member. McCartney no longer saw any reason why earnings from his first solo album, recordings by Lennon and Ono such as the unlistenable *Wedding Album* (1969), a covers collection sung by Ringo (*Sentimental Journey*, 1970) or whatever George managed to come up with should all be going into the same pot. One individual was clearly going to do worse out of that deal than the others.[20] McCartney had never trusted Klein in the first place. His qualms were vindicated when Klein was later charged with tax evasion, for which he was fined and served two months in prison.

In October 2021, *BBC News*, *The Guardian*, *USA Today*, *Rolling Stone* and many more media outlets reported that, in an interview for BBC Radio 4's *This Cultural Life*, Paul McCartney had 'revealed' that it was John Lennon who had instigated The Beatles' split. This was recounted and received as if it were some fresh scoop. It had been known for ages. Lennon admitted it himself in an autobiographical essay he'd written in the late 1970s, which was published posthumously in 1986. It was repeated in Barry Miles's *Many Years from Now* (1997). McCartney and Starr had discussed it in the *Anthology* book in 2000. George Harrison couldn't remember this happening, which isn't too surprising given he didn't attend the meeting when Lennon announced his decision. 'Everybody had tried to leave,' Harrison said, 'so it was nothing new. Everybody was leaving for years.'[21] That's a fair point, although in previous instances 'everybody' had been coaxed back. This final time, that didn't happen. 'I started the band. I disbanded it. It's as simple as that,' Lennon wrote.[22] McCartney's clarification, in 2021, over half a century since the event took place, was considered newsworthy because so many people, even Beatles fans among them, remained oblivious to the facts. Despite the availability of evidence, the public and media continue to possess and perpetuate misconceptions concerning what went on and who was responsible for what. Maybe they don't even want to know, like a cartoon ostrich with its head in the sand. Would certain parties simply prefer to blame McCartney? Because the truth was that The Beatles would never have lasted as long as they did were it not for McCartney's efforts in keeping the group together, especially after the death of Brian Epstein in 1967. As Ringo Starr quipped in the Abbey Road documentary *If These Walls Could Sing* (2022), 'If it hadn't had been for him [McCartney], we'd have made, like, three albums instead of eight.'[23]

Back in the early 1970s, with the ins and outs not known publicly, it had looked as though McCartney was taking his closest friends to court in order to permanently disband the world's favourite pop group, almost out of spite. This shaped the reception of McCartney's solo work. Greil Marcus edited *Rolling Stone*'s reviews at the time. He says he was persuaded by the magazine's co-founder, Jann Wenner, to alter a broadly positive review of the *McCartney* record – which Marcus considered to be 'wonderful: this rough, homemade one-man-band album' – to a far more negative analysis. Wenner spent three hours arguing with Marcus over the issue until the latter capitulated and then had to spend three more hours convincing reviewer Langdon Winner to rewrite his piece. 'We can't run it this way – he's just reviewing it as if it's this nice little record,' Wenner complained to Marcus. 'It's not just a nice little record, it's a statement and it's taking place in a context that we know: it's one person breaking up the band. This is what needs to be talked about.'[24] The published version did commend McCartney's latest songs as 'masterful examples of happiness, relaxation and contentment'. It also warned that the collection would disappoint many Beatles fans. Much background detail was included. Winner's piece discussed the album's sleeve, McCartney's press release and the nature of his promotional campaign. These were described in terms of 'unsavory vindictiveness' and 'tawdry propaganda'.[25]

*Rolling Stone* had more to answer for in its role in establishing the enduring 'John versus Paul' narrative. In January and February 1971, the magazine published an extensive two-part interview with Lennon, conducted by superfan Wenner. Bitter from the break-up and McCartney's lawsuit, Lennon took the opportunity to let off steam and proclaim himself the sole 'genius' behind The Beatles.[26] In the process, this cemented into public consciousness several myths that are, at best, debatable. Some were downright lies. Lennon falsely claimed, for example, that the Lennon–McCartney songwriting partnership had ceased functioning as early as 1962. As other evidence and eyewitness testimony demonstrates, this simply wasn't the case.[27] Wenner was such a fawning interviewer, in fact, that he sent his article to Lennon before it was published, allowing his subject to change and edit the text himself.[28] This is not what they teach you to do in journalism school.

Lennon also described McCartney as 'a good PR man', adding he was 'about the best in the world, probably'.[29] As Weber notes, the number of interviews McCartney conducted at this time paled in comparison to Lennon's. Paul was holed up in Scotland, licking his wounds and largely minding his own business. Of those in which McCartney did participate, three interviews made scant mention of The Beatles.[30] Lennon and Ono, meanwhile, were known for courting the press endlessly with their often well-intentioned but somewhat self-important stunts, including the infamous 'bed-ins for peace'. These kinds of events were already becoming tired by 4 February 1970 when Lennon and Ono met the Black Power leader and civil rights activist Michael de Freitas, known as Michael X, on the roof of the Black House commune on Holloway Road in north London, to ceremoniously exchange some cuttings of their hair for a pair of Muhammad Ali's blood-stained boxing shorts. Despite news reporters' presence on the day, recalled Apple press officer Derek Taylor, the story failed make the newspapers. 'I definitely should have had the wisdom to call a halt to the daily press conferences they were giving,' he remembered. 'Every day there was a new campaign, a new cause. This was the final proof that they were overexposed.'[31] Maybe that's partly what John had in mind when he spoke of Paul's PR skills. The latter was capable of turning it down a notch.

That said, McCartney didn't always triumph when shirking the spotlight. Because McCartney didn't want to talk to journalists, who would usually bombard him with countless questions about The Beatles, the notorious *McCartney* press release took the form of a Q&A transcript. In it, the world-famous musician didn't come across very well at all. Its tone is stiff, monosyllabic and embittered. Recalling the incident in 1984, McCartney said Derek Taylor had asked him 'some stilted questions', so he had provided his answers in the same spirit. Taylor's memory differed. He had asked McCartney for some information about the album. In its place, he'd received an interview that the musician had conducted with himself.[32] Whichever the case, 'good PR' it was not.

In terms of relations with the press, Lennon was rarely challenged by his often sycophantic interviewers. His claims in *Rolling Stone* and elsewhere helped to reinforce John's reputation as the edgy, experimental, politically radical, bluntly honest and generally more dangerous Beatle, as opposed to the conservative and commercially minded Paul.[33] There were times when McCartney could be blunt and volatile himself. He irritated his fellow musicians during the tense recording sessions for *Let It Be* and *Abbey*

John Lennon and Yoko Ono promoting world peace while on their honeymoon in Amsterdam, 1969.

*Road*. At one later low ebb, when presented with a letter requesting he delay the *McCartney* album because EMI didn't want it to clash with the release of *Let It Be*, he literally attacked the messenger, who was none other than the amiable Ringo Starr.[34]

Lennon would renounce his 1971 *Rolling Stone* interview and downplay its significance. In the interview itself, he had claimed he was clean of drugs. Lennon later confessed to George Martin that he'd been completely stoned at the time.[35] Speaking to *Playboy*'s David Sheff in 1980, Lennon admitted he had been lying to Wenner out of spite.[36] It has also been suggested that Wenner either did not understand, or was reluctant to indicate in clear terms to his readers, any of those moments when his interviewee had been speaking in ironic, sarcastic, tongue-in-cheek or hyperbolic terms, as Lennon was prone to do.[37]

Wenner perpetuated the misleading claims when he decided to publish the interview in book form, under the title *Lennon Remembers*, in autumn 1971. At this point, Lennon wrote to Wenner to complain about the republication. His objections proved futile.[38] The book has since been published in several subsequent editions, thereby making less ephemeral all of Lennon's exaggerations, unsubstantiated opinions and barefaced fibs. This further encouraged readers and writers to choose sides between Lennon and McCartney and helped to propagate an apocryphal Beatles story. This version of events quickly became what Weber calls 'the prevailing Orthodoxy'.[39] It was repeated endlessly in the music press of the 1970s and continues to cloud judgements today.

Wenner insisted that *Lennon Remembers* contained 'the truth', even thirty years after he conducted the interview, wilfully ignoring any evidence that contradicted Lennon's account, including that provided by the man himself.[40] That might be expected of Wenner, who would want to save face professionally. He was also friends with Ono, whose own reputation and career benefited from the claims made in the interview. Worse are those people who have written about The Beatles since, quoting verbatim parts of Lennon's *Rolling Stone* interview as a handy, revealing and ostensibly reliable primary source, without ever questioning its flaws and credibility.

As early as 1972, Lennon and McCartney met up and called a personal truce. The public's habit of taking sides did not ease in the same fashion. And despite tempers having cooled, shortly before his death Lennon was still bending the truth in interviews, often to the ongoing detriment of McCartney's character. In the 1980 interview he gave to *Playboy* to promote the *Double Fantasy* album, Lennon insisted he didn't follow Paul's career, saying in no uncertain terms: 'I don't give a shit what Wings are doing . . .'[41] Years later a letter was published, written by Lennon to his personal assistant in 1980, asking him to pick up the latest Wings album, *Back to the Egg*.[42] In *Lennon Remembers* he had claimed to have written at least 'a good half' of 'Eleanor Rigby' from 1966's *Revolver*. In *Playboy* this was upped to '70 per cent', presumably out of envy that one of The Beatles' most widely loved songs was, at root, a McCartney composition.[43]

While keen to claim 'Eleanor Rigby' as his own, Lennon liked to dismiss as 'granny music' the McCartney songs he considered too twee, safe and apparently beneath him. It is another insult that has been absorbed and regurgitated by the anti-McCartney brigade. There will be many more examples of Paul's non-granny music in the following chapters. As for Lennon, there's plenty of polite and pretty material in his own oeuvre, from his moptop days right up to the end. 'If I Fell' from *A Hard Day's Night* (1964), written primarily by Lennon, has a soft, lullaby quality to it. With Lennon and McCartney's joint harmonies sung into a single microphone, it achieves the desired Everly Brothers effect. Lennon considered this track to be his first sincere attempt to write a 'proper' ballad, and he saw it as the 'precursor' to *Rubber Soul*'s 'In My Life' (1965). 'And it's semi-autobiographical, but not consciously,' he told *Playboy*'s David Sheff. 'It shows that I wrote sentimental love ballads, silly love songs, way back when.'[44] The song's melody and its approach in general sound distinctly McCartneyesque, all things considered. Interestingly, McCartney would echo Lennon's attempt at 'Rigby'-grabbing when insisting the pair wrote 'If I Fell' together. They may well have done this, as the pair were still frequent collaborators back then. Nevertheless, as McCartney said to the same interviewer, 'If I Fell' showed that Lennon was just as much a writer of gentle ballads as he.[45]

Fast-forward to Lennon's final album, 1980's *Double Fantasy*. The tracks alternate between those sung by John and the ones led by Ono.[46] To listeners less invested in the John-as-edgy-genius narrative, Ono's tracks have stood out as the record's more captivating pieces, both musically and lyrically, whether this be by accident or design, or perhaps a by-product of Ono's unusual voice and creative approach. As for the Lennon-sung numbers, these are quite clearly a collection of 'silly love songs', smitten as they are with his wife, their son and the comfort of family life. There is nothing necessarily wrong with that, even if some critics did object to the overriding schmaltz factor.[47]

## Spreading Wings

It is understandable that Paul did not exactly nail his *McCartney* press release given the pressure he was under at that time. His beloved Beatles had fallen apart, finally. He had a family to support, and his finances were tied up in the messy Apple business and legal disputes and therefore inaccessible to him. A significant portion of the press and the public already had him pegged as somebody who would soon be washed up, or at least not at full force, without the other three musicians by his side.

From the moment they drew any media attention, The Beatles had been asked, on a fairly regular basis and often by men in suits with posh accents, what they intended to do afterwards. Almost by definition, pop music was a faddish thing and careers within it were seen to be inexorably short-lived. Beatles fandom was viewed as a teenage phenomenon. Girls and boys would mature and move on. Few old-school interviewers could foresee much longevity in either the music or the hysteria it attracted. Back in August 1963, as Beatlemania was starting to spread across the British Isles and in same the week that 'She Loves You' was released as a single, Ringo Starr said he hoped he might earn enough money by the end of it all to open a chain of hairdressing salons to be managed by his wife, Maureen. 'I figure it would be a good business move,' he reasoned. 'Girls will always want their hair doing . . . I could go round from time to time saying, "Is everything all right, madam? A cup of coffee, perhaps? Or would you like a tot of whisky?"'[48]

You'd think, therefore, that by 1970 Paul McCartney might have done some mental preparation for The End. By all accounts he was a shambles. He struggled to leave his bed. He refused to answer telephone calls. He drank too much and couldn't be bothered to shave. He was hesitant to make any new music at all, what with the incomparable pressure of having to follow The Beatles. He had scant idea what to do with himself. He would look back on this time and compare it to going through a grieving process or suffering from withdrawal.[49] The thing that hurt the most was surely the fracturing of his friendship and working partnership with one Beatle in particular. During Beatlemania, McCartney hadn't envisaged opening salons like Ringo. If – or when – his group hit the dust, McCartney speculated back then, he and Lennon would continue to write songs together, for other artists to record. Were he no longer with The Beatles, he would still be with John.[50]

Once Linda had helped Paul to pull himself together, the rest of the decade was defined by personal stability – the occasional bust for soft-drug possession notwithstanding – as the

McCartneys settled into raising their kids and living on their farm. McCartney's 1970s were artistically erratic, however, his career seemingly guided in large part by impulse. Having taken swipes at Lennon's political posturing on *Ram*'s 'Too Many People' (1971), McCartney had a go himself with 'Give Ireland Back to the Irish', a response to Bloody Sunday that has been aptly described as 'inappropriately chirpy'.[51] Its sentiment was controversial enough for the single to be blacklisted by the BBC.[52] McCartney followed this, either misguidedly or knowingly so, depending on who you ask, with a version of a nursery rhyme. 'I was coming off the road after three years in America with Joe Cocker,' reflected Wings guitarist Henry McCullough, 'and I ended up playing "Mary Had a Little Fucking Lamb".'[53]

From their formation in 1971 to the band's final rehearsals in 1980, Wings operated with similar open-mindedness and eclecticism to The Beatles, albeit without quite the same quality control as the Fab Four, and with less consistency in terms of chart success, critical plaudits and band personnel. The only members to last the duration of Wings' existence were Paul, Linda and Denny Laine, a former member of The Moody Blues. This gave the impression that Wings was, essentially, Paul McCartney as a solo act in all but name. On 1971's earthy *Wild Life*, the artist listed on the sleeve was, simply, Wings. The next two albums, *Red Rose Speedway* and *Band on the Run* (both 1973), were credited to Paul McCartney and Wings. For 1975's *Venus and Mars* they reverted to Wings and stuck with that for *Wings at the Speed of Sound* (1976), the live double album *Wings over America* (1976), *London Town* (1978) and *Back to the Egg* (1979).

As for the competition from McCartney's former bandmates, the solo careers of George Harrison and Ringo Starr peaked early. Their private lives also became chaotic, to put it mildly. At one sordid low point, Harrison started fooling around with Starr's wife, Maureen.[54] For Pattie Boyd, this was the 'final straw' in her rocky marriage to Harrison.[55] She telephoned Starr to tell him, 'Have you ever thought about why your wife doesn't come home at night? It's because she's here!', and when Harrison finally admitted in person that he was 'in love' with Maureen, Starr went into a feverish trance, repeating the words 'Nothing is real, nothing is real.'[56] Harrison's excessive cocaine use had changed him, felt Boyd: 'it froze George's emotions and hardened his heart.'[57]

John Lennon's career had its own peaks and troughs. Unlike McCartney, he never bothered to tour. After the birth of Sean Lennon in 1975, John devoted much of his time to hermetic domesticity. A big part of the problem faced by Harrison, Starr and Lennon was that they no longer had the restless and conscientious McCartney to rouse them from idleness.[58] Left to his own devices, McCartney worked harder and more prolifically than the other three, and it paid off. What's more, he actually enjoyed going on the road. While many would agree that Wings' output could fluctuate wildly, the band enjoyed a respectable number of hits.

With a Bond theme, a massive world tour and two UK chart-topping albums under his belt, by the end of the 1970s McCartney had confirmed his status as the most successful solo Beatle. What he hadn't managed was to shake off his reputation for being coldly calculating in sustaining his global fame. Despite – but also because of – his success, he was the ex-Beatle who was most routinely mocked, disparaged, disliked, targeted and treated with the intense suspicion that forms as a by-product of mainstream approval. Singles like 'Silly Love Songs' and 'Let 'Em In' had sailed, effortlessly it seemed, to the top of the charts. (Well, nearly: both reached number two in 1976.)[59] To the former fans who neither bought these hits nor had the curiosity to investigate Wings' deeper cuts, McCartney's works were viewed as flimsy ephemera. In realms beyond the commercial marketplace – within music criticism and academia, and in the minds of cross-generational hipsters – McCartney's reputation as a 'true'

McCartney rocking out with Wings in Montreux, 1972.

artist continued to sink while the 'coolness' of Lennon only rose, however unreasonably.[60] In numerous quarters, Lennon's quips against his former bandmate remained gospel.

## Noxious Fumes

Typical of McCartney's contrariness, as well as his disinterest in always being hip, Wings scored a number-one hit with the bagpipe-assisted ballad 'Mull of Kintyre' at the height of punk. A lot of people forget that this song, released in 1977, was one half of a double A-side single. Concerned that the Scottish waltz might be too quaint even for him, and well aware that it wasn't everybody's cup of tea, McCartney insisted it be paired with a rockier Wings number called 'Girls' School'. This ended up being played less frequently than its accompanying piece in the UK, although it did receive more airtime than 'Mull of Kintyre' in Canada and the United States, where the single didn't sell so well. Inspired by magazine advertisements for pornographic movies, the less remembered song appears to be set in a Catholic boarding-school-cum-brothel for sex-trafficked teenagers. In its third verse, some of the adolescents involved are drugged and then bashed over the head in what could be a call-back to 'Maxwell's Silver Hammer', McCartney's jaunty ode to serial killing on The Beatles' *Abbey Road*. Who says he doesn't have edge?

Whatever danger Wings did possess was lost on much of the punk generation. This rebellious and irreverent youth movement did not take too kindly to the dinosaur rock gods of yore. Malcolm McLaren, manager for New York Dolls and then Sex Pistols, was motivated in large part by 'intra-generational hatred', as Simon Reynolds puts it. 'He had an uncontrollable urge to pick fights with those figures who were in the mid 1970s coming to represent a sort of alternative establishment.'[61] To be fair to them, not all the leading lights of punk were as homogeneously hostile to The Beatles as we have been led to believe by hour-long documentaries on BBC Four. Ramones took their name from Paul Ramon, a pseudonym McCartney had used to check into hotels. The New Yorkers' dress code, and the decision to each adopt 'Ramone' as their new surname, evoked the uniformity and solidarity of the Fab Four's early years, first as Hamburg-dwelling leathered rockers and then as besuited moptops. In 1977, when Ramones arrived with Talking Heads to play a concert in Liverpool, the two American bands could hardly believe what they saw. The legendary Cavern Club they'd read about, where The Beatles had once wowed their earliest domestic audiences, had been unceremoniously demolished. 'I've waited all my life to see this place,' snuffled Talking Heads' bassist Tina Weymouth through the cold she'd caught.[62] Doing their best to mark the occasion, the four Ramones posed for photographs in front of the fenced-off rubble. The punk rock yoof didn't need to bury The Beatles after all.

English inner-city planning was doing that job on its own. There was no public outcry.

As for the home-grown movement, The Damned covered 'Help!' at breakneck pace on the B-side to their debut single, 'New Rose' (1976). On 1978's *The Scream*, Siouxsie and the Banshees put their prickly twist on 'Helter Skelter', one of the more infamous Beatles numbers since its appropriation at the hands of the Manson Family. The Banshees followed this up a few years later with a hit take on 'Dear Prudence' (1983). Sham 69 were prone to belting out their own rowdy version of 'Day Tripper'. Before forming Alternative TV, Mark Perry had been a member of The New Beatles. Alas, they split after a couple of rehearsals, no doubt avoiding future lawsuits. To some observers, these were iconoclastic acts of provocation. Fondness, and a sense of musical lineage, were also part of the equation. This is reminiscent of the Pop art painter Roy Lichtenstein, who became famous for lifting ideas directly from comic strips. In his signature cartoonish style, he often reproduced scenes by past masters like Pablo Picasso, Claude Monet and Vincent van Gogh. Call them 'cover paintings', if you like. 'In the parody there is the implication of the perverse and I feel this in my own work even though I don't mean it to be that, because I don't dislike the work that I am parodying,' pondered Lichtenstein in a 1964 radio discussion. 'The things that I have apparently parodied I actually admire and I really don't know what the implication of that is.'[63] The punks may have held similar uncertainties about their own perverse intentions.

It is true that the two most famous British punk bands did put sustained effort into distancing themselves from the 1960s, its music, culture and values. In the lyrics to '1977', The Clash boisterously rejected The Beatles, along with Elvis Presley and The Rolling Stones. They went on to celebrate the demise of Beatlemania, boldly dismissing it as 'phoney', on the title track to *London Calling* (1979). Explaining Sex Pistols' refusal to play at certain venues, drummer Paul Cook said, 'The trouble with pubs is you have to please everybody. If we wanted to please everybody we'd end up sounding like The Beatles.'[64] When bassist Glen Matlock was kicked out of the Pistols, the remaining members claimed it was because he was a Beatles fan. As such, according to vocalist Johnny Rotten, Matlock had wanted everything to be 'watered down'.[65] 'And what kind of reason is that for getting a guy out of a band?' Matlock asked when promoting his next group, Rich Kids. 'I hate the Beatles for the same reason as they did but anybody who doesn't admit The Beatles were great is dopey and if you feel that threatened by a band that broke up seven years ago . . .'[66]

In private, The Clash's Joe Strummer admired The Beatles. He liked John Lennon in particular, and to an extent modelled his own image on Lennon's more campaigning, outspoken and 'working-class hero' tendencies. In both cases, a hero *to* the working classes may seem a more appropriate title than a hero *from* the working classes, given the two gentlemen's backgrounds. This was especially true in the case of Strummer. The son of a diplomat, he had been sent to boarding school from the age of nine. Punk, as rock 'n' roll had done so many times before, provided ample opportunities for personal reinvention. In his later life as a campfire-dwelling Glastonbury regular, Strummer would claim that the ideals of punk rock and those of hippiedom (plus the newer rave scene) were more or less aligned.[67] This sentiment wasn't shouted from the rooftops in his punk days, mind. Unlike Strummer, John 'Johnny Rotten' Lydon stuck to his guns, blaming his hatred of The Beatles on overexposure from his parents' fandom.[68] Most of all, he objected to what he called McCartney's 'aspect' of the group. Having crossed paths a few times since (at swanky events such as awards ceremonies, one imagines), Lydon accepts that McCartney is 'a really friendly bloke', but he still feels the need to draw the line somewhere. 'You can separate the person from the work,' he says.[69]

For their own part, punk-promoting journalists were keen to chastise the 'boring old farts' who found Sex Pistols abhorrent.[70] They noted that although the older generation's musical heroes (the former Beatles, The Beach Boys, The Rolling Stones, The Who and so on) had once epitomized youthful rebellion themselves, most of the big hitters had converted into profit-oriented brands and lackeys of the elite.[71] Some of the accused would hardly deny it. As early as 1972, when a glitzy party was held in New York to celebrate the end of The Rolling Stones' widely documented U.S. tour, Keith Richards is said to have surveyed the scene (with guests including Zsa Zsa Gabor and Andy Warhol) and quipped to a friend, 'Right now is when you realise you're a product.'[72] Five years of big-tongued logos and supermodel seductions later, his band had become tabloid fodder for partying with Margaret Trudeau, then wife of the Canadian president. It was also around this time that Mick Jagger was rumoured to be having an affair with Princess Margaret. You could say they'd put their 'street-fighting' days behind them.

Incidentally, in the year prior to Richards's revelation, the writer and activist A. J. Weberman and street musician David Peel had been galvanized by their distaste at witnessing once radical artists pivoting to shallower-minded product hawkers. Together, the pair founded the Rock Liberation Front (RLF) in 1971. The group aimed to challenge musicians who they felt had abandoned or neglected political participation and radical forthrightness in favour of commercial self-interest. In other words, those who had sold out. Perhaps Keith Richards even had the RLF in the back of his mind when guiltily chinwagging with Warhol and Gabor. Having previously targeted Bob Dylan's widening distance from the counterculture, Peel and Weberman had then set their sights on other 'rip-off people in the world of rock'. Top of their list was

Paul McCartney, who'd had the nerve to release an album that was 'really inane and said nothing about what was happening on the street', as Weberman later told the writer Peter Doggett. 'He was supposed to be a representative of youth culture, but he was just a businessman. We reckoned he could use a wake-up call.'[73] The RLF may have misunderstood, perhaps wilfully so, the foundational motives of most musicians who end up famous. On the whole, these tend to be more opportunistic than community-minded. More than once in his official biography, McCartney recalls that the 'only reason' to start a group in the first place was to avoid having a proper job and, as he puts it, 'pull the birds'.[74] That was beside the point for the RLF. In August 1971 they staged a mock funeral for McCartney outside the Park Avenue apartment of Lee Eastman, his father-in-law and business manager. Neither McCartney or Eastman was there at the time, and passers-by were mostly nonplussed. The same goes for the media. 'Who cares?' shrugged Blair Sabol, reporting for *The Village Voice*, who noted the event was enjoyed only by the attention-seeking Weberman and his sycophantic pals.[75] One person who was amused when he heard about the stunt was John Lennon. After aligning himself with the RLF, it was through this connection that Lennon became involved with other causes and began contributing financially to the Irish Republican Army (IRA), although it didn't take long for him to lose interest in Weberman and his radical antics.[76] The Rock Liberation Front was a damp squib, ultimately, but its objections to and accusations of selling out have remained part of public discourse ever since. Naturally, these were inherited by punk bands and writers who were looking to oust the old guard.[77]

'On an individual level Paul McCartney and Wings is the only one [of The Beatles] to have maintained the tradition of an artist consistently performing for an audience,' wrote the pro-punk *Melody Maker* scribe Caroline Coon, 'and he speaks mainly to the generation he grew up with.'[78] This observation would not have permanent resonance. At the time, it seemed on the mark. Image was important to journalists, too. 'Soundcheck over, I approached the lead singer, ex-culinary artist Howard Wall, who is confident and wry, slim yet strongly built with cheery, cheeky features and black hair that looks short at the front but straggles a good few inches over the collar,' wrote *NME*'s Paul Morley after an encounter with Uxbridge punks The Lurkers. 'If the light catches him badly he resembles Paul McCartney.'[79]

Reputations were hardly enhanced by many of the musicians who most loudly championed The Beatles after the split, in interviews and through their songwriting and production preferences. If we're being honest, such artists often resided at the naffer end of the cultural barometer. The *raison d'être* of Jeff Lynne's Electric Light Orchestra was to fill the void left by the Fab Four. Unlike Sex Pistols, with their punkish qualms about where to play and who to please, ELO absolutely did wish to appeal to as many people as possible and tried to achieve this by mimicking The Beatles as closely as they could. They lifted copious tricks from the Lennon, McCartney, Harrison and Starr songbook, as well as the George Martin production sound, without really adding much to the various formulas.[80]

Steely Dan made a more persuasive claim on The Beatles' mantle. Formed by Walter Becker and Donald Fagen in New York State, Steely Dan had the talent, intellect and inquisitiveness to have gone down a prog rock or jazz route but found they had a knack for crafting, in a meticulous manner, what they called 'smart rock'. They insisted their work should be considered as 'compositions', not frivolous things like 'songs'.[81] 'I hated rock and roll,' Fagen once said of his adolescent interests.[82] You can still love The Beatles, though, even if you despise most rock 'n' roll. 'The Beatles had not long before set the example of concentrating on records and not touring, and we were arrogant enough to follow their example,' remembered Fagen of Steely

Dan's imperial phase. 'We never make a move without consulting the Beatle Chronology,' he added flippantly.[83] 'Yacht rock', as Steely Dan's style of smooth, radio-friendly, guitar-based pop came to be known, has been considered a perfectly reasonable and uncontroversial listening choice in recent decades, now that tastes are less tribal and fewer people subscribe to the idea that any musical experience should be considered a 'guilty pleasure'. There are still those, however, as there were back in the day, who consider Steely Dan's songs – sorry, their *compositions* – to be objectionably sophisticated, over-arranged, sterile and soulless. 'Too aloof and clever-clever, totally lacking heart,' complains my friend the ex-newspaper editor David Nicholson whenever the divisive subject crops up at the weekly pub quiz. Needless to say, Steely Dan was another act that left most punks unimpressed. 'I come over here and I switch on the radio and all I hear is the Eagles and Steely Dan,' grumbled Joe Strummer to The Clash's American audience in 1979, 'so I turn it to a country and western station.'[84] It didn't help that a lot of the extremely smooth music that dominated the airwaves at that time lacked the underlying edge that can be detected, sometimes, beneath the misleadingly slick surface of Steely Dan and Eagles. The English equivalent was perhaps 10cc.

On 1976's *Turnstiles*, an album steeped in nostalgia for older eras of popular music, Brooklyn's Billy Joel included a song about someone who sits around in abject misery, lamenting the lack of a Beatles reunion. Its sound has a resemblance to McCartney's occasional experiments in cod-reggae. Speaking of musical appropriation, the Bee Gees hit stratospheric success thanks to their reinvention as a disco act. The Grammy-winning soundtrack to *Saturday Night Fever* (1977), and the singles taken from it, sold like hot cakes, as did the hits that the Brothers Gibb penned for other singers. With that scale of chart dominance and cultural omnipresence, it was inevitable that people would mention them in the same sentence as The Beatles. Even those who were resistant to the charms of the Gibbs couldn't help but draw the comparison. John Rockwell of the *New York Times* considered the Bee Gees to be 'highly professional craftsmen who make catchy, appealing pop songs of no special value or profundity'. His headline, 'The Bee Gees are Getting as Big as the Beatles', read like a warning sign.[85]

The Bee Gees took their ceremonial role as the new Beatles to heart, with much hubris, when they followed *Saturday Night Fever* with the 1978 musical film *Sgt. Pepper's Lonely Hearts Club Band*. Peter Frampton joined them, playing the character Billy Shears. He was riding the success of his mega-selling double live album *Frampton Comes Alive!* (1976). Having initially turned down the role, Frampton accepted it when he was tricked into believing that Paul McCartney would be co-starring alongside him.[86] A similarly reluctant George Martin, who knew deep down that The Beatles would not approve, had to be persuaded by his wife, Judy, to produce and arrange the songs for the movie and its soundtrack, fearing that somebody else would make a hash of it.[87]

Robin Gibb had greater confidence, to put it mildly. 'Kids today don't know The Beatles' *Sgt. Pepper*,' he claimed in an interview with *Playboy*.

> And when those who do see our film and hear us doing it, that will be the version they relate to and remember. Unfortunately, The Beatles will be secondary. You see, there is no such thing as The Beatles. They don't exist as a band and never performed *Sgt. Pepper* live, in any case. When ours comes out, it will be, in effect, as if theirs never existed.[88]

The usurpation envisioned by Gibb was not the consequence of the now largely forgotten film in which Frankie Howerd plays the mean antagonist, Mr Mustard.

Rockwell's colleague at the *New York Times*, Janet Maslin, penned one of the many withering reviews of the Bee Gees' film, likening this 'ultimate multimedia mishmash' to 'a child's play' or an 'interminable variety show'. She noted how the Gibbs had recently escaped the Beatles comparisons that had dogged their early career by pursuing a different style. In the process, they'd hit new heights of fame. Yet here they U-turned back towards the old idols, making a bodge job of many of their renditions and dismaying their newer fans with the soundtrack's abject lack of disco. 'When whimsy gets to be this overbearing,' wrote Maslin, 'it simply isn't whimsy anymore.' She denied that it should even be considered art. Rather, it was 'a business deal set to music'.[89]

The Bee Gees' manager, Robert Stigwood, who conceived the project, had further transactions in his mind's eye. Alas, he was forced to abandon plans to build a *Sgt. Pepper* theme park and produce a TV spin-off.[90] Even though the ex-members of The Beatles had kept their distance from Stigwood's hare-brained schemes, such anaemically dollar-hungry projects helped to tarnish memories of The Beatles. A similar idea with comparable impact, the Broadway musical *Beatlemania* ran from May 1977 until October 1979, when the real Beatles and their lawyers, for once seeing eye to eye on something, had the production shut down. Its temporary run and cash-in cast recording has been blamed for souring people's respect for The Beatles and their music, especially among those who were young and cynical enough at the time to object to the show's nostalgic tackiness.[91]

Richard Mills, author of *The Beatles and Fandom* (2019), sees 1978 as a low point for the Fab Four's prestige. Wings were having hits, and people still purchased Beatles records, but they were not exactly fashionable. 'There was a [Beatles] fan convention in England around that time,' Mills told the journalist Tom Fordy, 'and there was hardly anybody there.'[92] Heather McCartney, Linda's daughter and adopted child of Paul, was unlikely to have been caught dead at a Beatles convention either. As a teenager she attended concerts by The Clash, The Damned, Billy Idol, The Stranglers and their contemporaries. It is said that, buoyed by Heather's enthusiasm, her parents considered jumping on the bandwagon by reinventing themselves as 'Noxious Fumes' and 'Vile Lin'. During the sessions for 1978's *London Town*, Wings demoed a vaguely punkish song called 'Boil Crisis', with an opening line about a certain spotty sod named Sid. It was never released in an official capacity as Paul feared the flak it would attract.[93]

After its initial bright flash, punk rock soon splintered and evolved. As it begat – and was displaced by – post-punk, hardcore, industrial rock, goth, new wave, synth pop and other subgenres, and as the new decade dawned, The Beatles seemed increasingly outdated.

The 1980s were, as one writer puts it, 'a confusing, passionless time for rock and roll' when many of the older generation of stars found themselves out of touch and 'lost in the shuffle'.[94] Among the adrift were even those who had sympathized with punk's 'year zero' moment and were also open to the futuristic keyboards of the new wave. Neil Young would dabble in synth work himself, without committing fully enough to pull it off convincingly. Next, he'd reinvent himself as a throwback rockabilly artist, or try to court Nashville in a country style. He'd end up pouring his own savings into pricey vanity projects like the *Human Highway* feature film (1982) and shambolic European *Trans* tour (1982). He would even find himself sued by his own record company for making music that was so unlike his own back catalogue it was deemed in breach of contract. Bob Dylan, meanwhile, would bemuse and frustrate long-term fans with his unwelcome Christian period, general patchy output and questionable production choices. In 1982 The Who played a 'farewell tour' (with The Clash in the support slot), initially hoping to plough on as a studio-only act just as The Beatles had done before. Instead, Pete Townshend bought himself out of the band's existing contract to concentrate on solo work, with diminishing interest from consumers.

Writing for *Record Collector* in 2022, David Quantick quipped that the 1980s were 'a decade when nobody was cool'.[95] On the next page of the same issue, another of its columnists, Luke Haines, wrote, 'No good records have been made on cocaine. I present the solo records of Eric Clapton – oh, and the entire 80s – as evidence.'[96] They're exaggerating, probably, yet this illustrates how that time and its related indignities tend to be remembered. Cocaine use among musicians had been rising steadily since the early 1970s, often coinciding with a creative downturn for the stars who were particularly partial.[97] As Rob Chapman writes of The Band's *The Last Waltz* concert film, recorded in 1976 and screened two years later, 'The overpowering stench of self-aggrandising coke bullshit hangs over the entire movie and the air lies thick with a powdery precipitation that all but threatens to clog up the lens.'[98] Its director, Martin Scorsese, was a heavy user at the time of production.[99] He had to be persuaded by Neil Young's manager, at a cost of thousands of dollars, to rotoscope out of the live footage a large rock of cocaine that had been dangling from the singer's nose.[100] In the 1980s this drug's popularity continued to grow among ex-countercultural hippie stars and entrepreneurial yuppies alike. As the comedian and actor Robin Williams famously quipped, 'Cocaine is God's way of saying you are making too much money.' He later admitted this remark had been donated to him by a friendly drunk he'd met in the street.[101] For many of the musicians in question, coke seemed largely to encourage laziness, empty bluster, reckless decision-making, spoilt tantrums and, in certain cases, sheer madness. In 1983 Young's occasional supergroup buddy David Crosby became a fugitive from justice when on bail for possession of cocaine and a loaded pistol. After turning himself in, he served a few months of a five-year sentence and was then released on parole. When asked why he'd felt the need to carry firearms in the first place, Crosby replied, 'John Lennon'.[102]

## Jealous Guys

Back in 1968, John Lennon had called an urgent meeting. He had something very important to tell his fellow Beatles and assorted key members of the Apple staff: 'I am Jesus Christ. I have come back again. This is my thing.' It could have been a joke. Tony Bramwell, co-manager at the company, considered Lennon earnest. Derek Taylor was worried that John had lost his marbles. The other Beatles were unimpressed. They had been dragged all the way into the office just to hear Lennon's latest acid-fuelled pronouncement. 'Meeting adjourned,' decided Ringo, 'let's go and have some lunch.'[103]

Lennon was no Lord and Saviour, yet his bugged-out messiah complex was prophetic in a sense. When he was shot outside New York's Dakota building by an obsessed fan on 8 December 1980, it brought Lennon close – perhaps closer than any rock musician has ever come or conceivably ever will – to sainthood. He was one of the most famous men in modern popular culture, whose life was cut short in an extraordinarily violent and senseless way. The historian Callum G. Brown provocatively pinpointed the end of Christianity in Great Britain to the year 1963, with The Beatles having played no small role in its demise.[104] It made a strange sort of sense that the void left by forsaking one messiah figure should be filled by another icon drawn from the secular world. The outpouring of public sorrow recalled reactions to the assassination of John F. Kennedy. 'When a rock star dies in a plane crash or from an overdose of drugs and alcohol, the accident may seem tragic or repulsive, but it is still comprehensible,' reflected Dave Marsh in *Rolling Stone*. 'When one of the finest artists and bravest men of our generation is shot down on his doorstep by a fan with a gun, the mind reels in disbelief.'[105] Crosby would certainly not be the only person affected. The ramifications were seismic.

David Hepworth's interpretation is that the killer, Mark Chapman, had been trying to escape loserdom: to 'obliterate the distance between his own puny life and the hero's life that he saw Lennon leading'.[106] Chapman's act of manic violence didn't exactly succeed in this mission, even if his name did gain permanent notoriety. Songs written about Chapman have included David Gilmour's folk-prog solo effort 'Murder' (1984), 'Andy Warhol Was Right' (1992) by Hollywood glam metallers Warrant, The Cranberries' clumsy 'I Just Shot John Lennon' (1996) and the more cathartic 'Mark David Chapman' by ...And You Will Know Us by the Trail of Dead (1999). For their 2023 album *Rush!*, Italian Eurovision rockers Måneskin wrote a song about a deadly stalker and named it 'Mark Chapman'. The band members were born twenty years after Lennon's death. In another form of popular entertainment, the 2007 biographical movie *Chapter 27* starred Jared Leto, who gained 30 kilograms (67 lb) to play Chapman. Thanks to such Stanislavskian commitment, the actor developed gout. *Slant* writer Nick Schager summed up the critical consensus when dismissing Leto's efforts as 'merely a Robert De Niro stunt in service of a pointless movie'.[107]

What the real Chapman did to Lennon had symbolic prescience too, argues Hepworth:

> His action foreshadowed in a uniquely terrible way our increasing desire to put ourselves at the centre of events, when our proper role should be as spectator or appreciative listener. It underlined just how big rock stars had become and how much some people still expected those rock stars to be able to mend their own broken lives. It wasn't anything to do with what the rock stars said or did. It was to do with what people expected of them.[108]

This echoes the thoughts, written in the immediate aftermath of the murder, of the writer and jazz singer George Melly. Refusing to even type the name of the 25-year-old spotlight-seeking culprit, Melly concluded: 'The boy is happy. He is, for a moment, as famous as his victim. What Tom Wolfe called "The Me Decade" has found its pathetic spokesman.'[109] If Wolfe and Melly thought that times had got grim enough already, the hyper-individualistic 1980s were about to take this up another notch.[110]

Lennon's murder also obliterated the prospect of any full Beatles reunion. Had Lennon survived and there been an eventual re-formation, however brief, grand, silly or cynical, it would likely have been anticlimactic. By 1970, the band had achieved all it needed. Anything afterwards would only have tarnished what Hepworth calls 'the most powerful franchise in pop'.[111] The tragic circumstances meant that, as a complete unit at least, The Beatles' position at 'the toppermost of the poppermost' (as Lennon used to call it) was reinforced. 'There they remain,' as Philip Larkin put it three years after Lennon's death, 'unreachable, frozen, fabulous.'[112]

'In the wake of pop music's JFK moment it seemed only right to regard the rock star's trade as a very serious business,' notes Hepworth.[113] This was reflected in Lennon's obituaries, which mourned the loss of a creative powerhouse. Even here, plenty of writers could not resist the chance to compare McCartney, unfavourably, to his former partner in pop. 'There was something over-cute and chirpy about Paul: he wanted to be loved not only by your mother, but by your grandmother too. Preferring Paul to John was like preferring Cliff Richard to Elvis Presley, or Donovan to Dylan,' sneered Martin Amis in *The Observer*.[114]

Writing in the *Village Voice*, Robert Christgau asked why it always had to be heroes, such as Bobby Kennedy and John Lennon, who got shot: 'Why isn't it Richard Nixon or Paul McCartney?'[115] On the day the news broke, Paul 'good PR man' McCartney had gone to work in the recording studio as usual. When a microphone was thrust under his chin by a reporter on the street, McCartney's closing response to the intrusive questioning about Lennon's murder was 'It's a drag, isn't it?'[116] McCartney has been asked to defend this statement so many times he must sometimes feel like he's the protagonist on trial in a novel by Albert Camus or Franz Kafka. Not prone to public grieving at the best of times, McCartney is visibly upset in that footage. He is still processing his feelings of shock and loss. Reported widely, the quote was seen as an insensitively glib comment from the 'cold' one.

Christgau penned another reflection, published two years later in an edited collection for *Rolling Stone*. In this piece, he hailed Lennon as the only true avant-garde Beatle. The other three 'hack' members of the band, he reckoned, did not have the same level of talent. He also blamed McCartney, Harrison and Starr for The Beatles' split, because they had failed to welcome Yoko Ono into their camp. By contrast, Christgau dismissed McCartney's wife as 'the amateur keyboard player who wore his ring'.[117] For the same volume, Christgau also co-authored an article with John Piccarella that insisted that 'John was The Beatles' chief composer and singer, edging Paul out statistically (by about fifteen percent) and thrashing him aesthetically.'[118] Lennon was the rock 'n' roller, while McCartney was more partial to 'fancy pop chords and corny pop tunes'.[119] Lennon had 'more energy, more conviction, more emotion, more humor, more ideas and probably more sheer talent'. In a parenthesized 'note to McCartneyites', they added bitchily, 'We said talent, not facility and/or technique.'[120]

Data scientist Dan Raviv calculates Lennon as the principal writer of just 1.5 per cent more Beatles songs than McCartney.[121] Besides getting the mathematics wrong, Christgau and Piccarella also overlooked the nature of Lennon's post-Beatles writing, which was often restricted, not enhanced, by his purist commitment to the principles of rock 'n' roll. In his book about music's debilitating obsession with its own recent history, Simon Reynolds diagnoses that by the 1970s Lennon had 'felt a desperate need to ground himself after a mid-sixties phase of constant LSD intake that had left him with a tenuous sense of self'.[122] Fifties rock 'n' roll had reminded Lennon of a pre-psychedelic era of innocence, before fame had transformed his entire life; a time when his distant mother, Julia, the Elvis fan who had taught her son banjo and purchased his first guitar, was still alive. Lennon's mission had become one of stripped-back, no-frills, direct authenticity: 'primal-scream therapy meets back-to-basics rock'n'roll', as Reynolds describes it.[123] It resulted in some sublime moments of musical catharsis, for sure, but also a conspicuous amount of disposable, standardized, uninspired, nostalgic filler.

It would take some time before Lennon's post-Beatles work could be recognized as so inconsistent. Criticism would have been deemed distasteful when the world was freshly grieving. The final John Lennon and Yoko Ono album, *Double Fantasy*, was released three weeks before the murder took place. When Lennon died, several newspapers and magazines declined to publish their already written negative reviews. Some editors commissioned respectful rewrites. For the time being, Lennon would be remembered, as he had once declared himself, as The Beatles' sole unquestionable genius.

The hallowed reverence awarded to dead rock stars did little to offset the disrespect levelled towards those still living. Rob Reiner's 1984 spoof documentary *This Is Spiñal Tap* is considered a watershed moment in laying bare the inherent absurdity of rock stars, especially those at a certain downward stage in their career. Thereafter, such figures became harder to accept as serious artistes.[124] *This Is Spiñal Tap* was not the first mockumentary to satirize the lives of popular musicians, however. As momentous as it was, Reiner's movie did not establish the format. You could say The Beatles had sent themselves up, in postmodern mockumentary style, in *A Hard Day's Night*. And six years prior to Spıñal Tap's movie, *The Rutles: All You Need Is Cash* (1978) had been aired. This was a feature-length extension of a sketch from Eric Idle's BBC Two series *Rutland Weekend Television*. Presented by Idle's hapless anchor, the film charted the story of 'the prefab four . . . who created a musical legend that will last a lunchtime'. The Rutles' songs were written by Neil Innes of Bonzo Dog Doo-Dah Band, whose McCartney connections had included a cameo in *Magical Mystery Tour* (1967) and a 1968 hit, 'I'm the Urban Spaceman', co-produced by the man himself. Innes's Rutles songs included 'I Must Be in Love', 'Let's Be Natural' and 'Ouch!' His musical parodies were so closely reminiscent of the (real) Fab Four's originals that the owners of the latter's catalogue took Innes to court, snapping up royalties and legally changing the songwriting credits to 'Lennon-McCartney-Innes' (and in fewer cases 'Harrison-Innes').[125] Consistently less enthusiastic than any of his bandmates when reminiscing about Beatlemania and the difficulties in escaping its shadow, George Harrison had been delighted by the idea of Idle's mickey-taking movie. To help shape the script, Harrison even gave Idle a rough cut of the proposed Beatles documentary that Apple's Neil Aspinall had been trying to complete. *The Long and Winding Road* never did get released. *All You Need Is Cash*, therefore, closely parodied a movie that few people beyond The Beatles' inner circle had even seen.[126] Harrison had a brief cameo in the film, and he later praised The Rutles for having 'liberated' him from The Beatles, 'in a way'.[127] John Lennon and Yoko Ono were said to be fans of the spoof, albeit at greater distance. When the former was asked about it, he would start singing The Rutles' psychedelic ballad 'Cheese and Onions'. Innes was told that Ringo Starr enjoyed most of the movie but the drummer became too emotional towards the end because it reminded him so vividly of the real band's break-up.[128]

McCartney was less pleased to be spoofed, particularly because journalists kept bugging him about The Rutles when he was trying to promote *London Town*, the Wings album that was released in March 1978; its timing happened to coincide with the mockumentary's broadcast. Such questions tended to receive a curt 'no comment'. According to Idle, McCartney did gradually warm to the comedy once Linda had persuaded her husband that it was genuinely funny, and affectionately so.[129] This is amusing in itself, given that one of the film's sequences shows its Macca equivalent, Dirk McQuickly, as a simperingly henpecked figure, doing everything he is told by his foreign bride (played by Bianca Jagger, no less). As affectionate as *All You Need Is Cash* had been, the band that it lampooned had become less of a sacred cow than before. The gloves were off, with huge implications for the member who would receive the most symbolic and satirical beatings in subsequent years. Needless to say, this was Paul.

Mockery of McCartney, whether fondly or considerably less so, would appear in Douglas Adams's novel *Life, the Universe and Everything* (1982), the biting TV series *Spitting Image* (begun in 1984) and countless BBC Radio 4 comedy shows, and that's before we even glance at the pages of the music press. Not that there's anything necessarily wrong with that. There are those who say that one of the worst national characteristics of the English is that we hate success. We will ridicule any person of notable achievement. We will strive to bring them down a peg or two, for little reason other than they have done considerably better than the rest of us. For the political cartoonist Martin Rowson, this is one of our greatest shared qualities. To laugh at our superiors, be they social, political, economic or otherwise, is therapeutic. It makes us feel better about ourselves. It is also an egalitarian process. Rowson sees this is as satire's most important function: its purpose, he says, 'to tear aside the fine raiments and the ceremonial clothing of the elite to show that they are sweating, stinking, shitting, pissing people just like us'.[130] Thus it gives us some power back over the politician, the celebrity, the tax-dodging business tycoon or whoever else is being lampooned. It helps to level out matters by jerking back down – if only symbolically – those who have ascended the hierarchy. It can be healthy for the satirized as well. McCartney likes to show how down-to-earth he remains, despite all his accomplishments, so some old-fashioned ridicule probably does him a bit of good by helping to keep that ego in check.[131] The journalist Tom Doyle observes that McCartney can be 'as slippery as a politician' when interviewed. He's well practised in skirting awkward questions and knows how to talk at length without giving much away. He can be prone to dishing out anecdotes he's told countless times before. Sometimes he appears a little bored by the whole palaver. 'At the same time,' observes Doyle,

> perhaps because he is surrounded by reverence most of the time, he seems to relish repartee, to enjoy measured mickey-taking. He is, of course, a man few ever dare to say no to, never mind lightly take the piss out of. But it's clear that he loves getting back in touch with the rougher, former working-class Macca, who is never too far away.[132]

Greater offence was inflicted by the more serious texts that were published in the aftermath of Lennon's death. Adding to the avalanche of anti-Macca reflections, obits and anthologies came Philip Norman's bestselling *Shout! The True Story of The Beatles* (1981).[133] Its critical and commercial success benefited from the unforeseen death of Lennon, which occurred a few months before the publication date. *Shout!* was the first major biography about The Beatles since Hunter Davies's authorized effort in 1968 and was extremely well received. Many still consider it to be one of the best books ever written about the band. In recent years, *Pitchfork* has praised the way *Shout!* places The Beatles' phenomenal work in the context of the 'tumultuous' 1960s period.[134] A 2020 listicle on *Rolling Stone*'s website says Norman 'nails the Hamburg period better than anyone'.[135] 'If you read one book about the Fab Four . . .' recommended *The Times* in 2021.[136] To the despair of experts such as Erin Torkelson Weber, more than 100,000 readers seem to have lapped up *Shout!* as legitimate history.[137] Under proper scrutiny, the 'true' nature of Norman's story unravels. As Weber demonstrates with calm and collected incredulity, *Shout!*'s major shortcomings are threefold: 'inadequate historical distance, lack of documentation, and deliberate authorial bias'.[138] Norman considered Lennon to be 'three-quarters' of The Beatles, as he declared when promoting the book, and its content reflects this partiality. Harrison's and Starr's contributions are barely considered, while McCartney is painted as the story's arch-villain. As Weber concludes, with insubstantial evidence to support its thesis, *Shout!* presents Lennon's 'creative inferior' (McCartney) as 'conniving, conventional, egotistical, shallow and manipulative: a Machiavelli with a gift for melody'.[139] Norman softened his views later, when hawking his 2016 biography of McCartney. The damage had set in long before. Successive editions and *Shout!*'s continued reputation as one of the 'best' Beatles biographies mean that Norman's inaccuracies have perpetuated various misconceptions about its subjects.

Decades after the publication of *Shout!*, observes Weber, much Beatles historiography faithfully followed the narrative set by Norman, and even today some of its fallacies are repeated as 'truth'.[140] Norman's narrative had itself borrowed heavily and unquestioningly from Wenner's *Lennon Remembers*. This text, as we have seen, had been renounced by Lennon himself in 1971 while Norman was working on his inaccurate biography. Alas, that inconvenience was ignored.

McCartney is said to have renamed Norman's book *Shite!*, although the source of this rumour may be the author himself, who has repeated it often as if it's a badge of pride. McCartney certainly wasn't happy with Norman. Nor was he impressed by the publications that followed, particularly those written by people who could cash in on their intimate relationship with The Beatles. They included books by sacked drummer Pete Best, early manager Allan Williams, personal assistant Peter Brown, and Pete Shotton, who'd once played in The Quarrymen and had remained friends with the others, especially Lennon, thereafter. Paul's brother dropped the pseudonymous surname 'McGear', reverting to Mike McCartney, and brought out the book *Thank U Very Much: Mike McCartney's Family Album* (1981), with him and Paul pictured on its cover. 'It's a pity, all that stuff,' Paul told *Music Express*.

> The worst thing about it is that it spoils immediate personal relationships. When I meet those people, I start thinking, 'Well, I've gotta watch what I'm going to say now because it might be in the next book.' You do get a feeling that they're sort of hanging on and living off you, which is not a nice feeling.[141]

He is said to have expressed this in more colourful terms in private. In that interview at least, he had some empathy for Mike's motivations:

> It's very hard for a brother of someone like me to cope without doing something like that, if he sort of needs some money. If someone asks him to write a book, why shouldn't he – especially if he's a good writer? It's difficult for him to turn down a offer like that.[142]

Goodwill was not shown towards Angie McCartney, the stepmother with whom Paul and Mike would eventually cut all ties. Their relationship had soured since the death of the brothers' father, Jim, in 1976. Five years later, Angie sold her story to *The Sun*, revealing 'the mean side' of McCartney. She accused him of refusing to help her out of debts incurred when trying to make it as a theatrical agent.[143] Paul also became dogged by paternity claims. Having found the information in Peter Brown's book, *The Sun* reported that Brian Epstein had once paid off Anita Howarth, who had claimed McCartney was the father of her son. 'He was a friend,' Linda said of Brown's betrayal. 'A man I trusted . . . Now it's like he doesn't exist.' The McCartneys didn't read Brown's book. Having received a copy and knowing what it contained, they burned it page by page as Linda took photographs of this ritual purging.[144] Another paternity claim, dating back to The Beatles' Hamburg days, was made by Erika Hübers and her daughter Bettina. Blood tests cleared McCartney as the woman's father, but the case dragged on as the claimants refused to accept the results had not been doctored.[145]

Characters from the Wings era resurfaced too. Both Denny Laine and his ex-wife Jo Jo sold stories to the press. In 1984 *The Sun* published a series of articles, headlined 'The Real McCartney', in which Denny described Paul and Linda as tight-fisted potheads who got their kicks from smuggling bags of weed through customs. (If they succeeded, that is, unlike when entering Japan in 1980 or returning from Barbados in 1984.) Both Laines described Paul as a 'mummy's boy' who would be lost without his ersatz mother, Linda.[146] Such pressures and stresses, compounded by the media, help to explain why McCartney was not at his most confident or robust in the period directly following Lennon's death.

## When He Wasn't Fab

The first Paul McCartney album to be released in the wake of Lennon's murder was *Tug of War* in 1982. Glad to hear that George Martin was producing McCartney once more, *Rolling*

*Stone* even awarded full marks to the album, albeit in a review that compared the title track to Lennon's 'Imagine' and spent two paragraphs discussing McCartney's tribute to his late friend, 'Here Today'.[147] Understandably, that song has endured as one of McCartney's most popular pieces from that time. It is a shame that *Tug of War*'s more curious cuts have been overshadowed by this as well as 'Ebony and Ivory', McCartney's hit duet with Stevie Wonder. Another Wonder-assisted song, 'What's That You're Doing?', is far groovier, as is the bizarre Latin-soul-funk number 'Dress Me Up as a Robber', whereas 'The Pound Is Sinking' is a three-minute, multipart rock epic based on a financial news headline. 'Ebony and Ivory' is seen as the epitome of McCartney's oversimplistic 'why can't we just work it out?' hippie mawkishness. In 2007 listeners of BBC 6 Music would vote it the worst duet ever recorded.[148] Katie Kapurch and Jon Marc Smith, researchers in English, accept that this 'horrifically cheesy ode to racial harmony' is well meaning. They also find it 'reflective of the post-1960s "color-blind" movement, which scholars such as Leslie G. Carr have argued is actually a racist ideology in that it seeks to absorb black Americans into a white hegemony.'[149] This kind of 'neo-liberal idealism', write Kapurch and Smith, is 'foundational to the post-racial American sensibility'. It 'obscures the recognition of ongoing political, social, and economic inequalities and injustice experienced by people of color'.[150] Whether analysing its lyrics that closely or not, for many listeners 'Ebony and Ivory' was the final nail in the coffin of Macca's credibility.

His next two studio albums were received less warmly, both critically and commercially. Including offcuts that hadn't made it onto *Tug of War*, 1983's *Pipes of Peace* was a smooth and fairly forgettable affair. Reverting to its traditional stance, *Rolling Stone* lamented the record's abundance of yet more 'silly love songs' and 'unforgivable doses of saccharine'.[151] Penny Reel insisted he didn't hold the same contempt for Macca as fellow writers at the *NME* and had zero interest in the 'envious considerations' of various Beatles biographers. Yet even this apparently objective ear heard only a 'dull, tired and empty collection of quasi-funk and gooey rock arrangements . . . with McCartney cooing platitudinous sentiments on a set of lyrics seemingly made up on the spur of the moment'.[152] As J. D. Considine of *Musician* magazine fretted, it seemed as though McCartney was finally succumbing to 'terminal cuteness'.[153]

*Pipes of Peace* featured another pair of duets, this time with Michael Jackson. When recording together, McCartney recommended that Jackson invest in music publishing. McCartney had done very well out of this himself since taking the same advice from Lee Eastman in 1969. Jackson soon purchased the rights to a catalogue that included most of The Beatles' songs. McCartney and Lennon had signed these away in their financially naive youth. Having long lacked possession of their own songs, the surviving Beatles now had to watch their legacy cheapened by, for example, the appearance of 'Revolution' in a marketing campaign for Nike footwear.[154] Such licencing also helped to perpetuate some of the who-did-what myths surrounding their work. A later magazine advertisement for the coffee brand Maxwell House featured a large illustration of John Lennon's signature spectacles, its rims formed from coffee-mug stains, accompanied by a quote from 'A Day in the Life' about falling out of bed, going downstairs and drinking a cup. These words were lifted from the verse written and sung by McCartney.

*Press to Play*, released in 1986, sold less well than any of McCartney's previous albums. The critic at the *Los Angeles Times* viewed it as 'basically just another in a long line (over 12 years!) of post-*Band on the Run* letdowns by a once almost unimaginably creative artist'.[155] In the days when it was difficult to hear much of a record without purchasing it yourself (or knowing somebody who had, or else waiting for the local library to stock a copy), *Press to Play*'s lower sales may have been impacted by its presentation. The front cover is a romantic portrait of Paul and Linda, photographed by George Hurrell in the style of the pictures he'd taken of Hollywood stars in the 1930s and '40s. Hurrell had recently done similar jobs for the likes of Midge Ure and Queen. Even so, this old-fashioned image of the McCartneys hardly indicated that here was an artist at the cutting edge. In its finer moments, *Press to Play* feels bold, experimental and futuristic, as on the unusual single 'Pretty Little Head', which sounds influenced by dark synth-pop princes Depeche Mode but, alas, failed to chart. At other times, the contemporary production impedes rather than elevates the songs, inhibiting any sense of timelessness and securing their fate as 1980s obscurities. With accompaniment by Pete Townshend and Phil Collins, 'Angry' is one such missed opportunity. Howled towards an unnamed foe, almost certainly an individual from the press, Paul's lyrics reveal that he took criticism personally and couldn't brush it off as breezily as he often made out in interviews. Sadly, the production dampens much of his pent-up rage. Eric Stewart of 10cc had co-written several of *Press to Play*'s songs, but he left the recording sessions after a disagreement with McCartney over the quality of the material. When Stewart finally received a copy of the album he'd walked out on, he felt that the immediacy of the co-writers' demos had been suffocated by excessive overdubs.[156] Producer Hugh Padgham, who had been appointed to modernize McCartney's sound, endured the tense sessions and later told biographer Howard Sounes that McCartney was boring, short-tempered, lazy, intimidating, indecisive and prone to smoking debilitating quantities of marijuana.[157] He also seemed (in Sounes's words, presumably based on Padgham's testimony) 'obsessed with what the public thought of him in relation to John Lennon'.[158] Can he be blamed on that front? When displayed by McCartney, the negative traits listed by Padgham are interpreted as a severe deficiency of moral character or indicative of a hypocrisy that reveals him to be not as down to earth and chipper as he likes to convey. Apply them to Lennon and they would feed into that tantalizing narrative of the 'tortured genius'. *Press to Play* is not considered McCartney's lowest point of that decade, however, and 'Angry' was likely inspired by the response to his big-screen turkey.

Paul McCartney has mastered many things in his lifetime. Film-making is not one of them. It started well with *A Hard Day's Night*, though he was but a player doing what he was told. Its follow-up was also a smash, albeit less so with the critics. By the time they were filming *Help!*, The Beatles had discovered weed and LSD. They weren't particularly interested in making another

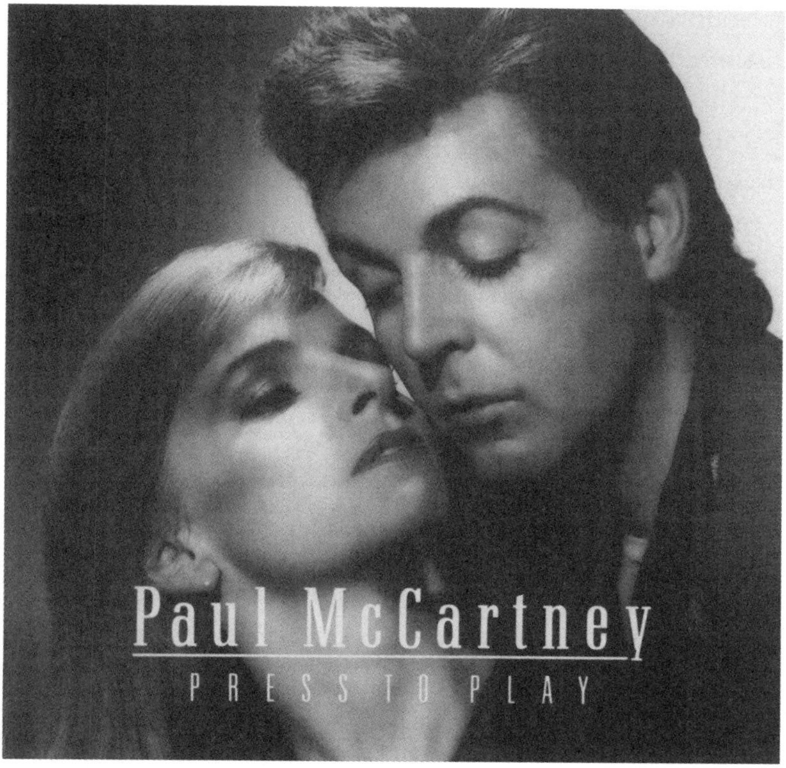


Paul and Linda pose as old-timey movie stars on the cover for *Press to Play* (1986).

movie and, unlike their more disciplined recording sessions, treated the filming like a holiday.[159] Paul was more hands-on with 1967's *Magical Mystery Tour*, later crediting himself as its driving force and de facto director.[160] It was 'in the spirit of the times', McCartney recalled, to make most of it up as they went along, improvising many of its scenarios and editing them afterwards into something they could just about sell to the BBC off the back of the band's popularity.[161] The movie continued the theme of the 'Strawberry Fields Forever/Penny Lane' double A-side single, released earlier that same year, in that it drew inspiration from acid counterculture and the avant-garde arts movements of the 1960s as well as the ostensibly more mundane reminiscences of an upbringing in post-war Liverpool. Lennon and McCartney had fond memories of these day trips, which transported old folks, mostly, to some unknown location. If boarding the bus in Liverpool, Paul noted, the mysterious destination was likely to be Blackpool.[162] For the movie, they upped the surrealism by singing about (and dressing up as) walruses and whatnot, bringing to fruition a dream Lennon had experienced about shovelling spaghetti onto an overweight diner's plate, and introducing various other on-the-hoof hijinks. It has its fans. The strange and haphazard nature of the film displeased, confused and even angered plenty of viewers, however. Its reception wasn't helped by it being first broadcast in black and white on Boxing Day at 8.45 p.m. 'It was probably a mistake really in retrospect because those people probably wanted Bruce Forsyth,' McCartney reflected.[163]

*Magical Mystery Tour* is often cited as The Beatles' first flop. With that in mind, McCartney could have put greater care, consideration and preparation into 1984's *Give My Regards to Broad Street*. His minimal outline for *Magical Mystery Tour* had been presented on a single sheet of paper. On this, McCartney had drawn a circle, divided into different sections with vague ideas on what should happen in each part of the movie. While slightly more substantial than that previous effort, McCartney's 'script' for his new film was scribbled on any spare paper to hand when his car was stuck in traffic jams. It reportedly ran to 21 more pages than the outline for *Magical Mystery Tour* – still thin in industry terms and much less substantial than another script, ultimately rejected, that Willy Russell and Mike Ockrent had been asked to work on in the Wings days.[164] Those who'd been involved in these chaotic movie projects suggested that McCartney failed to grasp that making a film is a very different process from jumping into the studio to record an album of songs.[165] It generally requires greater collaboration, organization, time, money, energy, pre-production and planning. Unless you're the next Wim Wenders, shooting on the fly is rarely going to cut it.

The Bee Gees' *Sgt. Pepper* fiasco and the kitschy *Beatlemania* on Broadway should have acted as further omens. Perhaps McCartney thought that a musical starring the man himself – and not Peter Frampton – would prove to be the real deal. Instead, this 'aberration' has gone down in history as 'ill-advised', 'ill-conceived' and 'unwatchable'.[166] America's most famous film critic, Roger Ebert, advised readers to avoid the movie altogether and head straight to its tie-in soundtrack album. There was a caveat there, too, in that people were likely to own a lot of it already. It includes several Beatles songs, rerecorded in fairly close resemblance to the originals. As for the film, Ebert thought it harked back to the frivolous pop musicals that had pre-dated the freshness of The Beatles' filmography. With 'paper-thin characters', it was close to being a 'nonmovie', he wrote, full of 'long musical interludes that have been photographed with a remarkable lack of style' and 'idiotic dream sequences'.[167] Paul Grein of *Variety* compared it to three recent features of similarly poor repute: Olivia Newton-John's *Xanadu* (1980), Rick Springfield's *Hard To Hold* (1984) and, yes, the aforementioned Bee Gees blunder.[168] 'There are only 50 shopping days till Christmas, so let's go out on a limb – *Give*

*My Regards to Broad Street* is the worst movie of the year,' opened Paul Attanasio's review for the *Washington Post*. The film was 'egomania run riot', and Attanasio wasn't convinced by its hero's allegiances: 'McCartney claims the moral high ground by taking sides with the little people against the corporadoes – but just what does he have against big business? Coming from one of the richest men in the world, it sticks in your craw.'[169] According to Eric Stewart, the movie's Leicester Square premiere was met with an awkward silence as the end credits rolled.[170] As reported in an item on the Channel 4 national news, the film had taken two years to make and cost $9 million, some of which had come from Paul's own purse. In the United States it opened in 311 cinemas. Four weeks later, this had fallen to 28.[171]

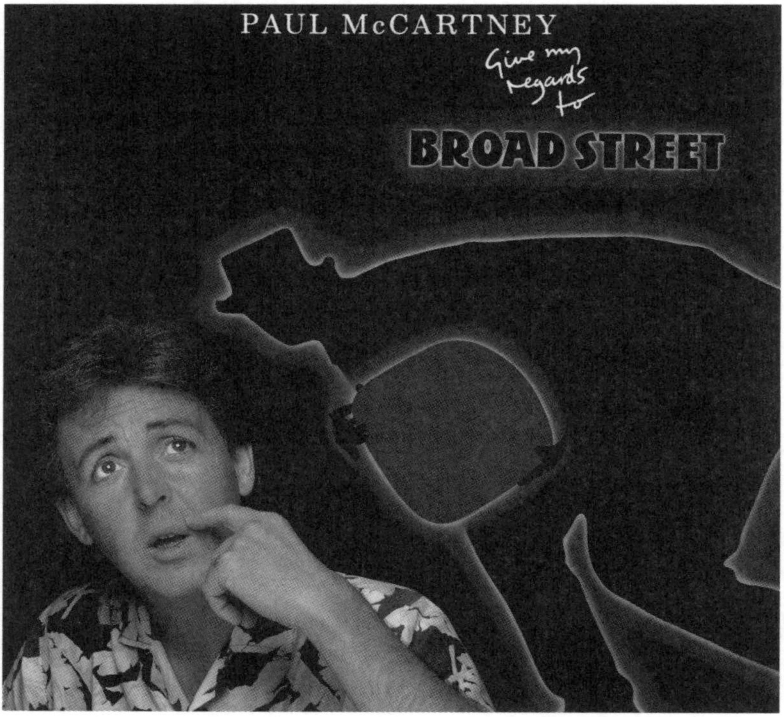


McCartney seems haunted by something on the cover of the *Give My Regards to Broad Street* soundtrack album (1984).

The extensive publicity campaign turned into an exercise in damage limitation for McCartney and his funders, 20th Century Fox. 'It hasn't been badly received, actually,' McCartney claimed in a TV interview with Russell Harty. 'But with me, if there's, like, 25 per cent bad criticism, that becomes the story. There's actually been 75 per cent very good reviews, but you don't notice them. It's not as good a story.'[172] If that was the correct ratio, the three-quarters of positive write-ups remain harder to track down than those in the alleged fault-finding minority. Asked by Harty whether he took such criticisms to heart, McCartney's brave mask slipped: 'Well, I mean, I'm glad there's 75 per cent good reviews . . . Erm. You can't . . . I care. Yes. 'Course you do. Everyone cares.'[173] After this moment of vulnerability, McCartney went on to complain about exaggerated media reports of his immense wealth and parsimonious nature. This may have stuck in more people's craw.

In a 1987 article for the *Popular Music* journal, Henry W. Sullivan offered a rare, more generous assessment of *Give My Regards to Broad Street*, one that draws on the work of Jacques Lacan and other psychoanalysts. Accepting that the film was aesthetically unsuccessful, Sullivan sees it as 'a fascinating failure' nonetheless.[174] For Sullivan, *Give My Regards to Broad Street* shows McCartney working through emotionally 'unfinished business', psychologically speaking and subliminally so.[175] Most overtly, the film's main character (who is a blend of the real McCartney and a fictionalized version) visits an elderly man named Jim, played by Ralph Richardson. 'You're always running around. Don't get a chance to see anybody,' Jim tells him. 'If you didn't run around so much, you might get a better view of the world.' McCartney has said this character was based on *Hamlet*'s Polonius, but it is clearly an opportunity for Paul to re-engage with his late father. Jim McCartney had died in March 1976 and, as reported in Mike McCartney's *Family Album*, Paul had not attended the funeral. In a less obvious reading, Sullivan sees another character, Harry, who is a shady ex-convict suspected of stealing Paul's latest master tapes, as a 'surrogate' for John Lennon.[176] Like Lennon, Harry is more of a tearaway than the politer and better-behaved McCartney. The missing tape box represents the idea that, on breaking up The Beatles, Lennon had 'absconded with their common genius'.[177] As for McCartney's unresolved feelings about Lennon's violent end, the Harry character is 'clubbed three times in the movie; thrown once and stabbed once: a total of five blows'.[178] This equals the number of shots fired into Lennon by his killer. Thus, the film's 'foggy Dickensian back streets' symbolize the towering Dakota building.[179] McCartney was not consciously aware of his real reasons for making the film, poses Sullivan. It's a convincing case nevertheless, especially when you consider McCartney's tendency, it seems, to avoid handling loss head-on. There's his non-presence at funerals. The 'It's a drag' controversy comes to mind. Then there's his enthusiasm for story-based, character-driven, poetic, abstract or even nonsensical lyrics, rather than delving into his deepest feelings and foregrounding these for all the world to gawp at, as Lennon was prone to do.

You don't have to buy into Sullivan's Lacanian interpretation to gauge where McCartney's head was during this time. The plot's missing master tapes could also be channelling his frustration with The Beatles' publishing rights being owned by different parties: Michael Jackson and others before him. This was an ongoing nightmare in McCartney's professional life, and the movie makes use of dream sequences, after all. In 1973, while working in Lagos, Paul and Linda had been mugged at knifepoint and had all their demo recordings stolen. Wings triumphed over this adversity by completing *Band on the Run*, but the assault could still have been in mind, post-traumatically speaking. To circle back to punk, McCartney said the film's plot was inspired by a conversation with Chris Thomas, who had cut his teeth assisting on The Beatles' self-titled 'White Album' before going on to produce acts including Sex Pistols. The master tapes for 1977's *Never Mind the Bollocks, Here's the Sex Pistols* had been mislaid, Thomas informed McCartney. The latter used this anecdote to mould his own story's premise. As such, he could also have been wrestling with the desire to recapture his fashionableness from the younger punks who'd pilfered it.[180]

Partly, I think, *Give My Regards to Broad Street* acted as a substitute, inadequate as it was, for McCartney's lack of live activities since the disbandment of Wings. He and Linda were busy raising their kids, with no nannies involved and education provided by the local comprehensive school, as their interviewers were often reminded. While this made for better-adjusted children, it wasn't natural for McCartney to be away from the road for so long. Before The Beatles split, he had hoped they would return to live performance at some point. Others in the group could not be persuaded beyond one short concert on a Savile Row rooftop in January 1969. McCartney had been keen to get Wings in front of spectators before they were even fully ready. On their debut tour, Wings had freewheeled up and down Britain, turning up at universities and asking to play, with a similarly impromptu approach to accommodation. Their repertoire at that point was so limited that if audiences wanted more, the band had to repeat songs they'd already played earlier in the gig.[181] Given the circumstances of Lennon's death, McCartney could be forgiven for his greater reclusiveness. He worried that his own assassin could be lurking around any corner or in the audiences at his concerts, were he to book any.[182] Paul's cousin, Mike Robbins, observed that McCartney had fretted about kidnappings, too, since he and Linda had started their family.[183] During *Give My Regards to Broad Street*'s promotion, newspapers reported that, about a year earlier, Scotland Yard had foiled a plot to kidnap Linda and hold her to ransom.[184] Back when The Beatles had tired of touring, they'd sent music videos to television studios so they could promote their singles without having to travel around the world to perform them personally.[185] *Give My Regards to Broad Street* follows the same philosophy in that, whether intentionally or not, it is less of a fully realized motion picture with a successful plot and convincing performances than a few promo videos for fresh versions of old songs (plus a couples of newbies), strung together with a requisite premise. 'Don't go in there expecting some kind of huge sci-fi blockbuster or something with incredibly deep meaning,' McCartney warned at a press conference for his movie. 'Just go for a pleasant evening out, and I hope you come out of it with a warm glow.'[186] This sounds quite like his attitude towards delivering crowd-pleasing concerts.

One of McCartney's few live spots of the 1980s took place at Live Aid in 1985. The benefit concert, held simultaneously in London and Philadelphia and broadcast widely across the world, raised millions for famine relief in Ethiopia. At the Wembley Stadium leg, Status Quo opened with gusto ('Rockin' All Over the World' being the perfect start to such an event). U2, complete with Bono in the role of Lennon's rock-saviour successor, relished the opportunity to leap a few rungs up the ladder of superstardom. Queen stole the show (sorry, Bono).[187] And Paul McCartney suffered a microphone failure so that nobody in the stadium or watching at home could hear the words to 'Let It Be'. He had to overdub his vocals for the VHS release.

For *Give My Regards to Broad Street* McCartney insisted that all the songs be performed live, which made the production more costly and time-consuming than your average Hollywood musical. In interviews from that time, he talked often about the 'live' elements and popular song choices. 'Either we were going to create a new musical with a whole new score or we were going to think of it as a live show,' he told the press conference in Chicago, pointing out that when people go to see Mick Jagger perform they expect 'Satisfaction' and not a whole setlist of unfamiliar material. Seeing as The Beatles stopped touring after 1966 and only a handful of their songs were introduced into Wings setlists, people had never heard McCartney perform songs like 'For No One' in this way before. That, he figured, 'was a good enough reason to sing them again'.[188] Interviewed briefly about the critical backlash by Peter Sissons on *Channel 4 News*, McCartney acknowledged the difficulties in combining music with plot. 'The people who liked it weren't expecting too much,' he said, 'so that the slight plot that it has – my fault because I wrote it – it really doesn't get in the way of the music. I think personally that it's okay and the more you see it, the better it is.'[189] Given that most reviewers had few qualms about McCartney's music, a straightforward concert film in the spirit of Wings' *Rockshow* (1980) would have been better received. Alas, McCartney was not touring at this time. As it was, in light of this big-screen misstep, the posing of Paul and Linda as classic Hollywood icons on the cover of *Press to Play* looked even more absurd.

Remembered more fondly, by some, was 'We All Stand Together' from the short animation *Rupert and the Frog Song*, which preceded cinema screenings of *Give My Regards to Broad Street*. Using pop-psychology, some have analysed this as McCartney's desire to return to the cocoon-like comfort of his own early childhood. Although McCartney had read some of the stories in his early years, Rupert Bear was of no great significance during his upbringing. As discussed with Harty, McCartney became more interested in the adventures of the scarf-clad bear when reading bedtime stories to his own kids.[190] MPL, the umbrella company established in 1969 to oversee Paul's multiple business interests, had bought the film rights to Rupert with the aim of producing a full-length feature similar to those of the Disney empire. 'But that's not easy to do,' as McCartney told Harty in a rare moment of clarity regarding the complexity of the film-making process.[191]

'We All Stand Together' is a song for children, taken from a kids' cartoon, and on those terms it succeeds wonderfully. It has a comforting theme of fraternal support, lush orchestral arrangements guided by George Martin and Kenneth Sillito, Elena Durán guesting as the froggy flautist, the surprising sound of kazoos at about 3:20, and some of the most unique backing vocals ever to grace the singles charts, so ranine at times they're positively burp-tastic. Still, it was used by many as proof of McCartney's descent from vibrant icon to vanilla dad-rocker, prone to knocking out novelty singles. This coincided with Ringo Starr finding work in narrating the children's TV series *Thomas the Tank Engine and Friends*. Both *Thomas* and *Rupert* were nominated for Best Short Animation at the 1985 BAFTAs, with the bear and his frogs triumphing over the Fat Controller's anthropomorphic train set. 'It's just mind-blowing that Thomas is so big in this day and age,' marvelled Ringo. Created in 1945, Thomas the Tank Engine was 25 years younger than Rupert and another comforting product of an earlier age. 'It used to be "Look! There's Ringo" in the street. Now it's "Look! There's Thomas",' enthused the storyteller of his latest gig. 'Would you believe there's hordes of screaming three-year-olds outside the house?'[192] Critics of these projects had forgotten that The Beatles had also been heavily marketed towards children, *Yellow Submarine* (1968) being far from the only example.

It's worth noting that Rupert was a particularly loaded character to champion because the cartoon bear had featured prominently in the obscenity trial of *Oz* magazine in 1971. Central to the case was the magazine's 'schoolkids' issue, edited by fifth- and sixth-formers. The fourteen-year-old Vivian Berger had contributed illustrations that spliced Rupert into the lewd strips of the underground cartoonist Robert Crumb. It presented an entirely new and sordid adventure in which the once wholesome bear engaged in graphic sex acts. *Oz*'s grown-up editors, Richard Neville, Felix Dennis and Jim Anderson, were subsequently charged with conspiring with younger people to create a publication so obscene as to be morally corrupting. They had been part of the counterculture movement associated with, and promoted by, The Beatles in the 1960s. John Lennon and Yoko Ono marched in protest to the trials and recorded a single with the 'Elastic Oz Band' to raise funds and publicity for the editors' cause. For people who held the same kinds of views towards McCartney as those who made up the Rock Liberation Front, it was disappointing that someone who had once championed titles like *Oz* and Barry Miles's *International Times* was now marketing Rupert in the more traditional manner.

Less remembered, in any capacity, than 'We All Stand Together' is McCartney's 'Spies Like Us' single of 1985. At the time it reached number seven in the U.S. *Billboard* chart and number thirteen in the UK. It came from a comedy film of the same name directed by John Landis. Like McCartney's title song, the picture fared better commercially than critically or in terms of posterity. '*Spies Like Us* is a comedy with exactly one laugh,' complained the *Washington Post*, 'and those among you given to Easter egg hunts may feel free to try and find it.'[193] Despite poor reviews it managed to gross $77.3 million worldwide, but it hardly secured itself a permanent place in the pantheon of great American comedy flicks. Playing most of the single's instruments himself, McCartney came up with a patchwork of obscenely reverbed and monotonous drum beats, a nothingy chant in place of much vocal melody and an intermittent guitar riff that harks back to 'Hey Bulldog'. The final minute is more enjoyably up-tempo, yet it's too little, too late, and the song sits many rungs below the grandeur of Wings' 1973 Bond theme 'Live and Let Die'. A fan of Landis's video for Michael Jackson's 'Thriller' (1983), McCartney had apparently contacted Warner Bros. himself and volunteered to make the theme song free of charge. It was an offer the studio executives couldn't refuse. Landis was flattered. He also thought to himself, 'What the fuck am I going to do with this song?'[194] He stuck it in over the end credits, and it wasn't even included on the official soundtrack album (original score by Elmer Bernstein). Also directed by Landis, the promotional video for 'Spies Like Us' featured Macca and the movie's stars, Chevy Chase and Dan Aykroyd, larking around at Abbey Road. Further hinting that McCartney's well could be running dry, the single had as its B-side 'My Carnival', a previously unreleased song recorded by Wings a decade earlier.

The promotional campaign for *Give My Regards to Broad Street* had coincided with the launch of Julian Lennon's solo career. His debut single, 'Too Late for Goodbyes', reached number six in the UK singles chart. (He hit that position again five years later, with 'Saltwater'.) In the United States, Julian's debut album, *Valotte* (1984), charted higher than Paul's *Give My Regards to Broad Street* album. *Press to Play* performed even lower. Despite the fact that his father had kept their relationship distant, Julian's voice and mannerisms were uncannily similar to John's. This appealed to some of the baby boomers who'd matured, settled down and were too busy raising kids to keep track of recent trends such as post-punk, new wave, synth-pop or new romanticism. Julian's was a weirdly middle-aged sound for a chap in his twenties. If anything, it inflicted further damage on The Beatles' already depleted street cred. 'People are reassured by how much Julian resembles John,' *Creem*'s Mitchell Cohen explained. 'It's comforting, and gives a sense of continuity that they don't get from Yoko's records.'[195] Others were harsher, such as the self-styled 'dean of American rock critics', Robert Christgau. 'Aside from the eerie vocal resemblance,' he wrote of *Valotte*, 'this is bland professional pop of little distinction and less necessity – tuneful at times, tastefully produced of course, and with no discernible reason for being, more Frank Sinatra Jr than (even) Hank Williams Jr.'[196] This is how Julian's career tends to be remembered, regardless of the odd hit.[197] While their output doesn't bear comparison, in some ways Julian suffered from the same problem as Paul. Neither one of them was John.

Published at the end of the 1980s, Chet Flippo's biography of McCartney was hesitant to write off the man completely. It was acknowledged that he had bounced back before, with *Wings over America* and 'Mull of Kintyre', when he had already 'been ruled out as an old fart'.[198] McCartney had then been in his mid-thirties. He was now pushing fifty. 'Gone now are those boyish good looks,' lamented another biographer, Chris Salewicz, 'in their place is a face deeply etched with lines.'[199] Any subsequent comeback would be a taller order and, in the 1980s, was tougher to envisage. Flippo diagnosed an 'erosion of [McCartney's] musical judgement, with an attendant decline in his musical self-confidence'. These were exacerbated by, according to an anonymous ex-employee cited by the unofficial biographer, 'the effects of long-term marijuana use'.[200]

The irreverent writers at *Smash Hits* nicknamed the ex-Beatle 'Fab Macca Wacky Thumbs Aloft', which may have contributed, as identified by Ian Leslie at the beginning of this chapter, to his perceived similarity to a game-show host. As the end of the 1980s neared, nobody predicted that Paul McCartney would go on to headline Glastonbury at the age of eighty in the unfathomably distant future of 2022. Nor did they expect him to headline there in his early sixties, which he did in 2004. The unbelievers were wrong. McCartney's story wasn't over yet. John Lennon was frozen. The Beatles were frozen. Paul McCartney was not.

# 2
# Off the Ground and Back on the Road

As a new decade loomed, Paul McCartney's mojo began to creep back into business. Reeling from the shaky 1980s, and having abandoned a whole album's worth of material recorded with multiple Grammy-winning producer Phil Ramone, McCartney went back to basics by recording a collection of oldies. The sessions were completed, live in the studio, in just two days. McCartney's management considered the project too similar to John Lennon's *Rock 'n' Roll* album of 1975, which is exactly how it would have been received had it been released in a conventional manner. Instead, it was licensed to the Russian label Melodiya under the title *СНОВА В СССР* (which translates as 'Back in the USSR'), the nature of its release making it a collectable export and curio deemed worthy of positive reviews. This reception was not lost on McCartney, who said he was now considering making an album that wouldn't be released at all: 'I'll just have one copy buried somewhere in Ohio.'[1]

In 1987, the same year he recorded *СНОВА В СССР*, McCartney agreed to another backwards-looking project in the form of a greatest hits package. This spanned the Wings era and solo years up to that point. The American edition had a slightly different tracklist, demonstrating the popularity of certain songs in different territories. There was, for instance, no 'Mull of Kintyre' or 'We All Stand Together' on the U.S. version. Americans were also spared the newly recorded 'Once Upon a Long Ago', an omission for which they might have been grateful. Culled from the Ramone sessions, the song was reportedly rejected from inclusion on the soundtrack to *The Princess Bride* on the grounds that director Rob Reiner found it too slushy.[2] McCartney preferred to think of his soft-rock ballad, featuring saxophonist Stan Sulzmann and celebrity violinist Nigel Kennedy, as 'quite a haunting thing'.[3] The cutesy animated section of the promotional video suggested he was still daydreaming of turning MPL into the next Walt Disney Studios, a 'haunting' thought in some respects. By their nature, greatest hits compilations cash in on nostalgia. This one came quickly after the *Give My Regards to Broad Street* soundtrack, and there had already been a *Wings Greatest* in 1978. The latest collection's title, *All the Best!*, read like the sign-off at the end of a letter or a note of resignation, even. Some of McCartney's apologetic fans secretly hoped it might be.

In reality, Paul McCartney hardly saw retirement as a feasible option. He says he once fired a manager for even suggesting such an idea,[4] although encouraging a client not to work does seem a counterintuitive measure from the perspective of earning a worthwhile business percentage. It's especially unlikely that McCartney would have considered putting his feet up at the exact moment when George Harrison was enjoying his own startling comeback. In 1987 Harrison had finally followed up 1982's poorly received *Gone Troppo* with an album called *Cloud Nine*. Harrison needed it to sell well, as his HandMade Films production company was on the wane. Lo and behold, it did just that. The album included 'Got My Mind Set on You', a song penned by Rudy Clarke and first recorded by James Ray in 1962. Harrison's take was duller than a bucket of unseasoned soup. Its lines about how much money it will take to win over a prospective suitor were old-fashioned by then, and somewhat at odds with Harrison's habit of criticizing materialism (albeit from the confines of his mansion). Boosted by a widely broadcast video that ripped off Sam Raimi's *Evil Dead II* (released earlier that year), minus the gore, the bland single reached number one in Australia, Belgium, Canada, Ireland and the United States. It was kept off the top spot in the UK by T'Pau's infinitely superior 'China in Your Hand'. Another hit single was found in 'When We Was Fab', a song about The Beatles that sounds like a Kid606 remix of 'Pole Grinder' by Revolting Cocks. Only joking. It sounds like The Beatles circa 1967. It's even got Ringo on the drums. It was co-written and produced by Jeff Lynne, who'd specialized in the same kind of imitative style with his Electric Light Orchestra. Following *Cloud Nine*, Harrison and Lynne had further worldwide success in the Traveling Wilburys, their supergroup with Roy Orbison, Bob Dylan and Tom Petty. 'I don't really know if George's success spurred me on,' McCartney half-confessed. 'I'm not really aware of it, but there probably was a bit of that.'[5]

His next album, *Flowers in the Dirt* (1989), was hailed in some quarters as Paul McCartney's return to form. In retrospect, that was a bit too giddy, as it was more like a step in the right direction. Some listeners were impressed by, as co-writer on a handful of songs, the presence of Elvis Costello, who was of the punk generation but had never really been *very* punk. An acquired taste, Costello's nasally vocals also take co-lead on 'You Want Her Too'. The contrast doesn't work particularly well, other than to remind listeners of McCartney's superior golden tones, not to mention those of a certain ex-writing partner. A ridiculous number of individuals are credited with production on the album. Like *Pipes of Peace*, the recording is heavily glossed and lightly funky, with a little more chutzpah in terms of the songwriting itself.

The album's sales were given a large boost by McCartney's return to touring, a more significant factor in his revival as a creative and commercial force. He would have been wise to tour first, actually, so he could have road-tested the new songs, if brave enough to confront his audiences with such unfamiliar material. Then he could've laid them down quickly with the live band in the studio, à la *СНОВА В СССР*, once they'd had time to develop, breathe and bulk up a little. You can hear the difference when comparing the studio versions to those *Flowers in the Dirt* tracks that appear on the *Tripping the Live Fantastic* live album of 1990. There's a touch more oomph and a lot more life in them. 'I experimented with computers, and working with producers who take a long time over everything,' McCartney reflected a few years later. 'There are some interesting aspects to working like that but not enough to excite me.'[6]

## Get Out of My Way

Around this time, the quasi-religious reverence that had been applied to John Lennon after his death was beginning to ebb, even in the face of the continued efforts of Yoko Ono and others. This is reflected in reviews of the documentary *Imagine: John Lennon*, commissioned by Ono in 1986 and screened two years later. 'At its best, it's a sensitive tribute; at its worst, it's a hero-worshiping whitewash,' cautioned film critic Michael Wilmington.[7] The year 1988 also saw the publication of Albert Goldman's book *The Lives of John Lennon*, which was rife with unsubstantiated tittletattle. More than that, it was a sustained character assassination, designed to counter hagiographies of the past and the chumminess between musicians and those who mostly get to write about them. Goldman was an academic, not a music journalist, so he claimed to possess greater objectivity.[8] All the same, his book is far from impartial and fails to meet proper academic standards. It does contain a long list of sources (unlike Philip Norman's *Shout!*, for instance), but Goldman's text does not include citations, so its specific allegations are not fully verifiable.[9] Revising Lennon's public image as a peace-preaching Jesus doppelganger, Goldman portrayed him as a violent and megalomanic bully, pitiful drug addict, rapist and even murderer.[10] He claimed Lennon was an antisemite as well; one who was accused of enjoying a long-running homosexual affair with The Beatles' Jewish manager, Brian Epstein.[11] It was a 'piece of trash', according to McCartney, while Ono said it felt like she'd been punched eight hundred times.[12] The book ends on page 699, so Goldman managed to land multiple blows with some of his pages. Its final chapter has the unchivalrous title 'Season of the Witch', and you can guess who's being referred to there. *Rolling Stone* published an article, nearly 6,000 words long, exploring the dubiousness of Goldman's research and testimony.[13]

Thanks to its sensational claims, the book received lots of publicity and reached number two in the *New York Times* bestseller list. The cover of a later edition vaunts it as 'THE MOST TALKED ABOUT BIOGRAPHY OF THE DECADE'. The number of people who read *about* the hefty pathography and discussed its many contentions significantly outnumber those who actually ploughed through the whole thing themselves. Many people were still not quite ready to hear or handle such criticisms of Lennon, especially when it was so scathing and riddled with problems.[14] Goldman's act of iconoclasm did show that Lennon was not a saint in everybody's eyes and that he was no longer the sacred cow of yore. It opened up the possibility that there were alternative ways to assess the musician's life and work. Goldman's was an extreme example, and there would gradually appear more measured assessments, ones that accepted Lennon as a human being who had his flaws and could often be unpleasant company (to put it mildly). Lennon's first wife, Cynthia, and their son, Julian, also became more outspoken about John's shortcomings.[15] Whether separating the art from the artist or not, writers could evaluate Lennon's music in less reverential terms as the gulf widened between his death and the present. The narratives offered by

Jann Wenner's *Lennon Remembers* and Philip Norman's *Shout!* – including Lennon as the heroic genius and McCartney as the cute and opportunistic antagonist – were less broadly swallowed and regurgitated as gospel.

As with the *Imagine* documentary, a 1990 John Lennon tribute concert was received with less warmth than Yoko Ono had hoped. The event was held to celebrate what would have been Lennon's fiftieth birthday (albeit scheduled several months before the proper date) and to raise money for Ono's charity Spirit Foundation. Both Lennon fanatics and non-admirers alike could agree that the event turned out to be a bit of a farce. Taking place in The Beatles' home city of Liverpool, it was co-hosted by the Manchester-born radio DJ Mike Read and none other than *Superman* actor Christopher Reeve. The latter would help sell the footage to an American TV audience to screen on Lennon's actual birthday. Both men read stiffly from autocues, as did Yoko and Sean Ono Lennon. Many genuine locals, it was noted, were unable to attend owing to the expensive entry price. This helped explain why only half the projected 45,000 tickets had been sold. Some Liverpudlians gathered outside the open-air concert site at Pier Head to hear what it sounded like. This included one Jeannette Byers, who, while bottle-feeding her baby, told reporters, 'It isn't for the Scousers. Every Scouser is on the dole.'[16] Those in the arena found themselves bossed around by producers and hosts, like extras in a movie, to help make for a smoother TV edit. As for the celebs, Paul McCartney and Ringo Starr appeared only on-screen via videotape. George Harrison refused to have anything to do with it. Elton John, David Bowie, Bruce Springsteen, Madonna and Michael Jackson were all said to have turned down the opportunity to take part.[17] 'As it was, the sheer mediocrity of it all was as bad as the falsity. Kylie Minogue singing "Help" was not the worst of it,' observed Michael Gray for *The Times*.[18] In interview footage screened before Hall & Oates sat down to run through 'Don't Let Me Down', the one with the moustache said that neither of the duo had been influenced by The Beatles when they were teenagers ('We grew up on a slightly different kind of music').[19] Lou Reed deadpanned his way through 'Jealous Guy' and 'Mother'. More lively was Al Green. Cyndi Lauper wore a mad wig. The ex-singer from Foreigner sported real massive hair. Terence Trent D'Arby wasn't Prince. Lenny Kravitz wasn't Hendrix. Marti Pellow ground his hips and whipped off his jacket like a male stripper during Wet Wet Wet's 'I Feel Fine'. There isn't the space here to run through every aural catastrophe and the malapropos nature of many of the bookings. 'We're thinking of changing our name to The Token Scousers,' quipped Gary from The Christians. Harrison was right to stay away, and Lennon likely would've done too, as Gray's review concluded. In fact, had Lennon been alive and caught these bloodless renditions on his television set, 'he'd have felt like killing himself.'[20]

As Lennon's life and work continued to be celebrated, often dubiously, as well as assessed more critically than before, hatchet jobs on Paul and his reputation had become so passé that the McCartney-bashing itself became an object of satire. *Viz* magazine now ran an article lampooning dirt-dishing biographies of McCartney and the speculative hearsay on which they relied. The piece was written in the style of the sensationalist tabloid stories that would routinely appear in tandem with the publication of such books, complete with eye-catching subheadings including 'AFRAID', 'HATED' and the more absurd 'KAZOO'. Its anecdotes and quotations were said to be lifted from *Portrait of a Tight Arse* by a writer named 'Keith Twatt', published by Bollock Press at a very reasonable £185.99. Lennon's best song about his erstwhile bandmate was called 'Paul's a Bastard', it claimed, 'but it never appeared on any records'. Other revelations included McCartney's visit to EMI Records when he disguised himself as Lennon, 'in a wig and glasses', to try to get his paws on John's royalty cheques. Once

Wings started making money, McCartney would penny-pinch to the extreme, hiring Linda because she wouldn't have to be paid. A trumpeter who was forced to blow so hard in the studio that he lost the strength to drive himself home was offered a lift by McCartney. 'Mean McCartney' then charged the 'poor fellow' more money for the lift than he'd paid him for the session. An unnamed member of Wings was 'sacked on the spot' when he asked Paul for £10 so he could buy some new trousers. The article concluded by ridiculing the desperate lengths that some journalists would go to in their attempts to smear McCartney. 'Next week: The daughter of the lollipop man who once helped Paul across the road to school reveals: "Paul hasn't visited me in 25 years".'[21]

As time went on, McCartney would feel less like he was stepping on other people's toes, or causing unnecessary upset to Lennon fanatics, by taking (spiritual) ownership of old Beatles hits and countering what he considered to be misleading portrayals of the past. McCartney's return to the stage was often compared to the performances of The Beatles' friends and rivals The Rolling Stones, who were still plodding on. They were capable of making a heavier 'ruckus', noted Jon Pareles of the *New York Times*, who sensed McCartney's shows valued straightforward proficiency over any kind of 'rock spontaneity'.[22] Robert Hilburn of the *Los Angeles Times* preferred the ex-Beatle's efforts, which he felt made for a warmer and 'more emotionally satisfying experience' than the Stones, with 'stronger new material' to boot.[23] McCartney's sets contained plenty of solo and Wings numbers, plus older rock 'n' roll covers, but it was the number of 1960s tunes – about half the setlist – that made the headlines. Because The Beatles stopped touring from 1966, McCartney was playing and singing several of these songs in concert for the first time ever. Audiences were thrilled by this, as well as the warmth with which McCartney spoke of his old band. As recently as 1988, Paul had refused to attend the ceremony when The Beatles were inducted into the Rock and Roll Hall of Fame, citing unreconciled business differences.[24] On the tour, he dedicated a song to his 'three mates: George, Ringo and John, without whom it would not have been'. We probably shouldn't read too much into the fact that the tune in question was 'The Fool on the Hill'.[25] As an extra visual kick, McCartney performed it on the trippily painted 'Magic Piano' he'd used back in the 1960s. When the tour reached Birmingham, England, in January 1990, *The Times* hailed 'a man who has at last come to terms with his earlier accomplishments and is no longer afraid to rejoice in them'.[26] The run established the formula for all future Paul McCartney world tours, regardless of personnel. These have remained crowd-pleasing in nature by comparison with the equally admirable but more bull-headed tactics of Neil Young or Bob Dylan, for example. As McCartney told *The Adam Buxton Podcast* in December 2020, his agenda is to give the audience what they want, while also doing some things for himself, without trying too hard to be cool, edgy or difficult. He'd recently seen Dylan perform in New York. Like fellow audience members, he'd struggled to recognize even the most familiar and famous songs:

> When I suddenly hear a bit of a lyric, I go, 'Oh it's that one.' 'Like a Rolling Stone'. I knew that one. But he just changed the melody. And so I kind of have to admire that there's something brave about that. He's got a room full of people who love him and are coming to hear him do that song he loves. But he goes, 'Like a Rolling Stone/ Like a Rolling Sto-one'. And it's like, 'That's not it, Bob!' You know, if he's on a talent contest, you'd get booed off. But I love him. I love his uncompromising stance.[27]

By including so many older songs in his setlists, McCartney risked boxing himself in as an ex-Beatle and little else. However, the confidence he regained by returning to stadiums full of screaming fans helped to spur on the relentless and varied activities he got up to in the 1990s and beyond. He seems to have become (re)possessed with a drive that would keep him working restlessly, on a myriad of varied and often challenging projects, frequently simultaneously, for years to come. Time – since The Beatles' split and Lennon's death – was healing old wounds and insecurities were easing. McCartney's children were older now too. This meant, to borrow father-of-two Cyril Connolly's questionable aphorism, there were no prams in the hallway anymore, threatening to block the corridor of creativity. He had scores to settle, as well. The 'Thumbs Aloft' stereotype would be challenged and challenged again, even if it could never be fully refuted.

## Hope of Deliverance

Encouraged by the excitement of touring with a new band, for his next studio album McCartney was keen to use those same players. They were Hamish Stuart (ex-Average White Band), Robbie McIntosh (from The Pretenders' line-up of the 1980s), Linda McCartney (best known from Wings), Paul 'Wix' Wickens (the only person to have remained in Paul's live act ever since) and Blair Cunningham (another ex-Pretender, replacing drummer Chris Whitten, who'd jumped ship to Dire Straits). It's their feet, along with Paul's, that appear on the cover of 1993's *Off the Ground*.

Two of its songs were exhumed from the previous writing sessions with Elvis Costello. His voice, this time, did not appear. No silly love song, 'Mistress and Maid' is a bleak account of marital misery. 'The Lovers that Never Were', meanwhile, is a tale of unrequited romance with a threatening undertone that might suggest a stalker's obsession. For fans of McCartney's more traditionally romantic songs, there was 'I Owe It All to You', inspired by a visit to Provence's Cathedral of Images on Linda's birthday, and a characteristically pretty piano ballad in the form of 'Golden Earth Girl'. 'Peace in the Neighbourhood' provides another cheerful dose of McCartney's post-hippie optimism. Unfortunately, another plea for togetherness, 'C'mon People', doesn't quite land like McCartney must have hoped it would, despite George Martin's orchestral contribution. Likely written with visions in mind of several thousand cigarette lighters held aloft, when it was performed on the next tour it was reportedly one of the songs that had audience members popping off to the bar or toilets.[28] It is overshadowed, to be honest, by the album's closing moments: a snippet of the more playful 'Cosmically Conscious', which McCartney had written during The Beatles' 1968 trip to Rishikesh.[29]

Songs such as the shuffling character piece 'Biker Like an Icon' were – and remain – divisive.[30] It doesn't really matter how many of its tunes ring your bell, though. The important thing about *Off the Ground* is its relaxed, comfortable and loose feel. McCartney sounds delighted to be recording in an earthier manner, playing live in the studio with his band, to just one co-producer, following some of the more stilted, self-conscious and uncertain works of the 1980s. As well as pulling off the big, slick arena gigs, McCartney had enjoyed appearing with his band on *MTV Unplugged* in 1991. He'd found the prospect nerve-racking ('the nearest thing I've done to a pub gig for a long time'[31]) and had prepared seriously with weeks of rehearsals. Unlike many other acts who appeared on the show over the years, he insisted the set be fully unplugged in a strict sense.[32] No electric pickups or amplified instruments were to be used. Everything was to be played acoustically into microphones. And still it was a looser affair than the bigger gigs. McCartney was so pleased with how it had gone that a limited release of the set was put out as *Unplugged (The Official Bootleg)* with similar artwork to *CHOBA B CCCP*, suggesting a companion piece. Mistakes made at the gig were kept in the final edit.[33]

Match the feet to the band member: *Off the Ground* (1993).

*Off the Ground* received mixed reviews. By this time there was nothing unusual about that. Yet the album was clearly an important one for McCartney. He sees 'Biker Like an Icon' as one of its key pieces because its first take made the finished album. Other cuts, too, were taken straight from recordings of the band warming up:

> We were just kicking numbers around, so that the band would get to know how they went, and we just got a really nice casual take of 'Peace in the Neighbourhood'. We thought later that we could make it a little bit more professional and did try a couple of times but never got the same

> vibe again. It was getting a little bit too stiff so we listened again to the rehearsal take and it was fine. I really love the drum sound on it. As for 'Biker . . .', it's such a simple little song that you can ruin it if you go over it 50 times. Everyone understood how it went, and Robbie [McIntosh] must have had some idea what he was going to do on slide guitar because he just delivered a solo – I didn't tell him when to do it, he just felt it . . . we just did it and got lucky. And the more you listen to the album the more you get to feel that we were enjoying ourselves.[34]

McCartney compared this to The Beatles' early method of working hard and fast, recalling how his old band finished 'I'm Down', 'I've Just Seen a Face' and 'Yesterday' in the same working day. 'I mean, you never do three tracks in a day now,' he added. 'We did get near to it one day . . .'[35]

The approach to his latest set of lyrics was less easy-going, no doubt owing to past criticisms of McCartney's work as banal, superficial or nonsensical. Perhaps with Dylan in mind on this count at least, he took care in crafting words he believed in and of which he could be proud. He asked his friend Adrian Mitchell to vet the works 'as if he was an English teacher checking my homework', to help make them fully 'poet-proof'.[36] Given the political, satirical and pacifist nature of Mitchell's own poems, plays and novels, it made sense that this resulted in the more outspoken lyrics mentioned in my introduction. Mitchell would later endorse McCartney as a legitimate wordsmith when editing the book *Blackbird Singing* (2001). It compiled lyrics from various songs of McCartney's alongside previously unseen poetry. As Mitchell noted in his introduction, the original idea had been Linda's.[37] If anyone had Paul's back in terms of securing the respect that he's owed, it was Linda. Mitchell compared McCartney's output to the 'popular poetry' of Homer, William

Blake and Robert Burns, as well as name-checking modern poets such as Brian Patten and Carol Ann Duffy. It did McCartney no harm that he was 'blessed with one of the subtlest, warmest singing voices of our time', added Mitchell.[38]

Although still successful by most people's standards, 1993's New World Tour didn't go as smoothly as the longer-awaited comeback run of 1989–90. Management had difficulties in lining up sponsors and persuading the McCartney family to cut deals with them.[39] There were also complaints about the price and benefits of special tickets that were sold to help fund the establishment of the Liverpool Institute for Performing Arts, with some promoters giving consumers the misimpression that they would get to meet Paul personally.[40] Without the boost of the last tour's VISA-backed advertisement campaign, there were empty seats in the some of the U.S. stadiums and even in Australasia, a region the previous tour hadn't even touched. Having been hired to turn things around after 1986's relatively low-selling *Press to Play*, manager Richard Ogden now felt compelled to resign.[41] The next live album, *Paul Is Live*, had a humorous title, referencing the conspiracy theory that the 'real' McCartney had died in the late 1960s, and an eye-catching cover that pictured McCartney and his dog recreating that of *Abbey Road*. It's often cited as having failed to sell in the same quantities as *Unplugged (The Official Bootleg)* or *Tripping the Live Fantastic*, and for supplying largely redundant content in light of those. *Paul Is Live* wasn't necessarily intended as a must-have item. As with McCartney's subsequent live albums, it's a commemorative document of the tour, and listeners can take it or leave it as they see fit.

Fatigue with outright bashings of McCartney, as illustrated by the aforementioned *Viz* article, was accompanied by the sense that it no longer seemed such a big deal that McCartney isn't, wasn't and probably never would be objectively 'cool', whatever that means. Andrew Ferguson argues that at one point McCartney had been considered by many as 'the coolest man who ever lived'. This was in his mid-twenties, when McCartney dated Jane Asher and was cock of the walk in Swinging London. After this point, Ferguson diagnoses a rapid descent into 'an antique, unavoidable showbiz figure of long-ago achievement who pops up at every halftime extravaganza, charity concert, royal jubilee, White House PBS special, and lifetime award ceremony'.[42] As we've seen, it has never been as clear-cut as that, but there was a time when people seemed to have forgotten that McCartney had ever been remotely hip in the first place. In 1993 Chris Campling wrote in *The Times* that McCartney had always been 'fundamentally uncool', from his pre-fame boyhood to later superstardom. 'He could sing rock 'n' roll, and play it, and write it (after a fashion). But he did not live it.' By the time of *Give My Regards to Broad Street*, argued Campling, this fundamental lack of coolness had hit its most embarrassing levels of cringe-inducement. Even that writer accepted that one could never write off McCartney for good or deny his impeccable talent: 'he can play the fingers off anyone, sing the throat out of most, and would feel deeply embarrassed were any of his concerts anything less than technically perfect.'[43] Campling also noted how apparent it was that McCartney relishes playing live. He was not the only critic to be won over by this infectious – if uncool – enthusiasm. As McCartney entered his fifties, it mattered less that he did not fit the mould of the scowling, tortured, rock-star bad boy. People could vicariously enjoy that sense of agony from Alice in Chains or Nine Inch Nails, if need be, or else they could revisit Lennon's solo moments of bitter catharsis. 'McCartney still doesn't show much interest in the dark side, which has inspired plenty of criticism over the years,' noted Jon Young in *Musician* magazine, overlooking some of *Off the Ground*'s angrier and darker lyrics. 'Onstage, however, this chronic sunniness became an asset – when someone enjoys performing so much, it's hard not to smile back.'[44]

Ticket stub from the New World Tour, 1993.

Ironically, as McCartney's lack of coolness became less of an issue than ever before, he was about to grow hipper than he had been for a long time. This was not wholly down to his own restless activities, although they certainly helped. As we've already seen, it's not just what Paul McCartney does himself that affects the changing perceptions of the man and his work. It's also about what happens to be going on around Paul McCartney in broader popular culture.

# 3
# Britpop and Beyond

In his possibly unreliable or at any rate misanthropically amplified memoir, Luke Haines recalls a brief encounter with Paul McCartney at Abbey Road Studios. The year was 1995. Haines's then band, The Auteurs, were recording their *After Murder Park* album with engineer Steve Albini when Paul McCartney appeared, out of the blue, to have a cup of tea. 'Apropos of nothing', and not for the first time in his life, 'Beatle Paul' recited the tale of how he came up with 'Yesterday' in his sleep. Haines did find it endearing that Macca showed genuine interest in his band and how they were getting on at their recording session. Nevertheless, The Auteurs' leader refused to play McCartney any of the material, such as the recently completed track 'Unsolved Child Murder'. 'I don't want him to be the first person to hear these songs,' Haines thought to himself; 'they're too good for him.'[1]

Two years earlier, Haines's band had been one of the acts hailed by *Select* magazine as the nation's saviours from the cultural dominance of music imported from Uncle Sam. Its cover featured Suede's Brett Anderson exhibiting his pasty navel, with a Union Jack superimposed behind him. Although it may have been slightly tongue-in-cheek in the first place, Stuart Maconie's provocative intro to 'the new Best of British' evoked invasion (and *Dad's Army*):

> Enough is enough! Yanks go home! And take your miserable grungewear and your self-obsessed slacker bands with you. You're already twice as cheesy as baggyism, and at least baggy was British.
>
> We don't want plaid. We want crimplene, glamour, wit and irony. We want people who never say 'dude' or 'sidewalk' or 'Can I get a beer?' If 1992 was the American year (overweight, overrated and over here) then it's time to bring on the Home Guard. These, Kurt, are the boys who will stop your little game: Suede, Saint Etienne, Pulp, Denim and The Auteurs. Bands with pride![2]

If you look at editions of *Select* dating from that issue back to the first one published in July 1990, about twice as many of them feature British or Irish cover stars rather than American or Canadian ones, so the situation couldn't have been too bad in the first place.[3] When British musicians from that era claim, as they do in the documentary *Rock Family Trees: The Birth of Cool Britannia* (2022),[4] to have been responding to a dearth of bands who sang in their own accents, it doesn't take much time to come up with a long list of well-known acts that did exactly that in the years prior.[5]

Anderson was embarrassed by *Select*'s deployment of the Union Jack. It had been added without him knowing. Had the singer been asked about it, he says he'd have 'told them to fuck off probably. I had no desire to become a nationalist pin-up.'[6] As Suede and The Auteurs withdrew – or were willingly rejected from – this contrived movement, their popularity was surpassed by younger groups who showed greater willingness to flaunt the national flag and shamelessly mine for ideas the country's pop past.

Not everything about Britpop was regressive, it ought to be noted. Pulp's 'Mis-Shapes' from 1995's *Different Class* was written as a call to arms for all the outcasts and eccentrics who were fed up with being bullied, mocked, attacked, spat at in the streets and scapegoated by intolerant gangs of macho blokes, all dressed in matching short-sleeved shirts, who prowled the centres of England's cities (in Pulp's case, Sheffield).[7] As Britpop grew in popularity, singer Jarvis Cocker noticed that those same blokes, 'townies' as they were then known, were coming to see his band in increasing numbers and the sentiment of 'Mis-Shapes' had become moot.[8] Pulp had originally formed in 1979, so even though they didn't sell many records until breaking through in the mid-1990s, they were the product of an earlier time. Cocker's was a very different proletarian voice to that of a certain pair of Mancunian siblings – we will come to them shortly – who dressed like those townies Cocker feared. Oasis's rivals, Blur, had a greater claim than most big bands of that decade to being 'The Beatles of the '90s'. They progressed, quite dramatically, from baggy beginnings through knees-up character studies to artier break-up albums. Because they had formed in London and many of their songs were defined, for a time, by Damon Albarn's lyrical observations on the idiosyncrasies of the English, it felt more suitable to compare them to The Kinks.[9]

## What's the Story?

Britpop could often be crass, and crassest of the lot were Oasis. It wasn't long after the release of their debut album, *Definitely Maybe*, in 1994 that everything changed for the Manchester band. First sung on tiny stages in thankless support slots to few onlookers, 'Rock 'n' Roll Star' had once been a pugnacious, aspirational fantasy. Even then, the song's working-class protagonist is a 'rock star' for the evening only, mostly within his own mind, and in spirit rather than actuality. The night described in the lyrics is liberating, momentarily. After that, it's back to a bleak life in the city from which there is no easy way out. Performed on bigger and bigger stages, to thousands and thousands more people, its meaning became emptier and less universal. Tonight? You're a rock 'n' roll star every night, mate. And every day. Unlike the rest of us chumps. The same applies to the bluster and bravado peppered throughout every interview with Oasis. In light of your usual English self-deprecation or the limelight-shy musician hiding behind a fringe and mumbling about whatever sparks their imagination, it was refreshing to consume interviews in which these northern upstarts carelessly slagged off other bands, not to mention each other, and declared themselves the greatest thing since sliced Warburtons.[10] Once Oasis were having strings of chart hits, headlining successive nights at Knebworth and making appearances on every media platform across the land, their arrogance became less charming and its appeal diminished gravely. When receiving Oasis's Brit Award for Best Video in 1996, Noel Gallagher moronically mocked the multitude whence he'd risen: 'I've got nowt to say except for I'm extremely rich and you lot aren't. Ha-ha.'[11]

Looking back on that time, Paul McCartney said the worst mistake Oasis ever made was when they started saying they were going to be bigger than The Beatles. 'I thought, "Y'know, so many people have said that and it's the kiss of death." Be bigger than The Beatles, but don't say it. The minute you say it, everything you do from then on is gonna be looked at in the light of that statement.'[12] Not only did this misstep seal Oasis's fate, their Icarian ambitions infected the wider industry. According to Steve Sutherland (*NME* editor from 1992 to 2000), Oasis's decision to be the 'biggest' band around, rather than concentrating on being the 'best' one, shifted everybody's focus: 'They traded brilliance for numbers and it kind of wrecked the scene, because suddenly, if you didn't sell a million records, that meant you weren't as good anymore.'[13]

It has been claimed that Oasis were never overly keen on The Beatles in the first place. Chris Hutton sang in a group called The

Rain with Paul McGuigan, Paul 'Bonehead' Arthurs and Tony McCarroll. In 1991 the musicians would replace Hutton with Liam Gallagher, who suggested the new band name. Liam's older brother, Noel, joined the fold that August. It was he who had the songwriting talent, the discipline and the drive to make something of Oasis. Hutton was left behind, working in factories as he watched his old pals rocket to stardom. Just as certain Beatles acquaintances had done in the past, Hutton cashed in on his experience with the memoir *Don't Look Back in Anger: Growing Up with Oasis* (1997). Hutton had an agenda, so his words must be taken with a pinch of salt. Nevertheless, he raises some interesting points about Oasis and their fixation with The Beatles, as well as the media's. For one thing, Hutton says the name of his old band had nothing to do with 'Rain', the 1966 B-side to 'Paperback Writer'. Rather, it was inspired by Manchester's weather. If you've spent any time there at all, this seems highly plausible. 'In good Manc style, it both took the piss out of, and yet celebrated, the city's image simultaneously,' says Hutton.[14] The writer Paolo Hewitt (Oasis's friend and biographer) and other journalists assumed Rain was a Beatles reference and repeated this notion as fact. Hewitt may have been fed the 'Beatles bullshit', as Hutton calls it, by Oasis themselves, 'all of whom now seek to build up the Fab Four's role in their lives'. When Hutton was a member of The Rain, The Beatles 'meant almost nothing' to them because they were 'too pop, too Scouse, too old'.[15] The ditched vocalist goes as far to say that 'Mancunian pop and rock has largely been untouched by direct Beatlepower, which has tended to affect Liverpool, Birmingham and London much more notably. Since the Hollies, only 10cc and the Buzzcocks have shown any real sign of Beatlism in either their working methods or output.'[16] It would be mad to suggest there was any UK city impervious to Beatlemania and its legacy. Yet Hutton makes a compelling point. Liverpool and Manchester have noticeably different vibes. The former is 'a crucible for warm hearted, psychedelic and romantic music', as the Rainhill-born writer John Doran observes. It is an LSD and pot, space rock, acid rock and proggy place. Thirty miles to the east, Manchester is 'a factory for groups that are urgent, intellectual and dark-hearted such as The Smiths, The Fall, A Certain Ratio and Joy Division'. Drugs-wise, its urban populace is traditionally more partial to speed and ecstasy.[17] This generalization definitely has some truth to it. It is also worth bearing in mind that when Oasis's members were growing up The Beatles weren't even particularly cool in Liverpool. The Cavern had been demolished. Attendance at Beatles conventions had hit a low. The new bands forming there didn't want to be cast under shadow of its most famous export.

As such, Chris Hutton couldn't fathom where the Gallagher brothers' Beatles obsession had come from. Even The Stone Roses, he says, sounded like they were influenced to a greater degree by The Byrds, Simon & Garfunkel, Love and Manfred Mann than The Beatles. The latter comparison was applied by journalists because it was the easiest and most recognizable reference to the 1960s.[18] 'My religion is The Beatles,' Liam Gallagher would declare in 1994.[19] If so, his was a late conversion. Liam says he didn't appreciate music at all, preferring to play football, until he was about fifteen and a stranger attacked him with a hammer. When being treated in hospital, he heard music differently.[20] Nor does Hutton see The Beatles as having had any strong hold over Noel, which he believes is corroborated by the book written by the third Gallagher sibling, Paul (*Brothers: From Childhood to Oasis, The Real Story*, 1996).[21] Hutton contends that as late as 1989–90, when Noel roadied for Inspiral Carpets, Gallagher was more into The Who and The Stones Roses. Thus, 'The Beatles became a useful template for Noel and the rest, rather than a pre-existing, life-shaping force.'[22] Realizing he could write vaguely Beatlesesque melodies, with few rival local acts flaunting that trick at the

George Martin offers words of wisdom to Oasis's Liam Gallagher, 1996.

time, and keen to exploit the absence of The Stone Roses as well as the market opened by the Britpop forerunners, Noel Gallagher never looked back.[23]

The more that journalists mentioned The Beatles in the same sentence as Oasis, the more the band took to this habit as well. Writing in *The Face*, Cliff Jones dubbed them 'The Sex Beatles'.[24] Liam increasingly took his style tips from John Lennon's wardrobe and, in 1999, would name his first son Lennon Francis Gallagher. Oasis setlists often included a lengthy, rocked-up rendition of 'I Am the Walrus'. Their 1996 single 'Don't Look Back in Anger' opens with the piano riff from Lennon's 'Imagine', an appropriation that Noel hoped would both annoy people and encourage his young fans to discover the music of Lennon.[25] Famously, Noel's sticky-fingered songwriting also dipped directly into the catalogues of T. Rex, Gary Glitter, Wham!, The La's, Cliff Richard and more. Neil Innes, once taken to court for his Beatles parodies with The Rutles, won a successful plagiarism case after the melody from his song 'How Sweet to Be an Idiot' (1973) was used in Oasis's single 'Whatever' (1994). The writer Alex Niven likens Gallagher's approach to sampling in hip-hop, which seems a bit generous.[26] For others, such as Taylor Parkes, Britpop's pillaging of the past was never adventurous enough to even qualify as postmodern. It went beyond mere derivativeness and into the realm of neophobia. Certain musicians – 'bozos', as Parkes sees them – were loath to stray from recycling familiar harmonies and ancient riffs despite the contemporary leaps that were being made in the field of music technology.[27]

Oasis are by no means the first rock band to take something old and turn it into something new, and they wouldn't be the last. However, they could at least have disguised it more subtly or been fresher with their approach. A song that began life as a motif pinched from The Stooges or The Doors would be transformed beyond much recognition by the time The Fall had finished with it.[28] When it was recorded, Julian Cope's 'World Shut Your Mouth' had little left in common with its starting point of 'Louie Louie'.[29] *Definitely Maybe*'s 'Shakermaker', on the other hand, sounds an awful lot like Oasis covering 'I'd Like to Teach the World to Sing' by The New Seekers, a fact not lost on the novelty tribute band No Way Sis, who did exactly that and broke into the Top 30 in December 1996.

Noel Gallagher said The Beatles were 'the greatest band in history'.[30] He always seemed more smitten with their sheer popularity and ability to get away with what he called 'a cheap-shot melody' than interested in the Fab Four's yearning to experiment and evolve, their philosophies and beliefs, or sponge-like absorption of different cultures, ideas, instruments and sounds. Oasis's 'whole new world of grey' is described by *The Quietus*'s Taylor Parkes as 'the most disastrous misunderstanding of The Beatles since Charles Manson'.[31] It's as though the ambitious and gobby young man focused less and less on any of his contemporary rivals (Blur being an exception), instead sighting as his main competitors a band that had split up when he was a toddler. 'We're not embarrassed by our success because we deserve it,' Noel informed Cliff Jones, 'and if you don't want to be as big as The Beatles, then it's just a hobby.'[32] When Oasis booked tribute act The Bootleg Beatles to open for them at places like Earls Court and Knebworth, it was the closest the Gallaghers could get to headlining over the real thing and – in their minds – blowing them off the stage.

Oasis became hugely popular at home but never globally like The Beatles did. The Gallaghers' egos were already too big, with Noel's prior discipline loosening daily, by the time they failed spectacularly, on more than one occasion, to conquer America. There they made shambolic, drug-addled performances. Audiences were insulted. Band members went AWOL in the middle of gigs or in between. Venues remained half-empty. Dates got cancelled. With a single principal songwriter who was hardly culturally curious, Oasis never had the creative legs to keep up with The Beatles. All the boastfulness in the world would never change that. Nor would acts of iconoclasm, such as the time Liam caught Bonehead buying a Paul McCartney biography at an airport bookshop, mocked the guitarist for wanting to read about 'Quacka the wanker', wrestled the offending text from the guitarist's hands and threw it over a balcony.[33] Oasis were of the moment. The Beatles – and 'Quacka' – surpass such mortal limitations.

## Roll with It

Britpop was the musical component of a wider renaissance known as 'Cool Britannia'. This spanned fashion, food, film, TV, comedy, literature, various other areas of the media and the contemporary art scene. The cinema hits included *Four Weddings and a Funeral* (1994), *Trainspotting* (1996) and *The Full Monty* (1997).

In the art world, the group known as the Young British Artists (YBAs) made their names. After failing to secure a sponsor and thus being temporarily abandoned in 1990, the Turner Prize was given primetime TV coverage the following year by its new patron, Channel 4. Over the next few years, the prize gained extra publicity due to the widely discussed and controversial nature of its nominees and winners. These included Rachel Whiteread's *House* in 1993 (she was also awarded that year's 'worst artist' prize by the K Foundation, an outlet for the artistic impulses of Jimmy Cauty and Bill Drummond after they had called time on dance project The KLF), Damien Hirst's animal carcasses preserved in formaldehyde (1995), Chris Ofili's paintings containing elephant dung (1998) and Tracey Emin's unmade bed (1999). As much as it aroused heated debate about what does and doesn't constitute 'proper art', the YBAs' output tended to be big, bold, bright and – most crucially – accessible. They could make you think (a bit), and at the same time 'You didn't need to read Foucault to understand it,' as curator Gregor Muir put it.[34] The YBAs succeeded in engaging the eyes and minds of the general public, making British contemporary art more popular than it had ever been before. Many of the YBAs became celebrities. In special cases, such as the YBA contemporary and saucy potter Grayson Perry, they would gradually and perhaps surprisingly ascend to the status of national treasure. By 1997, the YBAs were being exhibited in London's Royal Academy of Arts, in the *Sensation* exhibition. In May 2000, the Tate Modern was opened by Queen Elizabeth II, and it proved a bigger hit than anybody expected, attracting millions of visitors year after year.

In November 1996, *Newsweek* ran its cover 'London Rules: Inside the World's Coolest City'. The following month, *GQ* published 'The Great British Issue' with Jarvis Cocker on the front and the magazine's name printed in the design of the national flag.[35] 'London Swings Again!' announced *Vanity Fair* in March

1997, using an image of Liam Gallagher in bed with his fiancée, the actress Patsy Kensit from *Lethal Weapon 2*. For the purposes of the photoshoot, the couple's pillows and duvet were printed with the Union Jack. Noel Gallagher thought the cover made his brother look like 'an absolute fucking idiot'.[36] He may have been jealous of the attention. Noel himself owned a Union Jack-painted guitar. David Bowie had a Union Jack coat designed by Alexander McQueen, seen on the cover of 1997's *Earthling* album and worn onstage. At the same year's Brit Awards, Geri Halliwell of the Spice Girls wore a Union Jack dress. The following year her outfit was auctioned at Sotheby's for over £40,000.[37]

Some saw such iconography as an act of reclaiming and repurposing the flag, returning it to the arguably more wholesome symbol it had been in the 1960s, when mods had it painted on their scooters, The Who draped themselves in it, England won the World Cup and the British cultural 'invasion' of America was in full flow. Others remained uneasy owing to the connotations the Union Jack used to have – and, let's face it, still did – with far-right extremism and parochial jingoism. In a modern and multicultural society, how appropriate was it to be waving around this relic of empire? Some have even gone as far as to draw a direct line between the flag-waving Britpop scene and the United Kingdom's referendum on its EU membership in 2016.[38]

The phrase 'Cool Britannia' brought together different parts of the country's arts and culture boom under one Union Jack-coloured umbrella, making it easier to sell all this stuff to the media and to foreign audiences, with America targeted in particular.[39] It was encouraged by New Labour, who were elected to government under Tony Blair in 1997. As opposed to Tory governments before and after, New Labour's politicians more readily recognized the spiritual, intellectual and economic value of the nation's culture. To be fair to John Major, who was ousted from office by Blair, when he was prime minister he had created the cabinet position of Secretary of State for National Heritage, as fusty-sounding as that was. The first person appointed to the post was Putney's MP, David Mellor, who differed from other Tory MPs in that he actually followed football. So much so, in fact, that he enjoyed wearing the strip of his beloved Chelsea FC when he made love to his mistress, as exposed by the tabloid sex scandal that contributed to his resignation five months into the job. (A decade later, the woman in question revealed that the football shirt detail – among other juicy aspects of the story – had been made up by publicist Max Clifford.)[40]

The architects of New Labour understood the marketing and popularity potential of culture more willingly than the Conservatives, who'd struggle to look cool in a refrigerator.[41] In opposition, Blair would attend concerts by David Bowie and in 1996 presented that same hero with his Brit Award for Outstanding Achievement. Collecting Oasis's award for Best British Group at the same event, and perhaps hoping to make amends for his wealth-gloat earlier in the evening, Noel Gallagher praised Blair (alongside his own band and its manager) for 'giving a little bit of hope to young people in this country'.[42] Blair and his press secretary, Alistair Campbell, arranged meetings with popular figures such as Blur's Damon Albarn to gauge the views of young voters and to show how in touch they were, or at least to give the impression of being so. With all that has happened since, and his current resemblance to the most haunted cabbage at the back of the greengrocer's, it's easy to forget just how much goodwill greeted Blair on election. The BBC's Nicholas Jones had to keep reminding himself that people were talking in such adoring terms 'not about a pop star but a politician'.[43] After Labour's landslide victory, Noel Gallagher was invited to a party at Downing Street, where other guests included Neil Tennant of Pet Shop Boys and the soap actor Ross Kemp (then married to Rupert Murdoch's right-hand woman, Rebekah Brooks). 'Secretary of State for National

Heritage' was changed to 'Secretary of State for Culture, Media and Sport', with Chris Smith appointed to the newly named role.

New Labour did not invent or initiate Cool Britannia. As Smith points out, his Conservative predecessor, Virginia Bottomley, had used the phrase several times herself.[44] In 1996 the Tory MP John Redwood wrote an article praising the 'number of good bands carrying the sounds of Britain around the world, just as they did in the 60s', for *The Guardian* newspaper. 'The Lightning Seeds reassure us there is still an England under that English sky,' the Eurosceptic politician enthused.[45] In terms of credibility it was too little, too late. There are those who see the Cool Britannia generation as 'Margaret Thatcher's children', even if those in question would scoff at such labelling. 'They have all of the innate drive and entrepreneurialism of the yuppy era,' believes journalist Bidisha Mamata.[46] Those who got off the ground thanks to Thatcher's Enterprise Allowance Scheme, which was designed to lower her government's shameful unemployment figures by funding people to start small businesses rather than pay them dole money, included Alan McGee (the Creation Records founder who signed Oasis), the artists Jeremy Deller and Tracey Emin, and Luke Haines of The Auteurs. 'I wouldn't be what (ever?) I am, had it not been for the dole in the 80s and the Enterprise Allowance Scheme,' wrote Haines in 2018. 'It is of course small beans given the cruelty the woman reigned over, but I'd like to thank you Maggie, for giving me the opportunity to make lots of art that, in your artless, anti-intellectual, incurious Tory way, you would have no doubt found utterly appalling.'[47] In the art world, the YBAs had also benefited enormously from the patronage of 'a rich Tory moron', as journalist Tony Parsons put it on BBC Two's *Late Review*.[48] He was talking about Charles Saatchi, co-founder of the agency Saatchi & Saatchi, which had masterminded advertisements for the likes of Silk Cut cigarettes and the Conservative Party's 1979 general election campaign.[49]

However shallow or not you see the phenomenon as being, Cool Britannia gave Paul McCartney's reputation an enormous boost, especially at home. Oasis were one of the biggest bands of the era and by no means the only one obsessed with the country's pop past.[50] 'Fab Macca Wacky Thumbs Aloft' was suddenly the cool older bloke whom everyone wanted to namecheck and be photographed alongside. He'd been at the centre of the original Swinging London, after all. In Daniel Rachel's oral history of Cool Britannia, Ocean Colour Scene singer Simon Fowler and Creation Records' Alan McGee both recall that, in the years prior to Britpop, people would apologize for liking The Beatles. That was if they admitted it at all.[51] Meanwhile, those who did dare speak its name had risked having their love dampened by patronizing people with first-hand memories of Beatlemania. Keith Harris (the American journalist and editor, 'not the dead British ventriloquist', as his Twitter bio clarifies) remembers what it was like to be a young fan of the Fab Four during the 1980s. He compared the experience to 'trying to eat ice cream while weird older men insisted on lecturing you about the historical significance of ice cream'.[52] As a sign of how wildly things changed in the following years, by the time Gary Hall's book *Living Life without Loving The Beatles: A Survivor's Guide* was first published in 2003, the author wrote like he was the sole voice of reason in a world gone completely doolally to Beatles worship. By that point it was the nonbelievers who dared not voice their doubts in public, and Hall hoped to provide 'a self-help guide for an oppressed minority'.[53]

Once Oasis became huge with their retro sound and began namechecking the Fab Four in every other breath, Beatles fandom was relegitimized and reclaimed by a new generation.[54] This is how George Martin's son, Giles, sees it. 'I watched my dad go through it in the '80s, when no one wanted to work with him,' he told *NME* when promoting a fiftieth-anniversary edition of the

'White Album'. 'It upsets [people] when I tell them Oasis helped The Beatles to be cool again in the '90s. It's almost like blasphemy, but that's what happened.'[55]

By this time, the sense of existential dread that the Cold War had stirred until the end of the 1980s had faded significantly. The Soviet Union had dissolved and 'The End of History' had been declared. Deep down that was hard to believe, but for many it was a comfortingly utopic concept that was nicer to dwell on than the fear of atom bombs and life-threatening tussles over global power. As the misery for many that was the Margaret Thatcher era begat – via the greyness of John Major's prime-ministership – Tony Blair's rise to power, and with Britpop's rejection of grunge's ostensible world-weary cynicism, the national mood was better suited, once again, for McCartney's chirpier optimism.[56]

## Live Forever

McCartney was aware of his newly enhanced status, and he would have been flattered by it. What is noticeable, though, is that he also seemed to be very careful to keep Britpop at a distance. Amiable as ever, he was happy to pop into the studio to record a new version of 'Come Together' with Noel Gallagher and Paul Weller for the War Child charity in 1995.[57] 'It was a time-warp for me,' he said of the session, 'the room's full of young people being Beatles, or Small Faces or whoever they're being. I've never seen so many Epiphones together at one time.'[58] McCartney took Oasis's reverence as a compliment. He compared it, a little cheekily, to that of the similarly tributary ELO.[59] McCartney's generosity towards Oasis would shrink pretty quickly, however, not least on account of their decreasingly substantiated egotism. 'They're derivative and they think too much of themselves,' he told the *New Statesman* in September 1997. While still wishing Oasis the best of luck, he also issued an unheeded warning: 'I hope they don't make too much of it and start to believe their own legend because that can start to cause problems as others have discovered.'[60]

Whenever interviewers asked him which younger bands he enjoyed listening to or would be honoured to perform with, McCartney did not sing from the patriotic hymn sheet. Instead, he would often cite as his favourite 'new' band Nirvana, the most famous exporters of grunge, which the likes of Blur, Oasis and the UK music press had since turned against.[61] He even stuck to this long after Nirvana had ended, following the death of singer and guitarist Kurt Cobain in April 1994. 'Nirvana' was his answer, still, when McCartney appeared on Channel 4's entertainment show of the moment, *TFI Friday*, in 1997. You could say this exposes McCartney as being at least three years behind the zeitgeist. There could be more to it than that. It's an interesting interview in which McCartney does not look entirely at ease with being interrogated by the perma-grinning Chris Evans in the court of his whooping inner-circle studio audience. McCartney humours Evans's daft props and inane questions about farming and loyally defends George Harrison from the presenter's accusations of being 'a bit weird'.[62]

What was it about Cool Britannia that made McCartney slightly wary? What did this experienced cultural statesman realize, early on in the Britpop boom, to which Oasis and their contemporaries would remain oblivious in all their giddy naivety, until it was all too late and their pan had finished flashing? In some ways, McCartney had tried to warn them. Nobody was listening. They were all too busy having a right lark with Keith Allen at Soho's Groucho Club, worrying where the next wrap was coming from and convincing themselves that it would all last forever.

The late Neil Kulkarni, who wrote for *Melody Maker*, *The Wire* and many other publications, always considered Oasis to be 'racist homophobe dickheads' and 'a hugely damaging, regressive cultural force' whose rise equalled 'the cunts taking over'.[63] (Don't hold back in anger, Neil!) Britpop, he said, 'celebrated commercial success so long as it was for white blokes in bands'; it 'celebrated the mediocre so long as it was arrogant' and 'enabled a middle class media to homogenise its ideas about what counted as working class art'.[64] This monolithic and reactionary movement produced and pedestalled albums that 'could've been made at any point in the last 30 years', such as Kula Shaker's debut album of 1996.[65] It might be going too far to suggest that Paul McCartney shared the opinions of the furious Kulkarni or those of the *NME* editor who once informed Oasis's press officer that the band reminded him of playground bullies.[66] Besides his having witnessed so many pop trends come and go over his decades in showbusiness, you can understand why McCartney may have had some qualms, even if it was at the back of his mind, about nailing his colours too firmly to this phallic mast.

The sheer blokeishness of Cool Britannia was lost on few people. The sexual ambiguity and androgyny of Suede was eclipsed by the swaggering testosterone of Britpop Phase II. There was a pushback against the right-on political correctness of the 1980s alternative comedy scene as Frank Skinner and his contemporaries riffed on their sexual conquests. Jokes that might previously have been considered objectionably sexist could now be excused, executed and enjoyed under the clause of being ironic. The 'new lad', a term coined by Sean O'Hagan in 1991,[67] was applied to phenomena and ephemera throughout the rest of the decade, from the sitcom *Men Behaving Badly* to magazines like *Loaded* and *FHM*. The writer Nick Hornby and programmes such as *Fantasy Football League* helped to repopularize football fandom. Damien Hirst found it hilarious to whip his penis out in public places.[68] Fun-loving young women became known as 'ladettes', which was liberating up to a point. Britpop-era bands fronted by women included Sleeper, Echobelly, Elastica, Catatonia, Skunk Anansie, Kenickie and Lush. Unfortunately, as Sleeper's Louise Wener recalled, 'there was a sense that we were "apprentice blokes" rather than a movement in our own right. That was taken away from us.'[69] The term 'girl power' had been used by the early 1990s riot grrrl scene in Olympia, Washington, envisioning a feminist equivalent of Black Power. In 1996 the British power-pop duo Shampoo charted with a song called 'Girl Power'. This coincided with the rise of the Spice Girls, who used the same phrase as their slogan. 'Let the Spice Girls do what they want to do,' was Paul McCartney's vaguely diplomatic conclusion. 'I don't want to do that. Nor have I got the attributes to do that. But there's room for us all.'[70]

The Spice Girls' talents hardly compared to those of the girl groups once idolized, admired, emulated and covered by The Beatles. By the 1990s, McCartney had been monogamously married for twenty years. His days of promiscuous shagging were long behind him. With the idea of 'free love' and the introduction of the contraceptive pill in 1961, males' experience of the sexual revolution was different from that of the women who lived through that time. Wiser men realized this, if only after the fact (and their fun). The author Martin Amis, seven years McCartney's junior, spoke about this a lot when promoting his 2010 novel *The Pregnant Widow*, partly inspired by his younger sister's descent into alcoholism and depression, a situation he believed was compounded by her experiences of the sexual revolution. Sally Amis died in 2000. While sexual liberation was not a walk in the park for every boy either, 'the girls had to make all the difficult choices,' Amis reflected. 'And the girls suffered and some of them got a bit twisted out of shape.'[71] As the parent to three girls (and one boy), the mature McCartney did not encourage 1990s lad and ladette culture.[72] Too career-savvy to chastise the music industry directly, he hinted at his displeasure when discussing other subjects, such as the gutter press. 'In the sixties I used to call them loveable rogues, now they've lost the loveable tag and the whole [Princess] Diana thing shows that,' he said towards the end of the decade. 'There are a lot of them who are not good people. It's sad and it's in line with the very laddish phase we're going through.'[73]

Writers from the Left and Right have condemned the way British culture seemed to dumb down so deeply in this decade. 'By 1994, it was rather uncool to be bothered about anything much,' wrote Taylor Parkes in an anniversary piece – 'tirade' is a more accurate description – that laid much of the blame at the door of Blur.[74] They were among the Britpoppers who should've known better than to pose at the dog tracks in a mockney fashion, trade in pastiche and sing about the 'herd' holidaying in Greece: 'A whole generation playing dumb? Dunno what you're on about, mate. Cheery sexism? Shut up love, it's only a bit of fun. The armour-plated smugness of a new liberal bourgeoisie? Chill out you knobhead – have another line.'[75] Roger Lewis of the *Daily Mail* reflected on the 1990s too as the dawning of Britain's 'age of stupidity'.[76] Some of his examples of a country-gone-to-pot chime with Parkes's; others are more reactionary: the popularity of vacuous idols (Tim Henman, Posh and Becks, Harry Potter, Mr Blobby); the rise of cheap-and-nasty reality TV ('The new A. S. Byatt was People's Chav Jade Goody, the dental nurse from Essex who became rich and famous for her ignorance').[77] The 'mentally defective' comedy creation Mr Bean and his documentarian equivalent, David Starkey PhD, who'd rebooted the nuances of history into mere 'camp soap operas'. An artist's unmade bed in the Tate Gallery. Lad culture permeating everything from magazine publishing to the country's cuisine (see the matey 'Naked Chef' Jamie Oliver). Spice Girl-wave pseudo-feminism. The Archbishop of Canterbury and Chief Rabbi outing themselves as Arsenal supporters. Political correctness (this was the *Daily Mail*, after all) gone madder than ever before![78] (Notwithstanding the fact that quite a lot of those aforementioned cultural crimes were perpetuated, perhaps even subliminally so, as a pushback against the sterner political correctness of the previous decade.)

As for McCartney's ongoing allegiance to Nirvana, that's an interesting one. Other Nirvana fans of McCartney's generation included The Who's guitarist and songwriter. He was upset to read, in Kurt Cobain's posthumously published journals, the line 'I hope I die before I become Pete Townshend.'[79] The Kinks' Ray Davies considered Nirvana's *Nevermind* to be 'the most significant American rock'n'roll album since The Doors'.[80] Like McCartney, The Kinks' own fame and reputation were ameliorated by the scene from which they also kept themselves at a certain distance. Nicknamed the 'Godfather of Britpop', Davies preferred to think of himself as 'a concerned uncle'.[81] McCartney's son James grew up listening to Nirvana, so it's likely his dad's appreciation stemmed from there. Having said that, in the 1990s there were few people who hadn't heard about Nirvana besides a couple of Japanese soldiers who'd been hiding in the mountains, unaware that the Second World War had ended. As a perennially switched-on member of the music biz, McCartney Senior may also have been aware that, prior to Oasis's fame, grunge had already played its own role in reigniting interest in The Beatles.

The American punk, hardcore and post-hardcore scenes, from which grunge evolved, had never been as antithetical towards The Beatles as those in the UK. In 1984 Hüsker Dü and Minutemen risked having their hardcore membership revoked when both showed 'White Album' ambitions by releasing double LPs on the SST label. Others who'd been roused by punk began to move things in a more psychedelic direction. Take Butthole Surfers, for example, whose Paul Leary first took up guitar after seeing The Beatles' appearance on the *Ed Sullivan Show* in 1964. When like-minded oddballs The Flaming Lips compiled the albums they'd made between 1983 and 1988 into a three-CD box set, it was aptly titled *Finally the Punk Rockers Are Taking Acid*.

As the U.S. underground gravitated into the mainstream in the 1990s, Nirvana were not the only Seattle band to extol The Beatles.

The formula for most grunge music was, at root, The Beatles plus punk rock, multiplied by Black Sabbath. Grunge producer and Garbage member Butch Vig said the sound of the guitars and McCartney's voice on The Beatles' 'Helter Skelter' had pioneered grunge years before Seattle got around to it.[82] 'A lot of The Beatles' songs were heavier than most so-called metal tracks of the last 20 years,' said Soundgarden singer Chris Cornell, who'd been marvelling at The Beatles' fearless breadth of styles since he was nine years old.[83] Unlike Noel Gallagher, who admits he'd never played 'Come Together' before being asked to record it for War Child and found himself blagging it in the studio,[84] Cornell was long familiar with it. Soundgarden covered the song onstage and in the studio. They also knew their way around 'Helter Skelter', 'Everybody's Got Something to Hide Except Me and My Monkey' and 'I Want You (She's So Heavy)'. They were also prone to tacking a 'Hey Jude' intro on to their own tune 'Beyond the Wheel' (1988). Pearl Jam's Eddie Vedder has likened the 'White Album' to 'a textbook for someone born in 1964'.[85]

In 1994 the film *Backbeat* dramatized The Beatles' Hamburg days with its focus on Stuart Sutcliffe, who left the band in 1961 and died of a brain haemorrhage the following year. For its soundtrack, members of the contemporary U.S. alt-rock scene were recruited to recreate The Beatles' early 1960s sound. It contained only songs written by others that the young band had once covered, partly because that genuinely reflected setlists of that time but also because original Beatles-written numbers were trickier to license. *Backbeat*'s band featured Dave Pirner (Soul Asylum), Greg Dulli (Afghan Whigs), Thurston Moore (Sonic Youth), Don Fleming (Gumball), Mike Mills (REM) and Dave Grohl (Nirvana). Unlike past duds like the Bee Gees' *Sgt. Pepper's Lonely Hearts Club Band* or McCartney's own *Give My Regards to Broad Street*, *Backbeat* did rather well. It was premiered at the Sundance Film Festival, made nearly $2.5 million in the box office and was nominated for several awards. Sixteen years later, writer and director Iain Softley would adapt his screenplay into a successful theatre production, which was praised for offering refreshing darkness and depth in the midst of naffer jukebox musicals.[86]

The Backbeat Band played live at the 1994 MTV Movie Awards. 'Money' and 'Long Tall Sally' were ripped through violently, literally in the case of Thurston Moore, who leapt on Greg Dulli mid-song, inflicting a minor leg injury on his victim.[87] For the climax to the event, they also threw in a number from long after the Hamburg period: 1968's grunge progenitor 'Helter Skelter'.[88] The film, its recreated live scenes and the soundtrack revealed to younger listeners, while reminding older folk of, the almost proto-punk spirit of the early Beatles. It explicitly joined the dots between them and some of the coolest alt-rock musicians of the time (as well as that bloke from Soul Asylum).

The grunge generation were not immune from the Lennon-versus-McCartney narrative covered in Chapter One of this book. Paul McCartney saw *Backbeat* as having diluted some of his own 'rock 'n' rollness'. Portrayed by Ian Hart (lip-syncing to Dulli's vocals), Lennon was depicted as fronting a wildly thrilling version of Little Richard's 'Long Tall Sally'. This number had always been sung by McCartney. 'But now it's set in cement,' complained Paul.[89] 'I don't know who wrote what parts of what Beatles songs, but Paul McCartney embarrasses me,' Kurt Cobain once revealed to *Rolling Stone*. Unsurprisingly, his favourite Beatle was John Lennon. 'Lennon was obviously disturbed,' Cobain laughed. 'So I could relate to that.'[90] Cobain's signature howl was often compared to that of Lennon.[91] Mind you, when Brett Morgen was researching his documentary *Kurt Cobain: Montage of Heck* (2015), he found a home recording of Cobain singing 'And I Love Her'. Whether Cobain realized it or not, it was a song written primarily by McCartney. Cobain's favourite album by them remained the early U.S. release *Meet the Beatles!* from the cute, besuited, head-bobbing teenybop era. He also had a McCartney-ish pop nous when it came to his songwriting. This worked sublimely when paired with Nirvana's raw and visceral style of alternative rock, as *NME*'s Edwin Pouncey identified before most people had heard of them, when he declared them to be 'Sub Pop's answer to the Beatles'.[92] While Cobain may have been somewhat ashamed of this skill, it goes a long way to explaining why his band became quite as famous as they did. Mick Jagger, incidentally, complained to *Rolling Stone* that Nirvana were 'too angst-ridden for me . . . I'm not a fan of moroseness.'[93] (He preferred Pearl Jam.) That's the kind of attitude that certain people might have expected from Paul 'jolly optimist' McCartney. This darker side could also be exactly what attracted him towards Nirvana, compounded by the parallels that could be made between Cobain's demons and those suffered by another troubled man to whom McCartney was once drawn. Both Cobain and Lennon came from broken homes. Each was tormented by his own celebrity status. They struggled with hard-drug abuse. They met tragic and violent ends, one self-inflicted, the other at the hands of a mad fan. They were fathers who left young children behind. People have scapegoated both men's wives.[94]

The death of Cobain, and other ill-fated stars of the Seattle scene, has overshadowed the lighter-hearted and cheekier side of grunge. Defending his 'Yanks Go Home!' piece thirty years on, Stuart Maconie had this to say: '"Smells Like Teen Spirit" I know is a great record. For that one great record, boy you had to listen to some dreadful records. All these bands who looked terrible. They looked like they'd come to creosote your fence and they had nothing to say for themselves.' As for the Britpop bands Maconie had suggested to replace them, 'They seemed to have a certain British perspective. For want of better words: irony, sexiness, cleverness, maybe even a certain sense of self-deprecation.'[95] Few of these qualities had been absent from grunge, if you were paying attention. Maconie is an excellent writer, broadcaster and cultural commentator; nothing less than a national treasure in certain households (including my own). On this count, however, we will have to disagree. People who make sweeping statements like 'Grunge was so fucking negative and depressing'[96] ought to read the hilarious liner notes to the Mudhoney compilation *March to Fuzz*. Try listening to them too, along with the marvellously irreverent L7. Sarcasm, irony and wit flow through their lyrics. For sexiness (conventionally speaking or otherwise), you could look to Soundgarden or Hole. As for self-deprecation, that was a fundamental element of a scene that had risen from the post-hardcore underground, reacted against the pomposity of 1980s mainstream metal, condemned embarrassing displays of egotism and viewed most forms of success with utter suspicion. They were *persona non grata* by 1996 but, had they been invited to the party, grungers would have loved the sight of Jarvis Cocker crashing onstage to wave his bottom at Michael Jackson's Brits performance. It was as if the self-proclaimed King of Pop, arms outstretched and surrounded by small children dressed in rags as lowly urchins, had never even heard Soundgarden's withering 1991 single 'Jesus Christ Pose'.

Nirvana's own sense of humour was all over their final studio album, 1993's *In Utero*, from its cynical opening lines about teen angst having paid off well to sarcastic track titles like 'Radio Friendly Unit Shifter'. The band had been in good spirits when they recorded it. In their downtime, they made prank phone calls to other musicians and joined in giddily with engineer Steve Albini's penchant for setting his own clothes on fire.[97]

To view grunge as the enemy was to target something that was itself highly critical of many negative aspects of American culture and hegemony. Sure, grunge had its downsides and fair share of shoddier bands. It could be self-pitying and was regressive in its own way of harking back to the hard rock and heavy metal of the 1970s.[98] It was also predominantly white. Unlike Britpop, however, grunge was not a patriotic movement, nor was it a performatively masculine one. Several of its musicians used their voices to promote progressive causes and condemn the many wrongs they identified in their country's society and politics. To write off grunge on a nationalistic basis was a bit like objecting to 'America' because you didn't like George Carlin, Barry Crimmins or Bill Hicks, all stand-up comics who weren't exactly enamoured with their birthplace either.

In 1992 Nirvana had released *Incesticide*, a compilation conceived to capitalize on the success of their breakthrough studio album *Nevermind*. Some copies included a short essay in which Cobain ruminated on fame, fandom and 'the few really important things that I've been blessed with since becoming an untouchable boy genius'.[99] He champions female bands including The Raincoats and Shonen Knife. He recalls bringing ABBA tribute act Björn Again to the Reading Festival. He expresses his gratitude for being invited to perform at the first pro-choice benefit concert organized by L7. Kissing his male bandmates on *Saturday Night Live*, he reiterates, was designed to repel their less tolerant followers. 'At this point I have a request for our fans,' he wrote towards the end. 'If any of you in any way hate homosexuals, people of different color, or women, please do this one favor for us – leave us the fuck alone! Don't come to our shows and don't buy our records . . . Sorry to be so anally PC but that's the way I feel.'[100]

As with parts of the UK comedy scene, there were those involved in music who thought such battles had been fought, won and put to bed by the mid-1990s, or else they had never been especially bothered about them in the first place, and it was high time to return to a social and cultural climate of unashamed fun. This left a bad taste in some people's mouths. As an equality-championing Nirvana fan, was Paul McCartney one of them?

Seeing as much of Britpop was patriotic to the core, Oasis's obsession with the Fab Four can be viewed as an attempt to reclaim ownership from the U.S. grunge bands who had already made The Beatles trendy again. It's feasible, then, that the Americans sold The Beatles back to the UK, as The Beatles were once said to have reintroduced the blues to U.S. audiences. Before Britpop's resurgence of band-based 'indie' music (the quotation marks are needed here because an awful lot of it was released by major labels or subsidiaries thereof), grunge had also played a large part in washing away some of the more synthetic-sounding pop music and rock production of the 1980s to which McCartney had experienced trouble adjusting. This opened the door for the more live-sounding records that he enjoyed making in the Cool Britannia period.

Just as Noel Gallagher said he hoped they would, his own young fans did go back and discover the music of John Lennon, Paul McCartney, George Harrison and Ringo Starr. What those listeners found, as old as it was, sounded objectively superior to Oasis's apings of the formulas. The singing was better. Far less whiny, with harmonies to die for. The lyrics were more engaging and imaginative. The versatility and production tricks were still mind-blowingly difficult to fathom, decades after the recordings had taken place. There was so much more energy in The Beatles' studio output and footage of their live performances. They also contained a lot more love, love, love. Here was a band that, in just a few years, made astounding leaps forward by anybody's standards. (Yes, more than Blur managed.) The Fab Four were better-looking than Oasis. There was no denying that. Greater thought and care had been put into their artwork and presentation. People appreciated this. As funny as interviews with the Gallaghers could be, archive footage proved The Beatles were wittier. Scour websites like Reddit and specialist music discussion boards and there is no end of evidence that people did discover The Beatles through the gateway of Oasis, and then never looked back.

In one of his semi-modest moments, Noel Gallagher admitted he wouldn't be able to match The Beatles in the long run. 'If we were to sit down now and take John Lennon, Jimi Hendrix, Ray Davies, Steve Marriott, anybody's first two albums against my first two albums, I'm there. I'm with The Beatles,' he told *Q* magazine in 1996. 'If you ask me where I'll be after my eighth album in comparison to The Beatles then they'll piss all over me. Probably.'[101] He would disband Oasis after a backstage scrap with his brother in 2009. The band had made seven studio albums by then. The general consensus is they'd been treading water since their third, 1997's *Be Here Now*. Liam formed Beady Eye and then went solo. His brother has continued performing with Noel Gallagher's High Flying Birds. Thanks to the pedestrian nature of much of his music and his equally conservative views,[102] Noel has been branded by Luke Haines, whom we met at the start of this chapter, as 'Britain's Least Psychedelic Man'.[103] Maybe it could have been different, had Gallagher spent more time in Liverpool.

## Post-Grunge Postscript

Let's fast-forward for a moment to 2012, when Paul McCartney would record and perform with Dave Grohl, Krist Novoselic and Pat Smear. A jam between the four musicians, arranged as a tidy ending to Grohl's *Sound City* documentary, would turn into the song 'Cut Me Some Slack'. The quartet went on to perform it at a benefit concert after Hurricane Sandy, as well as on *Saturday Night Live*. They also dug it out, along with some Beatles numbers and Little Richard's 'Long Tall Sally', as the encore to a McCartney concert in Seattle. Two decades after grunge had exploded into the mainstream, McCartney fronted a band made up of the surviving members of Nirvana. What Kurt Cobain might have thought about this is as unclear as whether John Lennon would have approved of *The Beatles Anthology*'s 'Free as a Bird'. Cobain's widow, Courtney Love of Hole, voiced her objections. There has been much bickering over the years, financial and personal, between Love and her husband's bandmates. She was pleased, anyway, that they didn't perform any Nirvana songs. Love also confirmed her allegiance as a 'Paul person', recalling that she and Cobain used to have 'Paul and John fights'.[104] There was no doubting McCartney's delight in fronting what became known, in reference to his knighthood, as 'Sirvana'. 'It's a great power to have them on stage with you,' he said after that Seattle show. 'I mean, my band's great – but when you augment it with Nirvana, that's greater.'[105]

As much as Courtney Love might baulk at it, comparisons have been drawn between Paul McCartney and Dave Grohl, who have since become close friends. The drummer-turned-frontman's band, Foo Fighters, are virtually the Wings to Nirvana's Beatles. The two multi-instrumentalists are such similar characters that one wonders about the extent to which Grohl has deliberately or subconsciously moulded his own public persona in McCartney's image. People criticize both men for the same apparent failings. As Rob Sheffield puts it, 'Both got famous in bands where they played with a tortured genius who died young, and both moved on to long careers where they were almost freakishly untortured . . . We hold it against them.'[106] It could well be that any torment they do suffer is repressed, ignored, dealt with more healthily, funnelled less obviously into their work or tastefully hidden from public view.

Both men are proven workaholics who are usually juggling several different projects, musical and otherwise, at once. While they each receive plenty of help from the armies that support them, whose payroll relies on their activeness, their contemporaries have not matched such prolificacy or plate-spinning. 'We don't work hard, we play music, we don't work music,' McCartney has aphorized.[107] That said, there are few who could keep up with the 'play' rate of either him or Grohl. In the latter's case this came under scrutiny when Foo Fighters' Taylor Hawkins died in a hotel room in Bogotá, aged fifty, in March 2022. After complaining of chest pains, the drummer was found unresponsive. The autopsy found several intoxicants in his system. A couple of months later, *Rolling Stone* reported that Hawkins had been overburdened and worn out by Foo Fighters' intense tour schedule and three-hour concerts, and had felt under pressure to play a greater number of shows than he was comfortable with.[108] He is also said to have had a hyperactive personality himself, and certainly dabbled in his own share of multiple side projects.[109] His survival of a heroin overdose in 2001, which had landed him in a two-week coma, showed he had a prior record for partying as hard as he played. After publication of its piece, *Rolling Stone* was criticized by some of its interviewees, who felt their quotes had been taken out of

Dave Grohl joins Paul McCartney onstage at Glastonbury Festival, 2022.

context, misrepresented and manipulated into a sensationalized and misleading narrative.[110]

In June of that year, Dave Grohl made his first public appearance since Hawkins's death. He was invited to fly over as one of the surprise guests at McCartney's headlining set at Glastonbury Festival. To a warm and rapturous response from a crowd estimated at more than 100,000 people, McCartney introduced Grohl as 'My friend; your hero.' Yet this was no rock star moment. As Grohl ambled onto the stage to help out on 'I Saw Her Standing There' and 'Band on the Run', he still had the raw and shell-shocked appearance of the recently bereaved, that familiar broken look in his glassy eyes. There was a lot of love in the field on that night.

Occasionally, some disgruntled former band member or other kind of ex-associate will give an interview that contradicts McCartney's or Grohl's reputation as a 'nice guy'. With all the adoration they receive, it's incredible they've managed to remain remotely grounded. Both have been determined to avoid letting their ego swell to the size of Napoleon Bonaparte's, as it really – certainly in Sir Paul's case – has every right to do. That's the modest way of post-hardcore and grunge, where Grohl's background lies, so it's no wonder McCartney preferred Nirvana to Oasis or Blur.

# 4
# The Beatles Anthology

*The Beatles Anthology* is the name of a documentary series that aired on ITV and ABC in November–December 1995, a trio of double albums released between November 1995 and October 1996 compiling rarities, out-takes, alternative mixes and live performances, as well as a tie-in book. The latter was published in October 2000. It was delayed because Derek Taylor, who had been working on it, passed away in September 1997. The book might have sold in greater numbers had it been released, as one message-boarder puts it, at 'the height of Anthologymania'.[1] Fascination with The Beatles had hardly waned by the time it hit the shelves, however, and the hefty and hardly inexpensive tome still shot straight to the top of the *New York Times* bestseller list.

Postponed hardback aside, the *Anthology* campaign occurred at the height of Britpop. This was not some cynical attempt to capitalize on the country's moment of renewed coolness. It was more a happy coincidence for the Beatles brand. A documentary project had been mooted for decades. Apple staff had begun collecting footage and working on it when The Beatles were still together, and Neil Aspinall, in particular, continued beavering on it thereafter.

By the mid-1990s, with Aspinall now executive of Apple, a few things had fallen into place. Long-running legal disputes over royalties had been settled. Deals had been reached between The

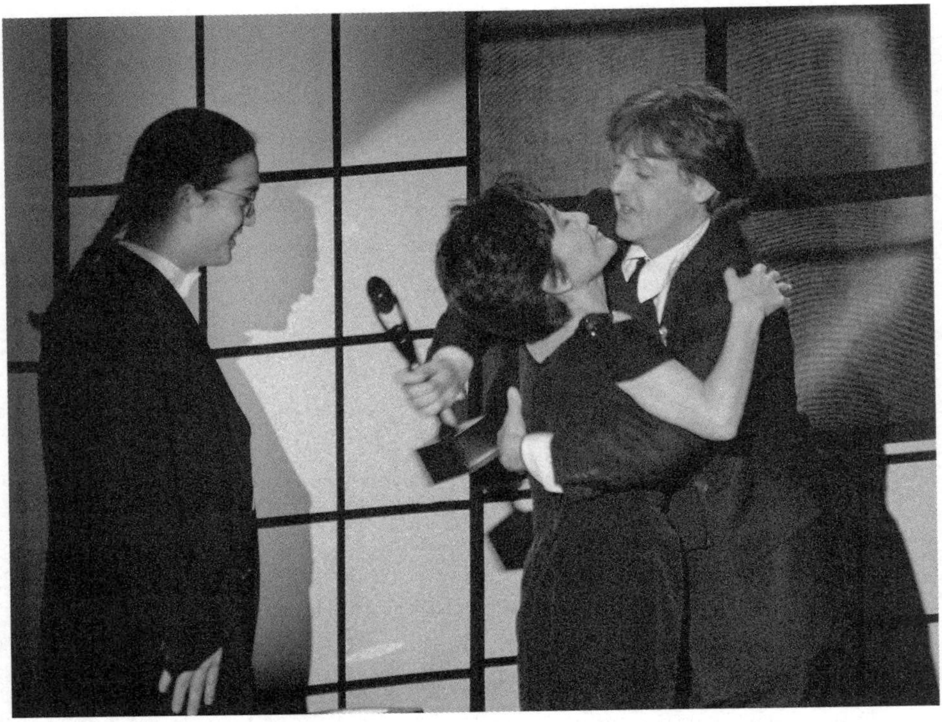

Paul McCartney embraces Yoko Ono while her son Sean Lennon looks on during the Rock and Roll Hall of Fame's Ninth Annual Induction Ceremony in New York, 1994, where Ono accepted honours for her late husband John Lennon.

Beatles, Apple and EMI. The band's Apple Corps, relaunched after a long period of inactivity, won legal actions against EMI, Sony and Virgin. In 1991 The Beatles' Apple took Steve Jobs's Apple Computers to court and won a payment of around $29 million.[2] The group's sessions had now been catalogued and digitized by the engineers at Abbey Road. The often fraught relationships between Yoko Ono and Paul McCartney, between Ono and the other Beatles and between McCartney and his ex-bandmates were warmer than they had been for some time.

Previously resistant to the idea of a Beatles documentary, George Harrison got on board. Following the collapse of HandMade Films, he was close to bankruptcy.[3] Ringo and his wife, Barbara Bach, had been to rehab and were now sober. Having initially pooh-poohed the idea of delving into the vaults of Abbey Road Studios, George Martin agreed to work on the three double CDs of unreleased material.[4] 'I am trying to tell the story of The Beatles' lives in music, from the moment they met to the moment they split up in 1970,' Martin explained in the press release for *Anthology 1* (1995). 'I have listened to everything we ever recorded together. Every take of every song, every track of every take, virtually everything that was ever committed to tape and labelled "Beatles." I've heard about 600 separate items in all.'[5]

Ever the professional, Martin did a fine job at telling that story through weaving together the songs, plus additional snippets of conversation. The earliest songs on *Anthology 1* are 'That'll Be the Day' and 'In Spite of All the Danger'. Recorded in 1958 when the group were still called The Quarrymen, the one copy of that single that was pressed is the most valuable record in existence. (It is currently owned by someone named Paul McCartney.) Six CDs later, *Anthology 3* (1996) finishes with a version of *Abbey Road*'s 'The End', onto which has been added the long and haunting final chord of 'A Day in the Life' for dramatic impact if not chronological correctness. In between, we hear teen skifflers blossom into Merseybeat superstars before evolving further into the most important, influential and innovative pop/rock/genre-defying band of their age and arguably any other. The *Anthology*'s first instalment received the most hype, inevitably. In retrospect it is the thinnest of the trilogy, its flow interrupted by too many excerpts of speech, presumably to help Martin's storytelling agenda. Mind you, those who favour the earlier stuff over The Beatles' later work may beg to differ. The two discs show off the group's catholic tastes, swift work rate, ability to play around with wildly different arrangements even when pressed for time, sense of humour, tightness as a live act, sheer raw power and capacity to wobble everybody's knees. The rendition of 'All My Loving' taken from the *Ed Sullivan Show* in 1964 is drenched in unceasing screams from the studio audience. *Anthology 1* also provides a sense of how savvy and firm The Beatles could be in trusting their own instincts and knowing when to say no. It includes their recording of 'How Do You Do It?', a jaunty tune written by Mitch Murray and proposed as the first Beatles A-side by George Martin, who promised them it would be a chart-topping smash. Early on in the documentary series, McCartney suggests they'd have been laughed out of their home town had they returned to Liverpool singing that song. It ended up being a number-one hit instead for Gerry and the Pacemakers.

*Anthology 2* (1996) charts how quickly The Beatles' compositions grew in sophistication, depth and subversiveness. It gives a sense of the pressures that fame had brought. 'Help!' Lennon sings immediately after McCartney's live debut of 'Yesterday', a companion song of mourning for simpler and happier times. There are excerpts of them muddling through concerts in America and Japan, where the screaming was so loud that The Beatles couldn't hear themselves play and the audience couldn't hear the band either. The group then cocooned themselves in the safety of the studio. From the many turning points that can be heard across the compilations, among the most thrilling is the first studio take of 'Tomorrow Never Knows', both swampier and stompier than the familiar *Revolver* version, which occurs halfway through disc one of *Anthology 2*. It's a shame when it fades out after about three minutes as it feels like it could loop along eternally without ever diminishing in appeal. Three different versions demonstrate the fascinating development of 'Strawberry Fields Forever' from Lennon's folky demo into a richer classic of psychedelia, here with additional drum madness from Ringo. Some of the cuts are composites of different studio takes, spliced by Martin ('Penny Lane', 'A Day in the Life', 'Lady Madonna' and others). This may have been one way to squeeze multiple different takes onto the two-disc capacity. It is one of the few things for which *Anthology 2* has drawn criticism. The tracks have been called 'artificial Frankenstein's Monsters of songs' by Jamie Atkins of *Record Collector*. 'The whole point of an exercise like this is to hear Beatles songs incomplete and with imperfections intact,' he writes; 'in creating "best versions" of the outtakes Martin was swindling fans with cosmetic revisionism.' Atkins hears triumphant moments elsewhere, when Martin sticks to the purer agenda. Among other highlights, *Anthology 2* offers versions of 'Only a Northern Song', 'Your Mother Should Know' and 'Across the Universe', which are, in turn, 'wonderful', 'bizarre' and 'delicate and spectral'.[6]

*Anthology 3* documents the final chapters of the band. Brian Epstein was dead. The Beatles were maturing and fragmenting. We now know that The End was nigh. Disc one features material intended or proposed for what would become the 'White Album' when The Beatles returned from their trip to India in 1968. There are acoustic demos and alternative takes that differ widely from the final cuts that made it onto the self-titled double album. Sadly, the slow and menacing twelve-minute version of McCartney's 'Helter Skelter' gets faded out at four and a half minutes. There's a run-through 'Hey Jude' with – would you believe it – fewer 'na na nas'. The second disc consists of material from the *Let It Be* and *Abbey Road* period. Once defined by Michael Lindsay-Hogg's *Let It Be* film of 1970, this tense time has since been subject to revisionism by Peter Jackson's *Get Back*, a much longer and seemingly more accurate account assembled from the same original footage and released via Disney+ in 2021. Jackson's cut still features George Harrison's strops, John Lennon failing to turn up on time and Paul McCartney getting on everybody's wick, usually from frustration that they were missing deadlines.[7] The overall picture is that everybody was having a nicer time, most of the time, than we were led to believe by prior accounts such as Lindsey-Hogg's and those that have been based on it. This version of events had been repeated so often over the years that those involved had become convinced of its reality. McCartney was surprised and delighted to see so much laughter in *Get Back* because even he had bought into 'the dark side of The Beatles breaking up'.[8] That being said, the truth is that The Beatles were nearing their final moments. On *Anthology 3* they can be heard tearing through oldies, including a medley of 'Rip It Up', 'Shake, Rattle and Roll' and 'Blue Suede Shoes'. Despite all the time that had passed since they stopped playing concerts, they hadn't lost their live chops and could still have a lot of fun jamming together. With hindsight, there is a sense of them trying to recapture something that had become out of reach. The tracklist for *Anthology 3* is sprinkled with songs that would end up being used on solo albums instead. There's the lullaby-like 'Junk' and 'Teddy Boy', both of which would appear on the *McCartney* album. There's also the song that would turn out to be the title track for George Harrison's triple album *All Things Must Pass* (1970). Harrison dug out 'Not Guilty', another number written by him, as late as 1979.

## You Can't Do That

Between The Beatles' split and the Anthologymania of the 1990s, there had been several attempts to repackage and reissue the band's material, to different degrees of success. The double albums *1962–1966* and *1967–1970*, usually referred to as the 'Red' and 'Blue' albums, had always sold pretty well since their release in 1973. Looking to capitalize on the nostalgia for the 1950s that was exemplified in phenomena such as *American Graffiti* (1973), *Grease* (the musical was launched in 1971, leading to the inescapable 1978 movie adaptation), *Happy Days* (1974–84) and the wider revival of rockabilly music, Capitol and Parlophone's *Rock 'n' Roll Music* of 1976 had compiled the 28 Beatles songs that were, as the writer Barbara Skelton puts it, 'least likely to annoy the Fonz should they suddenly vibrate the jukebox at Arnold's Drive-In'.[9] Its inner sleeve looks like it was the original blueprint for the Ed's Easy Diner chain of throwback burger joints. It depicts a jukebox, hamburger, glass of Coca-Cola, Chevrolet and image of Marilyn Monroe (who had died before The Beatles recorded 'Love Me Do'). The musicians themselves had not been consulted on the art, songs or running order. 'The cover was disgusting,' complained Ringo Starr. 'When we worked, we spent as much time on the cover as on the tracks. We didn't put some crap-house cover on something we'd done . . . It made us look cheap and we were never cheap.'[10] Flogging the dead horse further into the dust, the two-LP set was rereleased in 1980 as two separate albums, with another hideously uber-retro portrait of the Fab Four on each volume's cover. *Rock 'n' Roll Music*'s original release was followed, in 1977, by *Love Songs*. The sleeve this time looked a little more sophisticated than its predecessor's. It was unfortunate that the faux-leather brownness (to put it politely) suggested a fairly niche act of romance. Exacerbating this problem, the central image of the band made it look as though they'd been frozen within a squinting orifice. As for the music, grouping the ballads together served only to neuter the genius of The Beatles, namely the variety of their musical exploits and the astounding creative leaps they made within a decade. Who'd bother with it? Skelton imagines grown-up teenyboppers, now lumbered with commitments like full-time employment, mortgages and marriages, who dressed like the characters from Mike Leigh's *Abigail's Party*, already too past it for The Beatles' livelier numbers and appalled by the fresh raucousness of punk rock, using *Love Songs* as their smooching soundtrack after the kiddies had gone to bed (when not doing the same thing to the dulcet tones of Demis Roussos).[11] Although its cover was groovier, with an illustration that made it look as though The Beatles lived in a Lewis Carroll wonderland, 1980's *The Beatles Ballads* had a similarly homogeneous function. Two years later came *20 Greatest Hits*, a compilation of all the number-one singles in the USA and UK, as well as *Reel Music*, which featured selections from the different Beatles movies, packaged in yet more ugly artwork. Despite being released in the wake of Lennon's death, neither made much of a splash, in Beatles terms at least.

The back catalogue's fortunes were boosted when the *Abigail's Party* crowd were persuaded to swap turntables for CD players, dispose of their vinyl collections and repurchase all their old albums on the new, exciting and – as it was marketed – 'indestructible' format of digital discs.[12] Beginning in 1987, The Beatles' studio albums were issued on compact disc for the first time. The following year came two separate volumes of *Past Masters*, which featured commercially released songs that hadn't appeared on UK studio LPs. The 'Red' and 'Blue' albums reached CD racks in 1993. It was 1994's *Live at the BBC* that really whetted appetites for the *Anthology* albums, however. This included broadcasts recorded in the years 1963, 1964 and 1965, mostly cover versions with a few original compositions, and amusing snippets of dialogue. 'For one thing, these are the first known radio tapes where the talk is more precious than the music,' enthused Robert Christgau, 'in addition to everything else, they were the funniest rock stars ever.'[13] Other reviews warned that its 'charm' outweighed the low-fidelity sound quality.[14] 'No one is disputing that the Beatles were fabulously talented. Now can we let them lie?' pleaded *The Guardian*'s Caroline Sullivan.[15] There was fat chance of that happening given that *Live at the BBC* sold better than anyone had anticipated, including those at the record company. Although its two CDs were packed to capacity, *Live at the BBC* offered only the tiniest glimpse of archive material waiting for disinterment, lifted from a narrow period of the group's extraordinary career.

## Got to Get You (Back) into My Life

The other big news surrounding the *Anthology* was that The Beatles had 're-formed' to record 'new' material. The three members initially considered composing incidental music for the television series. They were also tempted to do something more substantial. 'Paul had a song, or George had a song, or I had a song,' claimed Ringo. However, they 'always hit a wall' in the process.[16] Like the walrus, the wall was Paul. McCartney would become increasingly apprehensive the closer they got to recording anything, fretting over whether a 'three-quarter Beatle record' really merited an existence.[17]

The solution was the acquirement of Lennon's home-recorded demo cassettes from Yoko Ono. The idea was to take a sonic sketch of Lennon's and turn it into a fuller experience. To take pressure off themselves, McCartney suggested they imagine that Lennon was on holiday: prior to departure he had asked the others to 'Just finish this track for us, will you? I'm sending the cassette – I trust you.'[18] Ringo was delighted with this scenario. In fact, in the drummer's mind Lennon was even closer. When later asked about Lennon's absence, Starr said, 'We got over it by feeling that he'd gone for lunch, he'd gone for a cup of tea . . . he was just around the corner – but it's a sadness for all of us because you know the three of us got pretty close again there, and still there's that empty hole, that *is* John.'[19] The more spiritual Harrison was less moved because he didn't believe that Lennon was dead. 'OK, your physical body falls off, but the soul lives on. We are going to meet again,' he told one interviewer.[20]

Writers and readers were eager to know what contemporary Britpop musicians made of the 'new' Beatles song. Having expected 'Free as a Bird' to be 'rubbish', Supergrass bassist Mick Quinn found it a 'fair-enough song' that was 'all right'.[21] Pulp's Jarvis Cocker felt greater unease. 'What's important about the

Beatles is that the timing was good,' he said. 'They stopped it just when they should have stopped it, and so their memory has not been violated in the same way that maybe the Rolling Stones' memory has been violated by some of the abominations that they've produced since then.'[22] Bob Stanley of Saint Etienne considered the whole idea to be 'really grim and distasteful'. Ono may have okayed it, but Lennon was no longer around to block it if he'd wished.[23] For Stanley, the *Anthology* took some of the 'magic' away from The Beatles' erstwhile 'perfect' discography. It didn't help that 'Free as a Bird' sounded 'like early ELO'.[24] John Power of Cast made the same comparison in more generous terms: 'I seem to remember a John Lennon quote once where he said, "If you ever want to know what the next Beatles album would sound like, then buy an ELO record."' Power doubted whether it would have any negative impact on the 'mystery' of the band. 'As long as you realise that they're not trying to change the world any more – because musically they've already done that – then it's OK.'[25] Martin Carr of The Boo Radleys thought the 'crap' single was just 'not good enough'. But he did enjoy the telly series.[26] Ian Broudie of Lightning Seeds couldn't understand why they'd even bother putting out a single that was less than phenomenal. To him it sounded too much like Traveling Wilburys. Instead of Jeff Lynne, it would've been smarter to use George Martin, 'even if he's a bit deaf'. He also questioned the wisdom of digging around Lennon's old demo tapes for the song's basis: 'If something's on a cassette and you haven't got around to putting it on an album, it's usually not your most inspired.'[27] That said, he was still disappointed when 'Free as a Bird' failed to reach number one in the UK singles chart. Paul McCartney must have lowered his thumbs and shaken his fists when it was kept off the top spot by his nemesis Michael Jackson with the sanctimonious 'Earth Song'. Oasis's Noel Gallagher, meanwhile, used the occasion to reiterate his standard cultural Luddism:

> If there was anything around at the moment that was new and was good, surely we'd be into that? You get repeats on the TV of *Match of the Day* and all that because the football games were better then. People now are into old bands because the old bands are better than the new bands. It's just as simple as that.[28]

Another song cribbed from Lennon's demo tapes was completed too. Included on *Anthology 2*, 'Real Love' was also released as a single, reaching number four in the UK (below Oasis, Robert Miles and Take That). The song received most of its column inches as a result of the controversy surrounding its exclusion from the BBC Radio 1 playlist. The Conservative MP Harry Greenway was so appalled by this decision that he pledged to push Parliament to intervene and reverse it.[29] Presumably this would have meant forcing the station to play the single. Had such measures been introduced, it would have set a terrifying precedent for the steering of popular culture by politicians with fingers so far off the pulse they may as well be gloved in blocks of cement.[30]

While accepting that The Beatles' careers would not be troubled by the snub, McCartney questioned Radio 1's decision in a letter to the *Daily Mirror*. He emphasized the band's popularity among licence fee payers (and the newspaper's readers) and pointed to the number of younger British bands ('like Oasis') who kept namechecking The Beatles. 'The station is being ageist,' complained the more forthright Francis Rossi, whose band, Status Quo, had recently gone a step further by taking Radio 1 to court when it declined to play 'Fun Fun Fun', their joint single with an extremely tired-looking Beach Boys. Radio 1 defended itself on the grounds that it focused on contemporary music enjoyed by younger listeners, which was fair enough. When he had taken over the station in 1993, Matthew Bannister had made several enemies for himself in his determination to win back an under-25 audience. Purged from the channel was its roster of veteran DJs who'd inspired the cringeworthy comedy characters Smashie and Nicey from *Harry Enfield's Television Programme*. Reflecting on it later, McCartney conceded that 'Real Love' had been a case of 'boiling your cabbages twice . . . You do a thing that's so exciting, you do it again and the novelty's ended.'[31]

Ian Broudie had wondered whether the hearts of the surviving band members had really been in it because 'Free as a Bird' sounded so much like it had been thrown together by Lynne.[32] It was Harrison who – by ultimatum – had insisted on the appointment of his Traveling Wilburys bandmate.[33] It was also Harrison whose heart was less in it than the other two Beatles.[34] Attempts to pad out further Lennon home recordings didn't work out. And when it came to trying out another new number, this one said to be co-written by McCartney and Harrison, the session was abandoned. The pair had never written together back in the 1960s, and the youngest Beatle had often complained that McCartney and Lennon had always been too dismissive of his own material and domineering when it came to collaboration. There had already been tension during the sessions for 'Free as a Bird' when McCartney had raised doubts over a guitar part that sounded reminiscent of Harrison's solo chart-topper 'My Sweet Lord' (1970).[35] Old habits die hard, and past insecurities festered on. McCartney would later attribute the mood swings and thorniness to those 'business problems' that Harrison had been weathering.[36] Neil Aspinall's working title for the documentary had always been *The Long and Winding Road*, and when certain parties objected to the use of a McCartney-penned song title, *Anthology* became a diplomatic, if slightly dull, compromise. Harrison also petitioned successfully to have the end of the documentary altered because its original version was 'too McCartney'.[37] The latter had his own hang-ups. Having received his test pressing of *Anthology 2*, McCartney had a last-minute wobble over the tracklist. This meant delaying the release so that new CD booklets could be printed at quite a cost, one McCartney apparently footed himself.[38] It is thought that 'I'm Down' was shunted from Track 6 up to Track 3 because McCartney had objected to the compilation opening with a succession of Lennon-sung numbers. Kinder speculators have argued that McCartney simply wanted to improve the flow by repositioning this up-tempo and more heavily rocking song.[39] Granted, it was one of his.

'Free as a Bird' did not fulfil Martin's prediction that it would easily reach number one 'all over the world'.[40] If Wikipedia's listings are accurate, it hit the top spot only in Scotland, for one week. Seven days later, The Beatles had dropped to number three, behind Jackson's 'Earth Song' and Boyzone's cover of Cat Stevens's 'Father and Son'. The fortunes of 'Free as a Bird' and 'Real Love', and those of the wider *Anthology*, are sometimes written about in terms of failure. That's what it's like for The Beatles. Anything less than sheer global domination can be interpreted as a flop, arousing schadenfreude in certain quarters. However, the *Anthology* can also be seen as a phenomenon.

In America, *Anthology 1* was praised for boosting retailers' spirits (read: profits) by getting people back into shops that sold records towards the end of an otherwise underwhelming year. The owner of San Diego's Off the Record said the documentary had 'revved people's interest again' and thanked it for bringing some 'buzz' back to his store. 'It's the kick in the ass that the industry needed,' he added.[41] In London and Liverpool, no doubt other cities too, people queued outside record shops to be the first to get their hands on *Anthology 1*.[42] The *Wall Street Journal* referred to the marketing campaign as 'Beatlemania II'.[43] According to *The Times*, The Beatles were 'pop music's latest craze' (again).[44] Reporting from New York, *The Guardian*'s Mark Tran wrote that Beatlemania was not only back but that it was 'even bigger than before'.[45] In the USA, an estimated 1.2 million copies of *Anthology 1* were shifted within the first week of its release, and sales of The Beatles' older albums were boosted in their tens of thousands.[46]

Reviewing the first instalment of the television show, Lynne Truss claimed its inherent problem was that 'everyone over the age of 30 knows this stuff already, and people under 30 are not interested.'[47] I could speak from my own and my friends' experience to counter this claim. Some people cheerfully embrace the music of their parents. Many shun it in favour of their own tribe. Young people in the 1990s seemed less eager than prior generations to reject the music of their mothers and fathers. Neil Young became hip again as 'the godfather of grunge'. Britpoppers emulated The Beatles, The Who, The Kinks and Small Faces. Older stars were also getting down with the kids. Or at least they tried to. Towards the end of the decade, Rod Stewart added to his repertoire songs by Oasis, Primal Scream and Skunk Anansie. Tom Jones duetted with the likes of Stereophonics, Cerys Matthews from Catatonia, The Divine Comedy and Space. In that respect it was a weirdly and perhaps uniquely noncombative time.

For many younger listeners, Anthologymania marked the beginning of their own lifelong Beatles fandom, one that's been passed down in turn to subsequent generations. To those who had been born long after The Beatles split, the *Anthology* CDs and documentary series gave some sense of the excitement they hadn't been able to experience for themselves. As for the accusation of everyone knowing everything in the documentary already, that isn't really the case. The series tries to clear up some misconceptions and either confirm or refute certain deep-set myths. As well as archive footage, it featured freshly conducted interviews with the surviving band members, producer George Martin, and Apple insiders Derek Taylor and Neil Aspinall. Like all human memories, their recollections will not always have been completely reliable. 'Despite their personal and at times clashing agendas, Lennon, McCartney, Harrison and Starr's *Anthology* accounts are among the most valuable sources in Beatles history because, unlike their biographers, they experienced and made history firsthand,' writes Erin Torkelson Weber.[48] She accepts that it is also an authorized history, so the account is sugar-coated. Some of the story's less pleasant moments are skimmed over or are absent entirely. It did have to squeeze a long, complicated, detailed, multifaceted, multi-charactered and richly sourced story into eight episodes, palatable to a TV audience with wide demographics. There are certainly worse official overviews in the history of the rock doc.[49]

Writing about the belated tie-in book, Ray Connolly noticed that one of the best things about the *Anthology* was its repositioning of Ringo Starr to the centre of the band's success story.[50] By the 1990s, Starr had long been the butt of jokes, like the one about him not being the best drummer in the world . . . 'Let's face it, he wasn't even the best drummer in The Beatles.' This gag is sometimes misattributed to John Lennon. As barbed as that man's tongue could be, he would have never said anything so disparaging about Ringo and his talent. Beatleologists said the line had been coined by the comedian Jasper Carrott. It is now thought to have first appeared in an episode of the BBC series *Radio Active*, broadcast in 1981.[51] All four Beatles had struggled to shake off the stereotype they'd each been assigned in *A Hard Day's Night* and *Help!* Ringo's was that of the underappreciated, almost childlike outsider. The *Anthology* provided a more rounded picture of the drummer than most people had known. The oldest member, who was last to join the band, Richard Starkey had come from the poorest background of any of The Beatles and triumphed against the odds. A sickly child, he had missed much of school. Growing up in the rough area of Dingle, he would get beaten up. He saw other people 'lose their eyes', witnessed stabbings and hammer attacks.[52] He was vital to The Beatles' sound and fitted beautifully into the group's social dynamics. The Beatles' success relied on so many pieces that happened to fall into place. If The Beatles had not met Ringo Starr, just as if they'd never come across and clicked with the likes of Brian Epstein and George Martin, their story – and that of the wider world – would have been a completely different one. With *Anthology 1*, Starr warranted reassessment from those who'd written him off or done him down. By comparing the *Anthology* material on which Pete Best drummed to those recorded after his firing, it's clear how much of a boost was provided by the reliable hand of Ringo. In one of his interviews for the documentary, McCartney indicates that the real 'beginning' of The Beatles was when Ringo joined the band. The documentary's archive footage is rich with clips and close-ups of Starr's powerful backbeats and inventive drum fills.

On the CDs, we also hear the boost that came when McCartney shifted from rhythm guitar to bass following the departure of Stuart Sutcliffe in 1961. The latter was not the greatest musician in the world and had always preferred painting. In the documentary, he is pictured with his back to the camera to conceal the fact he wasn't playing the right part. McCartney had not been desperate to get his hands on Sutcliffe's bass, as Philip Norman's *Shout!* had alleged.[53] Bass guitar had never been the sexiest role in a band. 'Forget it! Nobody wants to play bass, or nobody did in those days,' McCartney told his biographer Barry Miles. 'Bass was the thing that the fat boys got lumbered with and were asked to stand at the back and play . . . So I definitely didn't want to do it but Stuart left and I got lumbered with it.'[54] Over time, McCartney would grow to embrace and enjoy his instrument. With experience in guitar, piano and trumpet, an ear for melody and his natural inquisitiveness, McCartney would not be restricted by his default instrument's small number of strings or its standard tuning. He began listening closely to other bassists. He admired Motown players like James Jamerson ('I was nicking a lot off him') and became interested in how Brian Wilson might play in a different key to rest of The Beach Boys, 'just to hold it back'.[55] On the *Anthology*, McCartney can be heard moving away from the straightforward root notes that less adventurous bassists might have followed, liberating himself and his bass-playing admirers from such obedience. His parts grew in confidence, complexity and fluidity. They also became better recorded and more noticeable because they were placed higher in the mix. He'd sometimes put a capo on his strings to play in a different key or else down-tune his strings, a technique later embraced by heavy metal bands like Black Sabbath. Most impressively, he became known for playing independent melodies against the arrangement of the songs. It was a method, McCartney admitted, that jazz bassists already used. His father, Jim, had been an amateur jazz musician. In the 1960s it was not commonly heard in pop. His approach to bass playing, Paul felt, gave him more 'power' and 'control' than he would have had as a typical root-noter over the band, which was ostensibly a 'democracy', although one in which a couple of people were more equal than others. It was a power he wielded responsibly, without overshadowing his fellow members of the unit by making the bass lines too busy or dominant.

Some were surprised that McCartney came across so well in the documentary series. For those who were card-carrying members of 'Team Paul', it provided some long-awaited affirmation. Of all the *Anthology* participants, it was McCartney who most 'had his ass on the line', as Mindy LaBernz put it in the *Austin Chronicle*. 'I was a wreck every time he came on the screen, hoping to god he wouldn't come off too contrived, too nostalgic, too anything that would give the skeptics more ammunition.' Using the programme as the impetus to write over three thousand words in McCartney's defence, LaBernz showed how disbelievers had 'been duped into not appreciating him'. As for those who had been sniffy about Paul while glorifying John, they were accused of holding the same values as school bullies:

The Beatles' bassmaster performing with his band in Belfast, 1964.

> Make fun of the kid who does his homework – who at least attempts the problems on the blackboard or goes out for the school play – just because he's trying; everyone knows it's much cooler to sit in the back row making fun of the world, because if you try, you just may fail, and then you'd be the brunt of the joke. It's cooler to just not give a fuck.[56]

The McCartney of the *Anthology* could appear humble at times. He recognized his own failings and discussed certain situations he could've handled differently. He could also be funny, sometimes self-deprecatingly so, but also knowingly confident when he felt it was required: 'I'm not a great one for that, you know. "Maybe it was too many of that." Look. What do you mean? It was great. It sold. It's the bloody Beatles "White Album". Shut up!'[57]

## Hello, Goodbye . . . Hello!

'It is extraordinary that we now still listen to music from bands in the 1950s and 1960s, like The Beatles,' complained the documentary maker Adam Curtis in 2021. 'It is the equivalent of people in the 1960s still dancing to music from the 1890s.'[58] Curtis overlooks the fact that The Beatles are one of the exceptional examples. 'I'm the One' by Gerry and the Pacemakers has not been passed down the generations with the same degree of immortality. As for previous centuries, you can still pop into HMV And pick up a recording of Gustav Mahler's Symphony No. 3 (and dance to it if you wish). 'Much of modern culture has become like an ageing ghost that constantly haunts us and refuses to allow us to move on into the future,' says Curtis.[59] It's debatable whether ghosts can age, technically speaking, but that's beside the point. Nostalgia and sentimentality can be dangerous and debilitating national diseases. As someone who spends much of his life burrowing through the vast corridors of the BBC archive, Curtis ought to appreciate that historical culture can also be a healthy and even vital interest in which to be immersed. This is not mutually exclusive from people's simultaneous keenness to discover new art and artists, and to push things forward. It doesn't quite work like that. The artefacts of the past help us to understand how we got here and where we might be going. They connect us to our parents, grandparents, ancestors and forerunners. From the close study of old ideas, fresh ones often arise. Even the worst Beatles song has such potential contained within it. (That song, incidentally, is 'What's the New Mary Jane' from *Anthology 3*.)

On the subject of ghosts, 'Free as a Bird' was neither the first nor the only time that the voice of a dead person had been used to create new product. The 7-inch 'Peggy Sue Got Married/Crying, Waiting, Hoping' was completed by studio musicians from a solo recording after Buddy Holly died in 1959. Both tunes were covered by The Beatles. For their ninth and final album, 1978's *An American Prayer*, The Doors wrote fresh music to back the spoken-word recordings of Jim Morrison, the singer they had lost. It includes one of Morrison's poems about his own penis. Three years later, Patsy Cline and Jim Reeves could be heard duetting together on 'Have You Ever Been Lonely?' even though the pair never recorded together and had died in separate plane crashes about twenty years before. It became a number-five hit on the *Billboard* country chart. In 1988 Hank Williams Sr, who had died in 1953, posthumously duetted with Hank Williams Jr on 'There's a Tear in My Beer'. Natalie Cole also sang with her long-departed father, Nat King, on 1991's 'Unforgettable'. Because CDs couldn't sell fast enough, the music industry was booming, technology was evolving rapidly, the millennium was looming and it seemed like we had already reached 'The End of History', in the 1990s necro-songs prospered, with 'Free as a Bird' playing no small part in that. In 1995, a month before The Beatles' comeback single, Queen had released their chart-topping album *Made in Heaven*, which embellished vocals and music that Freddie Mercury had recorded before his death. The examples thereafter are too many to list. Elvis Presley and Lisa Marie Presley both singing on 'Don't Cry Daddy' (1997); Lauryn Hill performing with her partner's dead father, Bob Marley, on 'Turn Your Lights Down Low' (1999). Tupac Shakur must be the most prolific rapper from beyond the grave. By 2004, he'd released more albums since death than he'd made when still breathing.[60] To bring it back full circle to the Fab Four, on his first posthumously released album, *The Don Killuminati: The 7 Day Theory* (1996), Shakur sang of being 'free like the bird in the tree'.

In 1998 Prince (or The Artist Formerly Known As . . .) was asked whether he'd consider a digitally enabled 'jam' with any musical legend from the past. 'Certainly not,' he replied.

> If I was meant to jam with Duke Ellington, we would have lived in the same age. That whole virtual reality thing . . . it really is demonic. And I am not a demon. Also, what they did with that Beatles song, manipulating John Lennon's voice to have him singing from across the grave . . . that'll never happen to me. To prevent that kind of thing from happening is another reason why I want artistic control.[61]

Since Prince's death in 2012, his estate has issued plenty of material from his vaults (which, to be fair, were vaster than most artists'). Before the Super Bowl LII in 2018, there were rumours that Prince would appear in hologram form during the glitzy half-time show. Sporting facial hair that looked borrowed from a bearded Action Man figure, Justin Timberlake simply sang along to video footage of Prince that was projected onto an enormous curtain.

A clear line can be drawn between posthumously arranged recordings and the avatars of ABBA that were launched in 2022. These are destined to continue performing long after the deaths of the corporeal members of the Europop band, and probably long after the rest of humanity has been shaken off this planet – until, that is, the holograms' batteries run out (if that is what they run on and I'm not confusing them with the similarly energetic bunnies from the Duracell adverts). At Glastonbury 2022, when McCartney 'duetted' with footage of John Lennon from Peter Jackson's *Get Back* film, there was a hint that 'The Beatles' could re-form and carry on gigging even after the next two members have shuffled off this mortal coil.

As well as it sold, *Anthology 1* was kept off the top of the UK album chart by Robson & Jerome, two actors from the ITV series *Soldier, Soldier*, which gives us a picture of how the airwaves would soon be suffocated by the chart domination of people from the television who can sing karaoke. Robson & Jerome's success made the first fortune for Simon Cowell, who had pursued the pair so doggedly to make a record that at one point Robson Green was forced to scream down the telephone, 'Why are you harassing me and my family?'[62] Earlier in his career, the budding Svengali had shown similar levels of persistence in hounding Pete Waterman, the record producer who had first got into music after seeing The Beatles perform live.[63] Even if everything seems to circle back to The Beatles, we shouldn't blame the Fab Four for the Infernal One.

The *Anthology* records were a greater triumph in America. The first double-CD set entered the *Billboard* album chart at number one and went triple platinum within weeks. On that side of the Atlantic, as we have seen, the backlash against The Beatles in the late 1970s and the 1980s was not quite as severe as it had been back home. Some of the singles considered by his critics to be among McCartney's cringier works were less well known over there or not even released (see 'We All Stand Together' and 'Once Upon a Long Ago'). As for the comparable mockery it attracted, the *Anthology* documentary was ribbed lightly and with fondness on the ABC network by the 'Leftover Beatles Memories' sketch in the *Dana Carvey Show*. Britain's *Spitting Image* was, typically, more scathing. Seeking guidance on their next career move, its puppet caricatures of McCartney, Harrison and Starr were depicted trying to contact Lennon through a Ouija board. His answer? 'Leave-my-music-alone!-I'm-spinning-in-my-grave!-You-money-grabbing-bastards!'[64]

Some people – those around the same age as Adam Curtis, who was born in 1955 – were irritated because they had assumed that their generation had always been, and always would be, The Beatles' rightful owners. Suddenly their fandom had been commandeered by upstarts who couldn't possibly understand the music as comprehensively, or hope to relate to it as properly, as older folk. The reason being they weren't there ('man'). As Rob Sheffield has observed, the 1990s was the point at which The Beatles 'broke free of their era'.[65] The band's biographies were now less likely to have subtitles anchoring them to the distinct time when they'd been active, like *The Beatles in Their Generation* (the subtitle to Philip Norman's *Shout!*) or *The Beatles' Records and the Sixties* (from Ian MacDonald's *Revolution in the Head* of 1994). See the one written by Sheffield himself: *Dreaming The Beatles: The Love Story of One Band and the Whole World* (2017).

'Free as a Bird' is rarely played on the radio anymore. It hasn't matched the timeless magic of the classic hits The Beatles made together when they were all still alive. Jeff Lynne's production didn't help in this respect, providing as it does a sense of accidental self-parody. For some listeners, this impedes the song's emotional impact, though others found it to be very moving, aroused by the eeriness of hearing John Lennon's ghostly voice accompanied once again by his ex-bandmates, who were at the riper age he'd been so brutally denied. The sociologist Anthony Elliott considered it 'a noticeably mournful affair, caught between hope and despair'.[66] As *Mojo* reader Paul Hamilton enthused in the magazine's letters pages, 'the neat touch is the turnaround of the Lennon and McCartney roles; whereas in "We Can Work It Out", for example, Paul was Ollie Optimist and John was Frankie Fatalist, in FAAB (good acronym!) it's quite the reverse.'[67] The two men's roles had never been quite as cut and dry as that, but there was an emotional tug in the contrast between Lennon's unearthed verses and the freshly written, gap-filling bridge sung by McCartney (and by Harrison in its second, shorter occurrence). Elliott denies that this reunion was of the typical 'Hollywood' variety and sees it as a legitimate and artistic way of exploring and revisiting the past in order to better understand – and handle – the present.[68] The lesser-loved single 'Real Love' inspired Greil

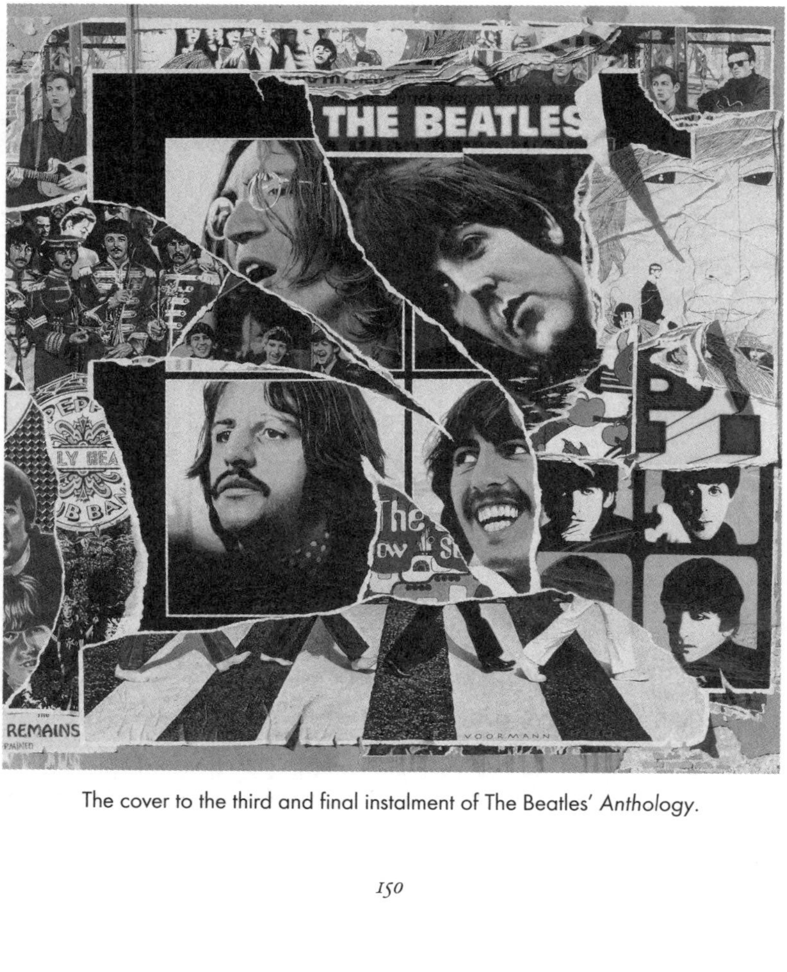


The cover to the third and final instalment of The Beatles' *Anthology*.

Marcus to write a lengthy reflection on how the sublimeness of the record made him 'swoon' and whether the sentimentality it stirred within him was something to be embarrassed about or not.[69] Even less likely to be heard on BBC 6 Music or Radio 2, that song has a questionable legacy in that it hit number seven in 2014 when sung by Tom Odell as the soundtrack to that year's John Lewis Christmas advert, which starred a computer-animated penguin.

There was a sense, at the time of its promotion, that the *Anthology* would be the last word on The Beatles. Advertisements for the third compilation trumpeted 'The final chapter in the story of the greatest band that ever was . . . or ever will be.' McCartney and Harrison joked about titling their next record *Scraping the Bottom of the Barrel*. 'And George Martin reckons if we put anything out after this, it'll have to be issued with a government health warning,' he added.[70] McCartney, Harrison, Starr and Ono seemed to be drawing a line under the matter; Harrison especially, since his financial predicaments had been resolved by the sales. The guitarist was said to be the 'chief architect' of a statement issued by Apple in November 1996 announcing 'The Beatles are no more. The official word is that Paul McCartney, George Harrison and Ringo Starr will never play together again as a group, and they have decided that there will be no more singles issued from their back catalogue.'[71] This announcement was echoed in 2023 when The Beatles released 'Now and Then'. As with 'Free as a Bird' and 'Real Love', the single was constructed around one of Lennon's demo songs, this time using artificial intelligence to clean up John's vocal and separate it from the piano track. Harrison was no longer around to object, if that is what he would have done. His widow, Olivia, and son, Dhani, said in the press release that George 'would have wholeheartedly joined Paul and Ringo in completing the recording of "Now and Then"'.[72] But then the estate would say that, wouldn't it? 'Now and Then' was billed as 'the last Beatles song'. With Peter Jackson's sound team on hand

and Giles Martin's eagerness to continue following in his father's footsteps, who's to say the cabbages won't get boiled again?

Little did Harrison realize that the *Anthology*'s success would pave the way for a limitless stream of subsequent Beatles products. The *Anthology* albums proved without doubt that there was an insatiable market for unreleased material, be they demos, live cuts, archive interviews or whatever else the barrel had to offer. This had implications not just for The Beatles but also for pretty much any artist with at least a few followers who had space available on their shelves.

The 'boxed set', as it was originally and correctly known (as opposed to a 'box set', which sounds like you've spent a lot of money on an extravagant set of boxes), is seen as the caviar of affluent, middle-aged, often male record collectors who have more money than they know what to do with. Better he spends his disposable income on boxed sets than a cherry-red Ferrari and extortionately priced tickets to see the testosterone-balded podcaster Joe Rogan at the O2 Arena, right? Simon Reynolds sees the boxed set as another symptom of our habit for cherishing music as 'memorial' and 'monument' instead of pursuing The New Sound. 'I can't be the only person who ferociously covets these box sets yet finds them strangely repellent once they've got them,' he observes. 'With its packaging resemblance to a coffin or tombstone, the box set is where an old enthusiasm goes to die: a band or genre you loved frozen into an indigestible chunk.'[73] Hardly any of these exhaustive packages, he adds, are able to hold one's attention from beginning to end. Perhaps that's right. You are allowed to listen to one disc in a single sitting and return to the others at a later date, Simon. Then again, Reynolds's complaint is bound to be the case. If we subscribe to 'Sturgeon's revelation' (also known as his 'law'), conceived in the 1950s by the writer Theodore Sturgeon to rebut common criticisms of the science fiction genre, then 'ninety percent of everything is crud'. This applies to 'cars, books, cheeses, hairstyles, people and pins'. In fact, it applies to 'all things', apart from 'the acceptable tithe which we each happen to like'.[74] Music suffers just the same. Most artists, albums, singles, concerts, genres and subgenres?[75] Crud! Utter crud. Boxed sets too. Yet there will be a certain minority of sets for which it is worth forking out, depending on personal taste and the state of your bank balance. The tracklists of boxed sets – appended by '(Take 4)', 'Instrumental Version', 'Studio Rehearsal', 'Early Version', 'Preliminary Demo', 'Orchestral Overdub' or 'Speech, False Start and Abandoned Intro to Take 5' – don't exactly lend themselves to the attention-deficit listening experience moulded by the algorithms of streaming services. They resist and defy this, encouraging a deeper, more attentive and reflective listening experience. They encourage us to continue to take music seriously, challenging the risk of relegating everything to the condition of background muzak or playlist-friendly moods. The physical sets also bring some much-needed revenue into the industry, whereas Spotify is infamous for paying a pittance for its plays.

Having come of age in the 1990s, I may be just another nostalgic dinosaur, pining for the golden age of the physical format. It's fairly likely that young streamers these days will mature into boxed-set buyers themselves. That's unless environmental or economic disasters prevent their doing so. The release of these boxed sets, deluxe editions and anniversary reissues encourages thoughtful reflection on the music, what it meant then and what it means today, if anything. See *The Quietus* website's regular 'Reissue of the Week' and 'Anniversary' features, where Public Enemy's *It Takes a Nation of Millions to Hold Us Back* is hailed as having even greater weight today than it did in 1988, unlikely similarities are drawn between The Offspring's *Americana* (1998) and the now hashtag-problematic sitcom *Friends*, and *Murder Ballads* by Nick Cave and the Bad Seeds is convincingly recategorized as a gansta rap record.[76] Peruse the monthly 'Boomerang' pages of

*The Wire*, where Simon Reynolds has praised at least one boxed set himself (*Trip II The Moon 2092* by 1990s breakbeat producer Acen).[77] Can the reissuing of every LP from the past and the endless curation of boxed sets serve a positive purpose beyond interminable (and terminal?) reminiscence for the good old days? For one thing, they can shine a light on artists whose contribution has not received the recognition it deserves. Light in the Attic Records' reissues of Betty Davis's pioneering hard-funk albums of the 1970s are in no way frivolous or inessential; they are important. As for The Beatles, it would come as a surprise if anyone claims to listen to *Anthology 2* more often than they drop the needle on *Revolver* or *Sgt. Pepper*. Because the material was previously unreleased and it still has less familiarity to most of us, it can make a rewarding and refreshing change from always revisiting the classic albums. Avoiding what could have been a more casual approach of thoughtlessly cobbling everything and anything together, George Martin's storytelling-through-the-music agenda, and the staggered release dates of the three compilations, meant that this wasn't a case of rare-material overkill. At this point, there was still the need felt to exhibit quality over quantity. As Jamie Atkins notes, 'While the opening of The Beatles' vaults was massive news back in 1995, today – with overdraft-threatening multi-disc sets for comparatively niche artists commonplace – *Anthology* increasingly seems like an exercise in remarkable restraint.'[78] And given this is The Beatles we're talking about, even their offcuts were as likely to sink into the 90-per-cent quagmire of crud as Bob Dylan is to perform one of his old songs in recognizable form.

Or, to paraphrase Paul McCartney, it was great. It sold. It's the bloody Beatles' *Anthology*. Shut up!

## How Do You Do It?

For better or worse, the *Anthology*'s success opened the floodgates. In 1999, to coincide with the film's thirtieth anniversary rerelease, the *Yellow Submarine* soundtrack was issued in newly remixed form. It was the following year's singles compilation, *1*, that really shifted units. Was it needed? Probably not. There were no previously unreleased songs this time round. Its concept, 27 singles that had gone to number one in either the UK or the USA, was slammed by veteran music journalist Charles Shaar Murray, who accused it of championing vulgar popularity over cultural significance. 'I'm really glad that most of the songs dealt with love, peace, understanding,' said McCartney at the end of the *Anthology* documentary (perhaps forgetting moments like 'Maxwell's Silver Hammer'). 'It's all very "All You Need Is Love". John's "Give Peace a Chance". There's a very good spirit behind it all.' Those who'd formulated *1*, 'by sacrificing story to statistics', were sending out a different message, complained Murray: 'that music powered by, and so perfectly expressive of, an overwhelming generosity of spirit and soul ends up being marketed with such blinkered cynicism. Still, them's the breaks.'[79] For *Record Collector*'s Pam Mitchell, it showed The Beatles' competitive edge remained fully intact, even after their second dissolution: 'In 1999, the Elvis estate had thrown down the gauntlet with their *Artist of the Century* box set campaign. One year later, *1* was a strategic Scouse "sod off" in response.'[80] Many wondered who on the planet didn't own all of its songs already. Even so, *1* sold phenomenally well. For its marketing, Neil Aspinall specifically targeted young people who might have been familiar with The Beatles but had not yet purchased anything by them.[81] They can't have been the only ones reaching into their pockets, though. It sold by the millions and went to number one in almost every country with an albums chart.

Releases that followed the success of the *Anthology* and *1* have included *Let It Be . . . Naked* (2003), which reversed the Phil Spector production on the original album, with which McCartney had never been pleased. Those who baulk at McCartney's saccharine side should note that he has his own sugar tolerance upper limit. Spector's string and choral arrangement, added to the piano ballad 'The Long and Winding Road' without its writer's knowledge or approval, resulted in a stern letter from McCartney to Beatles manager Allen Klein: 'I had considered orchestrating "The Long and Winding Road" but I decided against it . . . Don't ever do it again.'[82] In 2006 George Martin and his son Giles made *Love*, a remix album that mashed up loads of Beatles songs and sounds and was originally commissioned for a Cirque du Soleil extravaganza. Again some reviewers couldn't see the point. For its champions, it provided another new way of hearing The Beatles, shedding further light on how ahead of their time they were and proving 'they remain the act to beat', as *The Observer*'s Neil Spencer put it in his five-star write-up.[83] Once again, it sold handsomely. Martin Jr has since taken over the family business by producing the music on *The Beatles: Rock Band* (2009) video game, and he has overseen the succession of fiftieth-anniversary expanded, remastered and deluxe editions of The Beatles' studio albums. A seven-disc boxed-set reissue of the 'White Album', packed with demos, rehearsal takes, studio jams and instrumental backing tracks, may well be accused of barrel-scraping. Compared to products like *1*, it at least offers material most Beatles nuts beyond bootleg hounds won't have heard before. (Finally, the twelve-minute version of 'Helter-Skelter'. Hooray! Come on Giles, now give us the 27-minute one . . .) No one is being forced to purchase or listen to takes that were not deemed worthy of flogging to the public in the decade they were taped. They are there if you want to hear or own them. It's for the curious, I'd say, not the gullible. Is the public availability of art and music and archives really so heinous? Besides providing entertainment to willing consumers, freeing this stuff from the exclusive access of studio engineers means it can be of great use to musicologists and other scholars.

The individual members of The Beatles and the owners of their estates can be as competitive with each other as they are collectively towards Elvis Presley's legacy. *The Beatles Anthology* was followed by the unimaginatively titled *John Lennon Anthology* (1998), a set of demos, outtakes and rarities. In 2001 there was an *Anthology*-style documentary film on Wings called *Wingspan*. The tie-in compilation, subtitled *Hits and History*, included a few non-Wings vintage solo numbers too, without any appearances from Stevie Wonder, Michael Jackson or Rupert Bear. This release also goes to show how Wings' reputation recovered during the 1990s. There is a famous line from the sitcom *I'm Alan Partridge*, first screened in 1997. The haplessly uncool titular character, who resides in a Travel Tavern after his wife has left him for a fitness instructor, educates a younger concierge on the genius of Wings: 'They're only the band The Beatles could have been.' Cue much laughter from the studio audience.[84] By the time of *Wingspan*'s release, we see the likes of *Mojo* magazine seriously positing that 'for the most part these songs genuinely measure up to the standard of The Beatles' McCartney-penned tracks.'[85] However fun it is to read that sentence out in Partridge's voice, it doesn't make it any less viable.

Neil Innes's parody band The Rutles had got in on the post-*Anthology* action first, with 1996's *Archaeology*, a collection of 'lost' tracks that had been locked away prior 'to avoid bootleggers. And tax collectors.'[86] Whether joining in with the joke or deadly serious, Bruce Eder of AllMusic considered the pastiches to be better than any of the material that either McCartney or Starr had put out in decades.[87] The *Archaeology* engaged in plenty of silliness, but within this were occasional moments of real poignancy, not least on its final track, a parody of McCartney's more 'granny music' moments. The lyric to 'Back in '64' sees Innes's alter ego, Ron Nasty, reflecting on his glory days all those years ago, feeling mystifyingly disconnected from both the fresh-faced young fella that black-and-white footage shows he used to be and the grandchildren on his lap, from whom he disguises his sadness by regaling them with tales about how much fun was once had – stories in which the kids may have little interest in at all.

'Back in '64' raises the question of whether McCartney felt similarly melancholic to Nasty/Innes when watching clips of his much younger self and reflecting on those bygone days. As the *Anthology* project and subsequent endeavours – Beatles-based and otherwise – have shown, McCartney has not experienced Nasty's (fictional) failure to engage the hearts and minds of people his grandchildren's age. McCartney has in fact been able to travel backwards and forwards, often with the ease and energy of a particularly sprightly Time Lord. In the aforementioned spiel near the end of the *Anthology* documentary in which McCartney congratulated his old band, with a heavy tint of rose, on the warm-hearted peace-and-love nature of 'all' their material, another aspect he emphasizes is his belief in cross-generational togetherness and understanding. Hardly any of their work, he says, screams 'Go on, kids! Tell them all to sod off! Leave your parents!' That statement may not have made the then quinquagenarian look like the most rebellious rock 'n' roller of all time. For some it will have vindicated their image of him as a bit of a square. It also helps to reveal part of McCartney's genius. Paul the Time-Traveller has always been able to concurrently navigate living in the all-important 'now' while pushing forwards into the unpredictable future and also delving way back into the past. It's no wonder he find fans in every generation. He's able to jump around, back and forth, in his TARDIS.

In the 1960s McCartney demonstrated maturity beyond his years. He risked mockery for not writing 'sod-off' songs like The

Who's increasingly ironic 'My Generation' (1965). Part of the terribly sad and beautifully orchestrated 'She's Leaving Home' was written from the perspective of distressed parents whose daughter had run away aged seventeen. It was inspired by newspaper reports about the disappearance of teenager Melanie Coe, and its enduring power lies in its sympathy for the deserted couple as well as the young woman who has gone, in the middle of the night, to seek thrills elsewhere. The contrast is emphasized by John Lennon's backing vocals. Having once been quite the tearaway himself, Lennon can be heard on the chorus channelling the parents' memories of unappreciated sacrifice and feelings of abandonment. McCartney wrote it, intuitively, in the ancient Aeolian mode. This act of journeying backwards through time adds to the listener's sense of loss.[88] He was then only in his mid-twenties. Also on *Sgt. Pepper's Lonely Hearts Club Band*, which in 1967 was considered the cutting edge of long-form psychedelic pop music, McCartney imagined himself as an old man. He had composed the tune for 'When I'm 64' back when he was a teenager. Its writer considers the song to be tongue-in-cheek.[89] Ian MacDonald thought it was 'aimed chiefly at parents, and as a result got a cool reception from the group's own generation'.[90] That being so, McCartney's ambition – intuitively or otherwise – stretches beyond appealing solely to the narrow market of his similarly aged baby boomers.

The experience of listening to *Sgt. Pepper* changes as you get older. Different aspects of it reveal themselves to you, and they astound once more in hitherto hidden ways. Pete Paphides believes McCartney 'finessed' this ability on the same year's 'Penny Lane' single: 'a song which pauses the videotape of memory on a scene to which its creator can never return, and as a result, gets sadder with every passing year'.[91] *Sgt. Pepper* works in the opposite way to The Doors, notes Paphides, whose 'Dionysian pretensions' seem wise to the adolescent mind but become harder to take seriously in adulthood.[92] One doesn't need to have existed in 1967 to have such emotional attachment to The Beatles' material. (Paphides was born in '69.) When I rewatch the *Anthology*, happy memories are stirred of seeing it for the first time in the company of my parents (who were there in the 1960s and could offer their own reflections on the time and music) and my younger siblings. Others will reminisce of discovering The Beatles through *1* or *Rock Band*, or one of the many other entry points, and they will marvel in turn as people younger than themselves are drawn in by *Get Back*, 'Now and Then' and, in the future, the inevitable ABBA-style Beatles avatar experience directed by Peter Jackson, produced by Giles Martin, remastered by Rick Rubin and narrated by Idris Elba, or perhaps their nepo-baby descendants. And for all those listeners too, 'Penny Lane' will become sadder with every passing year.

McCartney's eagerness to cross generations stems partly from his childhood; his memories of wildly differently aged family members gathered around the piano to have a jolly good sing-song together. Intergenerational tension has often fuelled different stages and subgenres of popular music. In other forms, such as folk, songs are passed down through the generations much more readily. In another Beatles lyric, McCartney wanted everybody to dance together to a song that was a hit before your mother was born. 'Granny music', as Lennon and others might have dismissed it? Maybe. But McCartney wouldn't be the time-traveller that he is, were that all that obsessed him.

McCartney voiced enthusiasm about particular bits of the *Anthology* compilations, like Harrison's acoustic rendition of 'While My Guitar Gently Weeps', the unusable version of 'And Your Bird Can Sing', during which McCartney and Lennon burst into fits of giggles, and his own first take of 'Yesterday'. (He only performed two versions on the day of recording.) On a darker note, he compared the whole experience to death by drowning and 'your life flashing in front of you'.[93] In his more candid moments, not unlike Ron Nasty of The Rutles on 'Back in '64', McCartney seemed unsettled by it all. 'The scariest thing is seeing your life just laid out in front of you, it's like someone's written your memoirs,' he told Paul Du Noyer. 'And I don't particularly want to write my memoirs.'[94] There was still so much more work to complete.

# 5
# *Flaming Pie*

One of the ironies of the 1990s was that despite the anti-Tory momentum that had been building for years, when New Labour finally came to power towards the end of the decade Britpop was already in a severe state of decline. Another incongruity was that Labour used as their campaign song D:Ream's 1993 dance hit 'Things Can Only Get Better' rather than something current by The Boo Radleys or Dodgy.[1] The feeling of national optimism after the general election was undercut by the shocking death of Princess Diana at age 36 a few months later and the equally unexpected outpouring of pubic grief from people who didn't know her, hadn't met her and, if they had, would've shared little in common with the celebrity royal.

The expectation surrounding Oasis's third album could never be fulfilled, and certainly not by the overly long and underwritten material on *Be Here Now* (1997). 'No album in history has experienced such a swift and dramatic reversal of fortune,' observes Dorian Lynskey.[2] It received glowing reviews from many critics, who seemed determined to overcompensate for the lesser enthusiasm they'd shown towards 1995's *(What's the Story) Morning Glory?* That album, Oasis's second, had sold so spectacularly well it made some publications look like they'd got it wrong and were out of touch with the mood of the nation. 'This time around, the Yanks will get it,' raved Charles Shaar Murray.[3] Not exactly. The response on the other side of the pond remained cooler. In the UK shoppers queued in their thousands to buy *Be Here Now*, making it the fastest-selling album in British history. The problems arose when they then took it home to give it a listen; almost as quickly, it became a ubiquitous presence in charity shops. Something had gone badly wrong. Critics ought to be above worrying about what's already popular. By second-guessing this time round, they had committed an even more embarrassing misjudgement than underestimating *(What's the Story)*. More in sync with the general reception was a sketch on *TFI Friday* in which host Chris Evans wore a surgical mask and used a defibrillator to try to bring the album back to life. It was hopeless trying.[4] '*Be Here Now*'s reputation lasted only slightly longer than the effects of a line of cocaine,' continues Lynskey, an apt metaphor given that's what the band were on when they made it.[5] Noel Gallagher quit taking cocaine not long afterwards and has disowned *Be Here Now*, although it's not as if he's recorded anything better since.

'There's a fucking blizzard of cocaine in London at the moment and I hate it,' Damon Albarn had complained in 1996. 'It's stupid. Everyone's become so blasé, thinking they're so ironic and witty and wandering around with this stupid fucking cokey confidence. Wankers. I mean, I did it but I can't say I was a cocaine addict.'[6] He also dabbled in heroin. The latter substance informed songs including 'Beetlebum', from Blur's self-titled fifth album, released in 1997, on which one of the most outspokenly anti-American bands of their generation began lifting tricks from U.S. indie rock bands like Pavement.

That same year, Radiohead released *OK Computer*, which was even more existentially miserable than their previous work. One of its less comatose songs was the jangly 'Electioneering', a sceptical assessment of empty promises and political spin. Once wryly humorous, Pulp no longer possessed the defiant hopefulness they'd expressed in 'Mis-Shapes', the opening song on

*Different Class*. They followed that album with the much darker *This Is Hardcore* (1998), on which Jarvis Cocker, another man who'd ended up snorting too much coke and feared he'd turned into something he'd always despised, ruminated on the trappings of fame, the sordidness of showbiz, drug-induced panic attacks, ageing and regrets. Their most directly political song of that time appeared as a B-side. 'Cocaine Socialism' scrutinized the cosying up between pop stars and politicians, questioning the sincerity of both camps. Cocker's musings on almost any subject were usually more arresting than those of most rival lyricists. Lesser Britpop bands sounded burned out and weary: see the 1997 releases by Sleeper, Echobelly, Cast and others like them. Some acts went completely AWOL, such as Elastica, whose own drug intake totally crippled the band's productivity.

The Verve's *Urban Hymns* appeared a month after *Be Here Now* and benefited from its outstanding singles, which helped quench the expectancy that had been built, yet not satisfied, by Oasis's third album. Because The Verve split (not for the first or final time) before recording its follow-up, rather than lumbering on longer like Oasis, *Urban Hymns* also left its audience with a tantalizing promise of what might have been for Wigan's finest. This cessation has encouraged people to gradually erase from their memories the lacklustre nature of The Verve's late-1990s concerts, leaving rose-tinted recollections of singing along to 'Bitter Sweet Symphony' in a field full of fellow folk in fishing hats. Singles aside, the 75-minute album drags on for far too long. Dust off that compact disc for the first time in years and behold the surprising amount of urban yawns. That's if you still own it. It's another staple item of the second-hand shop.

While it lacked the sonic adventurousness of The Verve's earlier records, *Urban Hymns* had nothing on the mildness of many newer acts making the airwaves. The New Acoustic Movement, as *NME* dubbed it, owed a debt to the success of ballads like Oasis's

'Wonderwall' and Radiohead's softer moments, with less of the latter's wallowing despair. At the same time, this scene pushed back against masculine Britpop bravado with greater sensitivity. As commendable as that was, it could be hard to get feverishly excited about the background-friendly sounds of Travis, David Gray, Embrace, Coldplay and Badly Drawn Boy, even if their popularity proved that many people must have done. In his proudly unhip book on the subject, Tom Clayton writes about how this calm and gentle music made people feel a sense of comfort as they faced the uncertainty of the looming new millennium.[7] With Britpop's anti-Americanism on the decline as well, at the other extreme disillusioned kids could get into the hypermasculine genre of nu-metal, which combined hip-hop, metal, sexism, baseball caps and unfeasibly large shorts with heavy chains pulling down the waist to expose the wearer's boxers.

Paul McCartney was not about to jump on that bandwagon. There would be no Ross Robinson-produced album full of down-tuned riffs and guest rapping from Fred Durst. Given how things had turned out, McCartney had been wise to stay at a distance from Britpop. His next solo album put to shame most of the Britpop albums released around the same time. As comforting as the record was in places, it demanded and held the listener's attention more successfully than the acoustic-guitar muzak of the aforementioned New Acoustic balladeers. Packed with rich and catchy melodies that felt as though they had arrived very naturally, as if having appeared in McCartney's head as easily as 'Yesterday', the new album demonstrated that McCartney's pop sensibilities and innate songwriting nous were far from dimming as he entered his mid-fifties.

## Used to Be Bad

*Flaming Pie* (1997) proved to be one of McCartney's most critically acclaimed albums from any decade. It was assumed that revisiting the old days when working on the *Anthology* had rekindled his greatness. The references were there, after all. The record's title was taken from one of John Lennon's quips about how The Beatles had come up with their name. The lyrics to the opening track, 'The Song We Were Singing', harked back to the Swinging Sixties. Ringo Starr and George Martin contributed to the album. 'Little Willow' was written for Starr's first wife, Maureen, who had recently passed away.

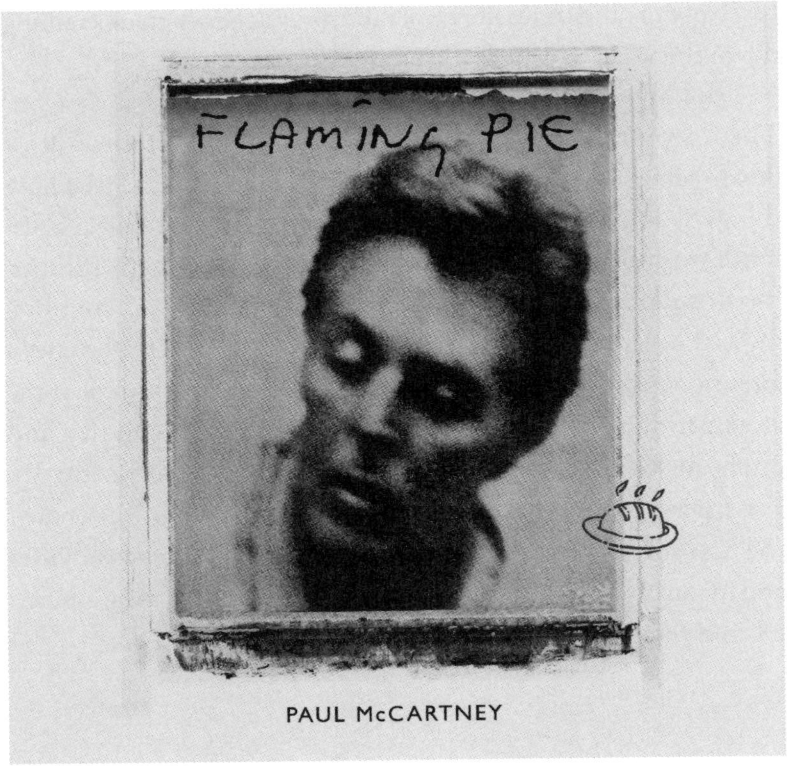


*Flaming Pie* (1997).

Journalists' leading questions elicited responses from McCartney that superficially confirmed that the secret to *Flaming Pie*'s merits lay in the *Anthology*. So did McCartney's own sleeve notes. These opened with a line about how he 'came off the back of *The Beatles Anthology* with an urge to do some new music', as if he hasn't possessed that desire for the whole of his life.[8] Reviews toed that line too, opening with statements like 'The Beatles' "anthology" projects clearly left Paul McCartney in a reflective frame of mind.'[9] The reality was less simple than that. This solo album could also be viewed as an exercise in maintaining the momentum that McCartney had been building before the interruption provided by the *Anthology* and its promotional commitments. McCartney said he would have liked to release an album earlier, if the record company hadn't pressured him to avoid a clash with the years-long *Anthology* campaign.[10] Several of *Flaming Pie*'s songs had been written back in the late 1980s and early 1990s. Some of them were nostalgic. Other lyrics were rooted firmly in the present.

McCartney asked Jeff Lynne to co-produce some of the tracks. They had got on well while working on the *Anthology*'s 'new' Beatles songs, 'Free as a Bird' and 'Real Love'. Yet McCartney was wary of falling into Lynne's usual, distinctive, recognizably ELO-ish sound. He suggested they find ways to avoid that or even subvert the formula.[11] Why did he appoint him in the first place, then? In one interview, McCartney said Lynne was 'sort of George's boyfriend, if you know what I mean, and, you know, you don't want to tread on people's toes'.[12] Still he did. Given the tension between McCartney and Harrison over the years, which had often spilled out into the press, and the awkward way in which the *Anthology* sessions had ground to a halt, it's tempting to see this symbolic infidelity as a slight towards George. Certainly it was a move that risked upsetting him further. The name of the third surviving Beatle was conspicuous by its absence in the credits to

*Flaming Pie*. 'I've rung him and maybe he hasn't rung back. No big deal,' McCartney explained.

> But when I ring Ringo, he rings back immediately, we're quite close that way. You know, I'll write George a letter and he might not reply to it. I don't think he means not to reply to it but it makes me wonder whether he actually wants to do it or not. And if you're not sure, you back off a little. But I love him, he's a lovely guy and I would love to do it. It'd be fun, he's good.[13]

Steve Miller contributed too. Despite the presence of some starry names, the album wasn't overcooked. McCartney played most of the instruments himself, including a variety of guitars, basses, keyed instruments, vibraphone and the trusty old 'knee slap'. Although the outcome was glossier than suggested by those reviewers who highlighted its 'down-home primitive miniaturist'[14] methods and 'organic, demo-fresh ambience',[15] it does share some of the freewheeling spirit of *McCartney* and *McCartney II*. He might even have got away with calling it *McCartney III*, but it made better business sense to use a Beatley title given the level of attention attracted by the *Anthology* campaign.[16]

McCartney's sleeve notes mention the speed at which The Beatles used to work and the amount of fun they had in the studio.[17] The approach this time was even more casual than the sessions for his previous studio album, *Off the Ground*, with its first takes, live feel, lack of preciousness and off-the-cuff moments that still made the final cut. In fact, *Flaming Pie* comes off the back of *Off the Ground* as much as it does the *Anthology*. This time, however, no band was used. It was made by 'a bunch of friends and family', but mostly the multi-instrumentalist McCartney, who wanted to 'not sweat it' and 'have a laugh, because it's just an album'.[18] While *Flaming Pie* supports the theory that McCartney produces some of his best work when he is not trying particularly hard, there is another angle to this in that he was also intensely focused on quality control. This was another thing, apparently, hammered home by the *Anthology*. The Beatles enjoyed making (most of) their albums. That's how McCartney remembered it, at least. At the same time, they set strict standards for themselves and the strength of their material.[19] McCartney wanted to be sure he was happy with each song that made it onto *Flaming Pie*. Anything that roused doubt was dropped. 'Bang, bang, every single one is a song you remember,' he said of the The Beatles' tracklists. 'I thought, I'm gonna make an album like that.'[20] The relatively relaxed attitude towards writing and recording, combined with fairly speedy recording methods that prevented overthinking anything, as well as a concern for the consistent quality of the material: these echo the making of *Off the Ground*. On the latter issue, see the 'poet-proof' policy discussed earlier. There are many differences between the two records, and on *Flaming Pie* the processes ultimately paid off better. Whereas there was an anger to some of *Off the Ground*'s environmentally conscious lyrics and a dark undertone to some of its character pieces (whether cloaked in typically pleasant melodies), *Flaming Pie*'s verses tend to stick to wistfulness and romance with the occasional bout of surrealism. Nevertheless, there is still a clear throughline between that record and the foundation set by *Off the Ground* that may have been supported but wasn't created by the *Anthology* and its reminders of The Beatles' glory days. Once more, it's as if McCartney was giving – pardon my French – less of a fuck in some respects and much more of a fuck in others, again reaping the benefits of such a contradiction.

## The Songs He Was Singing

*Flaming Pie* opens with one of its most nostalgic tracks, 'The Song We Were Singing', its position in the running order seeking to immediately satiate those *Anthology* customers who'd been drawn in by the album title and Beatles-referencing promo blurb. Naturally, this put other listeners off. Anthony DeCurtis chastised it in *Rolling Stone* because, as he saw it, the song 'suffers from the self-congratulation of that most cliched of genres, the boomer reminiscence'.[21] A more sympathetic evaluation is that, as on 'Free as a Bird', the songwriter is reflecting on times past to help make some greater sense of the present.[22] He sings about hanging out with his pals during the Swinging Sixties, staying up all night, drinking wine, smoking (weed, probably, among other substances), philosophizing speculatively, 'discussing the vast intricacies of life' and deliberating 'the cosmic solution'.[23] As McCartney explains in the album's booklet, 'It's that time in your life when you got a chance for all that.'[24] While it's not as melancholic as The Rutles' 'Back in '64', the subtext to 'The Song We Were Singing' has a mortal poignancy. That crucial moment in one's life has long since past. Although it can be remembered, it can never be revisited or recreated. Not accurately, at least, without some kind of midlife humiliation. 'That it will never come again/ Is what makes life so sweet', according to Emily Dickinson's poem of 1741. The 'cosmic solution', meanwhile, remains as elusive and inaccessible as ever. If it even exists at all.

DeCurtis was happier with the next song, 'The World Tonight', which he deemed 'a brooding track driven by a nasty electric guitar' and the best example of *Flaming Pie*'s 'needed edge'.[25] Linda McCartney could be thanked for this. She'd encouraged her husband to rock this one up a bit by not holding back on his guitar parts.[26] Paul compared his own style to that of Neil Young: 'a little naïve . . . not amazingly technical'.[27] He was also thinking of the more gifted Jimi Hendrix, whose live shows had blown McCartney's mind in the summer of 1967 and whom he's continued to namecheck in concerts, decades after Hendrix's death. Hendrix's short life resonates in the lyrics, too, as does the far lengthier one of the uncompromising Neil Young. The song's narrator observes a person whose fame and success has brought with it alienation, loneliness, unforeseen pressures and the beady eyes of the paparazzi. The Beatles had experienced this more than most. Early on, people told them that fame had changed them. Friends and acquaintances had wanted things from them, often out of necessity. Also, increasingly, in a more exploitative fashion. It could be tricky to pick out the genuinely needy from all the confidence tricksters. Likewise, press reporters stepped further and further over the boundaries of discretion and decency. 'It really alters your entire way of being because you know that around any corner there might be a long lens,' McCartney has said.[28] He seems to have handled being one of the most famous faces in the world better than most people would. Unlike McCartney and Starr's emphasis on 'love', George Harrison's parting words in the final episode of the *Anthology* documentary were less fondly sugar-coated: 'They [the fans] gave their money and they gave their screams, but The Beatles kind of gave their nervous systems. Which is a much more difficult thing to give.' When asked about this quote in 2021, and what his accomplishments had cost him, McCartney replied, 'Your privacy. That's kind of what you give up.'[29] He remembered thinking, when The Beatles were becoming well known in England, that he could always escape to Greece for anonymity, because when on holiday there the bouzouki band he'd met in the hotel had no idea who they were. A year on, that was no longer the case. 'I then had to make a decision. Okay. What are you going to do? Are you just getting out of music or are you going to live with this thing called fame? I decided I would live with it and I had to cope with what it brought. And that's sort of what I'm still doing. Coping.'[30]

It's no surprise, then, that McCartney also had Lennon in mind when working on 'The World Tonight':

> The lyrics were just gathering thoughts. Like 'I go back so far, I'm in front of me' – I don't know where that came from, but if I'd been writing it with John he would have gone, 'OK, leave that one in; we don't know what it means but we do know what it means.'[31]

McCartney considers this one of the best lines he's ever written, despite its lack of lucidity.[32] Singling out that same lyric, DeCurtis interpreted it as if McCartney were 'stunned to find himself still standing in the wake of grunge, rap, techno and every other sonic assault on the world since the '60s. It's assertive without being defensive, aware without being trendy.'[33] The line provides further evidence, straight from the horse's mouth, that Paul McCartney is a dimension-jumper to whom the usual, linear nature of time has never properly applied.

Speaking of which, 'If You Wanna' was written back in May 1993 during the New World Tour, when McCartney was promoting *Off the Ground*. It has a touch of that prior album's shuffling, live feel, even though a full band was not involved this time. All instruments were played by McCartney and Steve Miller. McCartney had Prince in mind when he wrote it in Minneapolis, home town of the dirty-minded musician with the androgynous falsetto.[34] You wouldn't necessarily gauge that from listening to it, as it's no riot of purple sex-funk. 'If You Wanna' is more in the alt-country vein. It's a love song that uses a road trip as a metaphor for courtship and commitment, with euphemisms thrown in for the resultant backseat activities. That last detail might be why Chris Ingham of *Mojo* considered the song to be 'slightly sinister', which seems a little prudish of him.[35]

The two following numbers were written at times when Paul's thumbs were twiddling. With Linda absent for a few hours on important vegetarian cookery business, Paul would assign himself the tight deadline to rustle up a song in the hope of having something he could play to his wife when she returned.[36] 'Somedays' was written in the B Aeolian mode and does not have a chorus as such, so its bridge (in the key of D major) acts as the uplifting accompaniment to the melancholic feel of the modal verses.[37] McCartney recorded it using acoustic guitar, Spanish guitar and bass. He then asked George Martin to add an orchestral arrangement, the outcome adding to the song's delicate gravitas. 'Somedays' has been compared to the mighty 'Blackbird'.[38] It was 'vintage Paul' and already 'a classic song', according to Martin. 'I think it's one of those simple ones, deceivingly simple, but so difficult to write,' he explained.[39] Because of the situation in which it was written, and the fact that it clearly deals with romance, it has been assumed that the lyric is a straightforward one in which Paul explores his adoration for the lovely Linda. When discussing it, the man himself seemed to consider 'Somedays' as one of his more detached character pieces:

> I'm not a great reader into moods: I don't naturally say that if I wrote a sad song then I was sad that day, or if I wrote a happy song I was happy. I wrote 'Ob-La-Di, Ob-La-Da' but that doesn't necessarily mean that I know a Desmond or a Molly. I compose songs like playwrights write a play. They don't have to know everyone in the play, they don't have to know anyone in the play, it's just a product of their imagination. I remember George Harrison saying to me once, 'I always have to write from something that's happened to me, something in my experience.' Well, that's certainly a good way to write but I'm more fluid, more flexible than that. Sometimes.[40]

Also written quickly while Linda was busy, 'Young Boy' has fewer fans than 'Somedays'. At the time, it did seem strange that one of the weaker tracks from McCartney's best solo album in years was selected as its lead single. Well, in the UK anyway. Maintaining Paul's standing as a cooler figure in the USA, the American market received the rockier 'The World Tonight'. 'Young Boy' was the song that George Harrison surely should have played on, had he been returning Paul's calls at the time. Writers then and since observed it could've been penned by Harrison himself.[41] It's another collaboration with Steve Miller. Believe it or not, Jeff Lynne went nowhere near it, which is surprising given its sheer Traveling Wilbury-ness. The earlier demo version that McCartney recorded alone with just an acoustic guitar is far more palatable. Unadorned by the radio-friendly production, layers of instruments, high-in-the-mix drums, animated backing vocals and theatrical ending to the album version, the 'Young Boy' demo has the hushed quality of a gentle and unassuming lullaby.

Surviving in a stripped-back form was 'Calico Skies', another song said to 'hold its own and more[!] with "Blackbird."'[42] McCartney had the older song in mind when he wrote it.[43] By 1997, 'Calico Skies' wasn't that new either. It had been written in 1991, during a stay in Long Island, New York, when Hurricane Bob had caused the power to cut out for days. Deemed unsuitable for the full-band arrangements that filled *Off the Ground*, McCartney had recorded it on his own in 1992, in a single session with Martin, and kept it in his back pocket until *Flaming Pie*.[44] It's that same five-year-old version that appears on the album. Its first two verses resemble a direct love song before the third and final one reveals a more political, anti-war sentiment. McCartney often keeps his cards close to his chest. Speaking about the third verse of 'Calico Skies', he said this: 'There are certain politicians, presidents, prime ministers we don't like, who can lie wilfully, and I've fought against them in my own way throughout my life.'[45] Given it was written in 1991, he may have been thinking of President George H. W. Bush and the Gulf War. McCartney also ties that verse to the history of military service.[46] He'd only narrowly avoided it himself. National Service in the UK was phased out from 1957, when it was decided that people born after 1 October 1939 would not have to be enlisted. Even after that, American participation in the Vietnam War (1955–75) made people – especially the young, fit and politically engaged – fearful that a similar military draft could be reintroduced in the UK. As a boy, McCartney had been so daunted by the prospect of being called up into battle that he tried to harden himself up by murdering frogs in the woods.[47] If anything, this adds a curious psychologically compensatory dimension to 'We All Stand Together' by Paul McCartney and the Frog Chorus.

More playful than 'Calico Skies' is the album's title track, on which McCartney riffs on that old Lennon line with his surreal lyrics. It's a piano-based rocker with a hint of 'Lady Madonna', bursts of electric lead guitar and an unexpected New Orleans breakdown that fades out a little too soon at the end. A darker undertone can be detected in its lyrics, seeing as they allude to mental and corporeal fragility. Among other bizarre physical feats, the man on the flaming pie removes his brains, stretches them on a rack and wonders whether he will be able to retrieve them again. It's very tempting to associate this with the effects of LSD. There's also a line about there being a simple explanation to everything he does. Is McCartney suggesting the same goes for this song too? Or is it a sarcastic comment on those who have speculatively interpreted the musician's life and works in certain ways, rather like Lennon did on The Beatles' 'Glass Onion'? The mystery remains.[48]

In certain ways *Flaming Pie* is an album of contradictions, and the final song written for it, 'Heaven on a Sunday', sounds more like it could have been produced in the 1980s than any of the others like it. It has that smooth feel of yacht rock (a term retrospectively applied to acts such as Kenny Loggins and Hall & Oates), which is apt because McCartney came up with it when sailing on his boat in America.[49] Alongside Jeff Lynne's presence and a French horn section, 'Heaven on a Sunday' is a family affair. Linda can be heard on backing vocals. James McCartney makes his first appearance on record by contributing electric guitar licks in the style of Pink Floyd's Dave Gilmour. The music's ambience was designed to reflect how calm and contented McCartney felt while on holiday. As were the words. If Sundays tend to be the most restful days on earth, how calm must they be in heaven, the most peaceful utopia imaginable? In one or two of its lines could be detected, as Vincent P. Benitez does, that 'something is awry'.[50] As in the final part of the nursery rhyme 'Row, Row, Row Your Boat', there is that idea that life is but a dream; so fleeting and hard to properly fathom as to be barely real. The recording's lush textures soften this blow and also make the song stand out from the rest of the album. Linda cried when she first heard it.[51]

'Used to Be Bad' was co-written by Steve Miller, who brought a bunch of riffs to the studio hoping to hear McCartney sing some good ol' Texas blues.[52] Jointly sung by the pair, it is, lyrically and musically, a blues-by-numbers affair and one that emphasizes *Flaming Pie*'s sense of carefree fun. It boasts a ZZ Top-esque groove that only the most killjoy muso would be able to resist. Much of this comes from McCartney's one-man rhythm section. If he remains underrated in general, 'as an artist and as a man', as Ian Leslie diagnoses,[53] then McCartney is certainly owed greater appreciation not only as one of the greatest bassists of our time but as an incredibly capable drummer (like Ringo, without being too show-offy).

Working on 'Souvenir', McCartney told Lynne and his engineers that they needed to retain the spirit of the version he'd demoed while holidaying in Jamaica. Specifically, he didn't want to impose 'an uptight feeling to something relaxing'.[54] Reading between the lines, it seems McCartney prefers that preliminary demo. However, it's not the done thing to include on one's finished studio album a song with a load of banging in the background and a landline telephone ringing.[55] That's not to deny the roaring success of its spruced-up form. Having been written with Wilson Pickett in mind, the song is embellished with several piano and guitar tracks, plus a three-man horn section. With a lyric exploring the healing power of love, it achieves its aspired soulfulness, with a slight psychedelic tinge around the edges and a comforting record-scratch sound on the fade-out, which gives a nod to McCartney's fondness for both his own treasured demo and popular music's rich past.

Although it was never released as a single, 'Little Willow' is one of *Flaming Pie*'s best-known songs. It was said to have 'just popped out' as soon as Paul heard the news that Ringo's first wife, Maureen, had passed away.[56] In place of writing a letter of condolence to her children, Paul wrote a song for them instead: 'I knew their kids would be missing her a lot and thought this might help.'[57] The small yet sturdy tree of its lyric is used as a metaphor for the unshakeable love that holds us up and keeps us going in the face of the often unexpected challenges and tragedies that life can throw at us.

Lifting the mood again, 'Really Love You' is another rockin' bop, this one cooked up from a jam session with Ringo Starr, with additional guitar from Lynne. The ever-humble drummer was surprised when informed the songwriting was to be credited to 'Paul McCartney/Ringo Starr' (the first time this had ever happened):

> because we did just make it up as we went along. He called me and said I was sharing the credit and I said, 'Thank you very much'. I wasn't expecting anything. It's like, 'you play on my albums through the years, and I'll play on yours.'

> I don't get union rate! You know, we usually have dinner and send each other flowers and that's it.[58]

For Benitez, 'Really Love You' is the weaker sibling of 'Used to Be Bad'. Restricted to a limited, three-chord pattern, the music is 'disjointed', its lyrics 'meaningless', with melody that 'lacks coherence'.[59] Other folk might find these supposed flaws appealing, such as adherents of the Neil Young and Crazy Horse philosophy of following the groove in the most primal and minimalist way possible in order to unlock and evoke true *feeling*. When McCartney played the finished mix down the telephone to Starr, the drummer's response was a delighted 'It's relentless!'[60] Besides the presence of that famous rhythm section, the song is notable for McCartney's ragged and widely ranging vocal performance. This, too, was a primal and impromptu affair. Paul recorded his vocals live, in the moment, making up his words on the spot, like 'the actor's worst dream, of being on stage but not knowing what play he's in'.[61] There was one verse, he admitted, 'that doesn't make any sense, which goes "I need your heart hopping on a plate"'.[62] It can't be the first of his songs to which that applies.

Ringo was also present on 'Beautiful Night'. This one had been written even longer ago than 'Calico Skies'. It had first been recorded ten years earlier, complete with the heavily reverbed and arena-rock drum sound of that age, for the album produced by Phil Ramone that never saw the light of day. *Flaming Pie*'s version of the piano ballad retains some of that bombastic spirit. Its earthier production liberated it from the decade in which it was written, however, allowing it to be considered one of the record's most ambitious pieces, a 'Beatley' number that's 'symphonic in scope' and, according to one reviewer, McCartney's 'best ballad since "Only Love Remains"' (from 1986's *Press to Play*).[63] Its reception was enhanced by George Martin's orchestration (overdubbed on Valentine's Day, no less) and a newly added coda that upped the tempo and rock factor towards the end, with joyous vocal accompaniment from Ringo. Linda is on backing vocals, too. It's a love song, of course, albeit another one that alludes to some of the heavy storms that must be weathered in any long-term relationship.

*Flaming Pie* draws to a classy close with 'Great Day', placed there as a gentler complement to the preceding orchestra-aided epic. In the same session as 'Calico Skies', it was recorded back in 1992. McCartney had been mucking around with this tune, usually in the private company of his close family, since the early 1970s. There's a lovely home-recorded version, included in the 2020 reissue, on which Linda and children can be heard tinkering and talking in the background and joining in intermittently. *Carpe diem* is the philosophy of the lyric, transmitting again that crucial and too easily forgotten subtext that life is but row-row-boatingly brief.

## Mind Out of Time

When this album was first released, some critics sounded cautious of getting too carried away. In *Mojo*, Chris Ingham ranked *Flaming Pie* as 'pretty good, nudging upper middle . . . probably on a par with *Flowers in the Dirt*', noting how strange it was that the songs involving Lynne sounded the least like they did.[64] Referencing the *Anthology* project and anticipating Oasis's decline, *Vox*'s Roy Carr wrote that it was time to 'Forget about that ubiquitous Mancunian bunch . . . The Beatles are still the biggest band in Britain.' As for McCartney as an individual, this was 'his best album in years', flaunting songs of such high quality that in another era he could've offered them for inclusion on the 'White Album'.[65] There was much talk of McCartney 'coming to terms' with the past or else being 'freed' from it. He'd learned that it was 'OK to be himself – a Beatle – rather than having to create an alternative persona,' suggested Carr. McCartney no longer had to compete with the glory of his Beatles days, argued *Uncut*'s Carol Clerk. Nor did he have to try so hard to escape it. 'Perhaps this is why *Flaming Pie* is the most relaxed album he's made in years,' she wrote.

> Macca doesn't have to try to change the world because he's done that once already. He no longer needs to make records at all, and if he's doing it just for fun, then at least he can allow himself to sound that way. This is a man simply pleasing himself, dabbling in this and dipping into that, as he assembles the musical equivalent of a diary, complete with family snapshots, half-nostalgic reminiscences and personal confidences.[66]

At the same time, *Flaming Pie* helped to separate McCartney from more recent events. 'For some years now, The Cute One has been less famous as an artist in his own right than as that sixties songwriter guy who inspired Noel Gallagher,' noted *The Guardian*'s Caroline Sullivan.[67] Whereas, back in 1993, Sullivan had McCartney pegged as 'an unabashed ham who hasn't written a great song in 20 years',[68] she admired the new album's 'classy simplicity' and avoidance of 'the sickliness of which he's capable'.[69] It wasn't up there with The Beatles, that impossible bar set three decades ago, but the 'duds' were few and far between: 'The return of the Macca as proper jobbing musician starts here.'[70]

Not all critics felt the same way. *The Independent*'s Andy Gill considered it all 'pretty woeful stuff . . . effectively a bunch of mash-notes to the wife, jams with old friends and family members, and throwaway doodles of songs mostly written on his holidays'.[71] Hatchet jobs like Gill's were few and far between, however. Most people who listened to 'Somedays' themselves and had even a passing familiarity with the back catalogue could not agree that this was a genuine contender for 'the worst song he has ever written' and might therefore have reasonably concluded that Gill doth protest too much when asserting that McCartney had 'never sounded less necessary'.[72] In the years since, *Flaming Pie*'s reputation has only grown. It makes regular appearances in discussions of McCartney's greatest post-Beatles works and is considered a watershed moment in his later career. As Howard Sounes wrote in his 2010 biography, its love songs are far from 'silly'.[73] They are sophisticated, with a new-found humility, often infused with feelings of mortality, loss and regret. Sounes identified a 'touch of winter' to it, comparing this to the same year's *Time Out of Mind* by Bob Dylan.[74] It was that record that *Flaming Pie* lost out to when nominated for Album of the Year at the 40th Annual Grammy Awards, along with fellow candidates Paula Cole, Babyface and Radiohead. *Bridges to Babylon* by The Rolling Stones didn't get a look-in, suggesting that wrinkling rockers who engage with and reflect on the passing of time are held in higher esteem than those hip-shakers who pretend their youth is perpetual.

Positive appraisals of *Flaming Pie* have become the consensus. Granted, it is much rarer these days, in general, to see negative album reviews of the likes of Gill's quoted above, owing to changes in the way music journalism is created, funded and consumed.[75] That being said, the reception that greeted *Flaming Pie*'s expanded reissue in 2020 showed how much love and respect there is for this record. *Rolling Stone* was among the publications giving it higher praise than they had the first time around. The original set was now 'a sturdy potpourri', as Kory Grow put it, and one of McCartney's best ever solo albums.[76] *The Independent* had changed its tune by this time too, listing *Flaming Pie* in the top ten of all Beatles solo works.[77] The new 'Archive Collection' version included McCartney's demos, recorded at home. To my ears, some of these sparse renditions are better than the professionally produced final cuts. McCartney's voice, at times, sounds frailer than usual but also earthier and richly lived-in. He hasn't

'The World Tonight' single (1997).

(yet?) made an acoustic album of alternative folk songs. It would sound a lot like this if he did, give or take the barking animals, familial interruptions and telephone ringing in the background. Much like watching Peter Jackson's *Get Back*, it's a goosepimple-raising experience, as if McCartney is in the corner of your own living room, figuring out what to play and how, debuting the material to you in private, playing softly enough as to not wake the neighbours.

For Howard Sounes, *Flaming Pie* marks the point at which McCartney puts his erstwhile need to be 'relentlessly commercial' behind him.[78] As the musician said himself at the time, 'I started to ask myself what's it all been worth – the Beatles, the money and fame – if at some point I can't go "Now can I have a good time?" It's do or die. It would be great if *Flaming Pie* is a success, but I really won't be frantic if it isn't. If I keep on going like some manic preacher for the rest of my life, it just seems so pointless.'[79] As we've already seen, McCartney may have grown more relaxed regarding commercial success, but he was still concerned with quality. The B-sides from around this time show how strict he was being. The cheerfully stomping 'Looking for You' and the catchy blues number 'Broomstick' could easily have been considered album-worthy. 'Love Come Tumbling Down' and 'Same Love' from the 'Beautiful Night' single are more jarring as these were unreleased cuts lifted directly from sessions in the late 1980s. In this case, it's almost as if McCartney is deliberately contrasting the garish production of his works from that time with his more organic modern sound, or perhaps even demonstrating his wisdom in abandoning that Phil Ramone-produced album in 1987.

McCartney may also have felt he had less to prove on receiving his knighthood. He had apparently been in two minds about accepting it. Fully aware that there was a certain prestige to be found in refusing a title from the Establishment, in the end he'd concluded in diplomatic terms that 'it was a very great honour that the people of Liverpool and the British people of my generation could share in.'[80] The ceremony took place in March 1997, making McCartney one of the first few pop stars to be knighted. Unless you count 'fifth Beatle' Sir George Martin, the one before McCartney was the decidedly naffer Cliff Richard, the rock 'n' roll singer turned evangelical Christian and recurrent Wimbledon pest. Before Cliff, Bob Geldof had been made a Sir (honorarily, as he's Irish), for his charity pursuits rather than Queen Elizabeth II's fondness for 'Banana Republic' by The Boomtown Rats. Sir Bob's subsequent career was another thing that worried McCartney: 'Got knighted, never sold another record,' he joked later. 'That was it!'[81]

McCartney's approach to *Flaming Pie*'s promotion was also largely defined by nonchalance. There was no tour to support it, unlike his previous two studio albums. 'I'm just too lazy at the moment,' he claimed.[82] He also spoke of (unnamed) fellow musicians on 'mega-campaigns' who looked like they were trying too hard to sell themselves, admitting he'd been guilty of this himself in the past.[83] It was time to stand up to 'the suits' that he said were 'back in charge' of the music industry and to give more freedom back to the talent.[84] He felt there was something 'subversive' in his resistance and didn't want those who were tasked with its promotion to overexert themselves. 'I don't want anyone sweating about this album,' Paul 'good PR man' McCartney told *USA Today*. 'It was conceived with no sweat and recorded with no sweat. It's a little homemade pie.'[85]

For all his talk of laziness, liberty, subversiveness and sticking it to the suits, there was another reason McCartney wanted to stay at home. In 1995 his beloved wife Linda had been diagnosed with breast cancer. This was the same disease that had taken McCartney's mother from him when he was a teenager. Linda died just under a year after *Flaming Pie*'s release. The air of sorrow and loss that had floated below the surface of some of its songs now made clearer sense. People could use it to support the (debatable) theory that McCartney produces some of his best work when weathering darker times.[86] Although 'Little Willow' had been written prior to Linda's diagnosis, it took on a new meaning. This was not lost on the McCartneys themselves. When Linda heard the song again during her treatment, she looked into Paul's eyes and said, 'Oh God, it's about me now.'[87] Taken before her time towards the end of the decade, Linda had also enjoyed a remarkable 1990s.

# 6
# Behind Every Great Man

Pity the plight of a Beatle's wife. Sure, you may have married one of the most famous people in the world, but is it really worth all the flak? The relentless ire of the envious fans. The snide potshots fired frequently from the media. All that criticism. All that scrutiny. The perpetual narrative that buries you leagues beneath your husband's genius while also blaming you for draining it like a vampire that feeds not on blood but on her partner's creative juices. God forbid you should want a career, voice or identity of your own. Oh, and just try dabbling in music yourself without becoming an absolute laughing stock.

There is not one person who experienced this as much as Linda McCartney. Well, besides Yoko Ono that is. In some ways, Linda attracted greater hostility than Yoko. While there are those who believe she is a literal witch, or an arch manipulator at the least, Ono also has her fair share of passionate defenders. Before she met John Lennon, Ono was an exhibiting Fluxus-associated artist in her own right. Despite her later pursuits as a 'professional widow', she has continued to make her own art and music – distinctive, out-there, challenging and playful as it is – with a sense of creativity unmatched by many of her peers. Her singing voice an acquired taste, she still has fans and collaborators in the form of Lenny Kravitz, Sonic Youth, Tune-Yards, Nels Cline, Nico Muhly, Peaches, The Flaming Lips, Cat Power, Porcupine

Tree and many more. She has been credited with helping to popularize avant-garde art forms and alternative music scenes.[1] The journalist-turned-award-winning-novelist Ben Myers has put Ono forward as 'the coolest' one of her husband's band, of which she wasn't actually a member despite her regular presence at the recording studio.[2] Rarer is it to find such champions of Linda McCartney, who was, to be fair, an official member of the chart-topping Wings.

There have been times when Paul McCartney has been accused by certain ex-associates, Denny and Jo Jo Laine among them,[3] of essentially appointing his wife as a replacement for the mother who died when he was young. This is unfair, bitter and unnecessarily cruel given the circumstances. It would require more than pseudo-Freudianism to hold up. Having said that, there is no denying that Linda acted as a solid rock for Paul when The Beatles were breaking up (and beyond). As McCartney was trying to ground himself during that particularly turbulent time, he did encourage Linda to take on the lion's share of the housework. Brought up in a privileged family, she had little experience of household chores and considered Paul's views to be curiously old-fashioned.[4] She went along with it nevertheless. 'Paul was saying that there's a lovely pleasure in laundering something and smelling it, or ironing something,' Mrs McCartney recalled in 1984.

> He remembers the smell in his house, of his mother, his auntie. And his mother died when he was young. So to have a wife who is intelligent, independent, artistic – but who also fills that role – was important. He thought I was missing something: I thought, come on, I want to be outdoors with my horse.[5]

Paul recognized this made him look chauvinistic, justifying it on the grounds of his own upbringing. 'In the kind of family I'm from, housework is considered a pleasure – the smell of ironing and the laundry,' he told an interviewer the following year. 'Where I'm from, once a week, the women would sort of get the laundry out and smell the washing and feel it and see it and iron it all, and they'd be chatting or listening to the radio. It was like a peasant thing. It was an event, like treading on the grapes.'[6] It's likely the McCartneys had more help than they liked to admit. At the very least there was, reporter Diane de Dubovay observed, 'a cockney cleaning lady' who called in once a week and also did some babysitting.[7] This was still nothing on the scale of Linda's upbringing, nor the *Downton Abbey*-like lifestyle of other celebrity families. Paul realized he wanted as few staff as possible after hearing Ringo Starr's son, Zak, say 'Hello, Mummy' to a nanny.[8] Linda could identify. She felt her own upbringing had prevented her from being as close as she would have liked to her own mother, who died in an aeroplane accident when Linda was at university. 'I never got to know her,' she remembered, 'as someone else was always giving me a bath.'[9]

The McCartneys also worked together, of course. Linda was a photographer by trade and had scant interest in polishing her own image. One sock up, the other down, carrying a tatty twelve-year-old handbag, always looking 'kind of a shambles', as Chrissie Hynde remembered her, 'she probably never had a manicure in her life.'[10] Linda didn't wear much make-up either. Back in the day, journalists and envious admirers of Beatle Paul had attacked Linda's lack of glamour and the fact that she didn't shave her legs.[11] In those interviews to which she did agree, Linda often looked uncomfortable. She felt happier and more at ease behind the camera. This is a difficult position to maintain when you've married Paul McCartney and agreed to join his band with no prior musical training.

As well as appearing on every Wings album and tour, Linda would feature on all of her husband's solo albums until the final one completed before her death, *Flaming Pie*. She contributed backing vocals at first, graduating to multi-instrumentalist. In some critics' minds, Linda's presence had little to zero impact on the material written and recorded by Paul.[12] Others believe she had a detrimental effect on her partner's post-Beatles output. Biographer Howard Sounes writes that on the *McCartney* album of 1970, Linda 'sang shaky backing vocals in the manner of a schoolgirl thrust reluctantly onto stage at her end-of-term concert'.[13] On the McCartneys' return to touring in 1989–90, Sounes considered Linda 'a flat note in the band, slogging her way joylessly through these shows to keep Paul happy'.[14]

It was apt that Paul's solo career should have kicked off with 'The Lovely Linda', *McCartney*'s opening number, even if it lasted no longer than 42 seconds and hardly matched the grandeur of 'Maybe I'm Amazed', which appeared later on the record. 'The Lovely Linda' was one of the *McCartney* songs chastised by *Rolling Stone* for having 'virtually no verbal or melodic content whatsoever'.[15] The follow-up album, 1971's *Ram*, was a proto-Wings project in that it featured Denny Seiwell and Hugh McCracken (plus David Spinozza) as drafted-in band members. It is the only album to be released under the artist name 'Paul and Linda McCartney'. Six of its eleven songs were listed as co-written by the couple. Paul insisted that Linda had been an active collaborator. Many struggled to believe this. The credits were also seen as a way for the McCartneys to keep extra publishing royalties for the record, so they were sued by Northern Songs and Maclen Music. 'Because Linda wasn't trained at the Guildhall, Northern Songs think it must mean she can't write,' McCartney told *Record Mirror* at the time. 'Northern Songs has got me under contract. I start writing with someone whom they don't have under contract – and they don't accept it.'[16]

The consensus on *Ram* has grown more positive with each passing year. When it first hit the racks, there were critics on both sides of the Atlantic who considered it the worst thing to which McCartney had ever put his name.[17] Speaking of names, the double-billing hardly helped its reception. Often Linda was belittled with outright misogyny. Exhibit A is a joke that did the rounds in the 1970s: 'What do you call a dog with wings? Linda McCartney.' (A variation on the set-up line was 'cow'.) Perceptions had hardly changed by the beginning of the 1990s. A bootleg tape was circulated featuring Linda singing along to 'Hey Jude' on which her isolated vocal parts sounded like an off-key karaoke singer. It was said to be taken from McCartney's Knebworth concert of 1990, recorded and circulated afterwards by a live sound engineer, perhaps as revenge for Linda or Paul's offhand treatment of him.[18] DJs such as the American shock jock Howard Stern played excerpts on their shows for a laugh.[19] There is even a rumour that the recording was a hoax that had been created by one such radio presenter.[20]

Whoever was behind it and whatever their motivation, it was a reprehensible thing to do. The incident was echoed in 2014 when Courtney Love was victim to similar treatment. Platforms including *Vice*, *Consequence of Sound* and *Uproxx* reported on a newly uploaded live recording of the re-formed incarnation of Hole, taken from a show in 2010. Love's guitar playing and vocals had been isolated to shame the singer by exposing her apparent lack of talent. The person who made it, J. M. Ladd, said he'd been hired to record the show and had never been paid for his services. The aforementioned websites emphasized the cringe factor of the footage.[21] 'Whether you think she's the worst or this just makes her all the more "punk rock" is for you to decide,' Ladd wrote beneath his YouTube post. 'I'm merely presenting the facts as they are. Make of them what you will.'[22] The problem with this is that male rock and pop stars rarely receive the same treatment. It implies that Linda McCartney, Courtney Love and pop stars such as Taylor Swift and Katy Perry, who have also been the butt of this kind of scenario, are fraudulent invaders of inherently male spaces. Love's isolated tracks are 'even worse than you'd imagine', laughed *Vice*.[23] Those of her husband, Nirvana's Kurt Cobain, however flawed, were usually described in terms of their raw emotion.[24] Scour the Internet for the latter and you're more likely to discover isolated *studio* vocals, usually the result of several takes, with effects like echo involved.[25] It's like sexist schoolyard bullying. It is also built on straw because, unlike studio efforts, live sound is a one-shot, in-the-moment scenario and the job of the concert-room engineer is to bring together the different noises coming from the stage so that the band sounds, well, good. As one such professional, Danielle DePalma, put it when asked to analyse the footage of Hole, all it really shows us is 'an incomplete sentence in a very complex novel'.[26] Ladd's treatment gives us two microphone signals from a total of 24 instrument signals, estimates DePalma. Unlike studio recording, the live engineer uses these to 'control, process and enhance the sound . . . to create a powerful mix through loudspeakers'.[27] Thanks to the full sound of the band and the way it was mixed on the night, Love's vocals would've sounded loud and powerful in the room. As for the erratic and out-of-tune nature of Love's guitar work, DePalma says it is not unusual for the frontperson to 'mimic' their playing, or to have their instrument turned down low, for the sake of bringing the musicians and the audience together and putting on a spectacular live performance.[28] Authentic or otherwise, plenty of front*men* do the same thing and yet do not find themselves exposed in the same way by disgruntled (also usually male) leakers. Returning to the case of Linda McCartney, her job during 'Hey Jude' at Knebworth was not to knock out studio-worthy backing vocals. It was to add keyboards, enthusiastically bang her tambourine and help to bring everyone together by na-na-na-ing along with the crowd.

'Paul's blind spot for his wife's lack of musicality, a symptom of his devotion to her, would characterise and mar his subsequent career,' Sounes says of *McCartney* and everything after, demonstrating how unkind history has been to Linda.[29] The idea of there being a genuine songwriting 'partnership' between the pair was 'a bad joke', according to the 1991 biography by Geoffrey Giuliano, who'd retained greater admiration for McCartney's brief and hardly fecund dalliance with Michael Jackson.[30]

As much as Britpop bands liked to namecheck The Beatles, their respect for Paul McCartney did not extend to his wife. At least two of the most famous female musicians from the scene were desperate to avoid any comparisons to Mrs Macca. 'I just thought it was better to be Pete Best than Linda McCartney,' Justine Frischmann said of her decision to leave Suede before going on to front Elastica.[31] Thinking back to one of her early, pre-Sleeper bands, Louise Wener recalled her frustration at being 'relegated to the Linda McCartney role, flapping around at the back with a cowbell and tambourine'.[32]

Does this underestimate Linda's importance? Did she undervalue her own contribution when comparing herself to someone who'd never played or sung a note agreeing to perform with Ludwig van Beethoven?[33] Or when she insisted this was not where her talents lay?[34] Was she more than a mere muse for her hubby's silly love songs?

One of Linda's loyal defenders is Pete Townshend. As leader of The Who, he understands a thing or two about the mysteries of creative practice. 'I know that there was something about Wings' sound which had a particular kind of quality to it that definitely came from the way she sang,' Townshend told Linda's friend and biographer Danny Fields.[35] He also challenged the notion that Paul would return to the studio to overdub all his wife's parts: 'I know it's bollocks, I know it's nonsense. 'Cause you can hear her . . . she's part of the sound and she's part of the character of it. I think when you're a composer, you work with the elements that are around you that are part of your human palette.'[36]

This idea was never given much consideration by most of those who examined Wings and the McCartneys' work beyond. Writing to the magazine after the sad news of Linda's death, *Mojo* reader David Simmons defied the consensus in a way that group-thinking rock journalists had failed to. Not only had Linda been the subject of many of Paul's most beautiful love songs, her own musical abilities had been 'grossly underrated' by press and public alike. 'I have always thought that she made an extremely significant, though subtle, contribution to Paul's solo output,' wrote Simmons. He pointed to Linda's 'sublime backing vocals' on the songs 'Bluebird', 'Magneto and Titanium Man', 'Letting Go' and particularly the coda to 'Long Haired Lady' from *Ram*, considered by Simmons (and by this time he was not alone) to be 'arguably Paul's best solo album'.[37]

Paul once said that the whole point of Wings was never to 'be cool and over-reach ourselves and try to be Pink Floyd'.[38] It was always supposed to be a lot more fun than Floyd and certainly never as pretentious or technically complex. Despite his apparent workaholism and the excitement that songwriting has always given him, McCartney tends to take his music less seriously than most of the people who choose to analyse it in depth.[39] Chart his career, delve into past interviews, and you'll soon notice his appreciation of innocence, naivety and primality when it comes to the creative process. Partly this harks back to his formative immersion in skiffle and early rock 'n' roll. As accomplished a multi-instrumentalist as he is, and as keen as he has remained to absorb different sounds and pick up new techniques, McCartney has always been reluctant to learn *too much* about music or to know *everything* about it, lest this ruin the 'magic' of music-making or result in overly precious or stiff-sounding material.[40] 'Primitive is a word I like very much,' he confirmed in 1993.[41] Linda was on the same wavelength. In the late 1960s, for instance, she'd enjoyed watching Blue Cheer. The San Francisco-based heavy rock band were accused, at the time, of compensating for their musical ineptitude with sheer volume. Linda loved them.[42]

Paul McCartney shares his attitude with some of the greatest minds in music history, from shambolic punk rockers to highbrow jazz masters. Band leaders in rather different disciplines, trumpeter Miles Davis and Mark E. Smith of post-punk pioneers The Fall both liked to regularly replace their members with young musicians who had relatively limited experience. They felt it helped them to avoid complacency and conventionalism. It kept things fresh and meant those leaders themselves had to stay on their toes. It pushed things forward. It encouraged risk-taking when there was the danger of treading water safely. Funk legend George Clinton is among those who view technical prowess with suspicion. For him, the all-important 'groove' is something that's captured in the early stages of a musician's training. As your practical skills improve, you risk losing that primeval way of playing, which is something you ought to hold on to, retain in your repertoire and be able to re-access no matter how much is learned thereafter.[43] Neil Young feels the same way. The members of his backing band, Crazy Horse, have been criticized for not being good enough, with a propensity to flub their parts. The mistakes – which sometimes sound exciting or engrossing because they are unexpected, raw and unusual – are 'a by-product of the abandon' with which Crazy Horse play, Young told his biographer:

> They're not organized. No matter how fuckin' much we practice the song, Billy can get so into the groove he'll forget to do the change, y'know? And Ralph may turn the beat around. It happens. Or I can start playin' the guitar, and Ralph can pick it up on the wrong beat and play it backwards – that happens all the time. Never happens with real professional groups. With *our* band this shit happens all the time. But what really happens all the time is that it *grooves*

> – even if it's not in the groove, it's in a groove. You hear it and you wanna hear more.[44]

McCartney has compared his own guitar style to that of Young, and the two have similar tastes.[45] Back when recording Beatles songs like 'Hey Jude', McCartney would irritate George Harrison by rebuking the lead guitarist's tendency to overdo it on the notes front instead of keeping things simpler (and better).[46] These tensions arose again in the 1990s when McCartney reined in Harrison on 'Free as a Bird', urging him to play 'a very simple bluesy lick rather than get too melodic'.[47] Despite all the incredibly inventive things McCartney has done with the bass guitar and other instruments, he told *Bass Player* magazine that he is 'one of the least technical people you're likely to meet'.[48] His love of simplicity, directness and intuition extends to the music he enjoys hearing. One of his favourite moments from the world of jazz, he informed Paul Du Noyer, occurs during a rendition of 'Duke's Place' when Louis Armstrong tells Duke Ellington to 'take it' and the pianist starts playing an outrageously minimal solo with one finger. 'It's almost embarrassing,' McCartney enthused, 'except it's just so ballsy. That is *good*.'[49]

In a sense this is similar to painters like J.M.W. Turner, Vincent van Gogh and Pablo Picasso, to whom in the last case McCartney has been compared as the musical equivalent,[50] about whose final words he wrote a song for *Band on the Run* and after whom the McCartneys named one of their cats.[51] Those artists' styles became less representative of visual reality, and their processes grew less reliant on traditional technique: more 'childlike', as some people saw their works. This allowed the painters to express themselves more freely, giving their paintings greater emotional resonance and aesthetic impact.

McCartney values spontaneity in terms of lyric writing and tends to follow his instincts in that field, as well: 'Who says words have to make sense? Certainly not poets. There is this thing called surrealism and many of us love it.'[52] McCartney was on board when Du Noyer brought up the maxim 'honour your mistakes'. It's one of the ideas from Oblique Strategies, Brian Eno and Peter Schmidt's card-based method of stimulating creativity.[53] 'There's so much of that,' McCartney agreed. 'It's like dreams, we're all so boxed in . . . There's so much in the unintended. "Mumbo" [off *Wild Life*] was an early version of that.'[54] McCartney may have been working in the field of pop music, but this enthusiasm for the accidental was shared by Fluxus-related creatives, including John Cage, La Monte Young, Terry Riley – and Yoko Ono. Determined to escape classical music's fastidious obsession with control, order and precision, such artists embraced chance, randomness and anarchic laxity.[55] People are sometimes surprised to learn that as one of the most successful songwriters in history, Paul McCartney never learned to read music. He said 'it seemed a bit too much like homework' when thinking back to his childhood music lessons.[56] He wasn't only deterred by the effort involved:

> I just couldn't get my head around reading music and being so regimented in what to play and how to express it.
>
> It seemed to go against something in my core – I wanted the freedom and the creativity. I didn't want to toe the line, and I don't think there are many musicians that do really. I do think it's about time I learned, but I guess I've done OK without it![57]

Among the other gnomic suggestions to be found in the Oblique Strategies card deck are 'Abandon normal instruments', 'Ask people to work against their better judgment', 'Balance the consistency principle with the inconsistency principle', 'Discard an axiom', 'Don't be afraid of things because they're easy to do', 'Emphasize the flaws', 'Look closely at the most embarrassing details and amplify them', 'Use an unacceptable color', 'Use fewer notes' and 'Humanize something free of error'.[58] Based on these tips, Oblique Strategies could just as well have included 'Ask a photographer who has no musical training to join your band.'

To weave a few of these threads closer together, a formative moment for the young Brian Eno occurred when he attended a lecture on the creative potential of tape recording at Winchester School of Art in 1969. Delivered by one Pete Townshend, it convinced Eno that he would be able to embark on a successful musical career as someone who was a 'non-musician'.[59] Townshend's penchant for destroying his instruments onstage, incidentally, had arrived when he inadvertently broke his guitar on the ceiling of a

Linda McCartney's posthumous compilation album, *Wide Prairie* (1998).

venue. He expected a bigger response from the crowd, who didn't seem to realize how precious this instrument was to the guitarist. Angered by those onlookers' indifference, Townshend leaned into it: 'I proceeded to make a big thing of breaking the guitar. I pounced all over the stage with it and I threw the bits on the stage and I picked up my spare guitar and carried on as though I really meant to do it.'[60] Repeated thereafter, this became a signature part of The Who's stage show and one of the things for which Townshend is most famous. Honour thy mistakes, indeed.

Now, I'm not going to spend pages here going over the madcap genius of 'Seaside Woman', written by Linda alone and recorded in 1972 with Wings under the pseudonym Suzy and the Red Stripes. I got enough stick for talking about *St. Anger* and *Lulu* at the expense of any better-loved Metallica albums in my last book, *Electric Wizards*. Suffice to say, 'Seaside Woman' is a gloriously wonky cod-reggae number in a similar spirit to 'Ob-La-Di, Ob-La-Da', which appears to be foreshadowing the skew-whiff genre-dabbling antics of the oddball's oddballs: Ween. Besides 'Seaside Woman', the posthumously released compilation of Linda-led songs, *Wide Prairie* (1998), includes dabbles in country, Dixieland jazz, romantic ballads in the style of the man with whom Linda was besotted, a couple of covers recorded with dub reggae legend Lee 'Scratch' Perry and other curios. Paul appears on it throughout. It was not warmly received by reviewers, who took the collection too seriously. By nature, it is slightly ramshackle. Two songs, 'I Got Up' and 'The Light Comes from Within' (the latter her final recording), provide a fine sense of Linda's resilience in the face of all the criticism she'd attracted through the years, the imperfect nature of her vocal takes only adding to the bold sense of defiance.

Linda McCartney played a greater role in her husband's music than has been recognized or appreciated. It may certainly have been subtle. Yet it was not insignificant. Nor was it identifiably detrimental. And if it helped Paul to avoid any self-indulgent Pink Floyd-isms then I, for one, am wholeheartedly behind it. She did improve, it has to be said, and she would impress Paul by mastering the 'really difficult stuff in the middle' of 'Live and Let Die' and 'synthesizing a whole orchestra on the tour'.[61]

Paul is known to have got frustrated, at times, by Linda's musical inexperience and amateurish abilities, yet these could also be a source of revelation and originality. They offered unusual and impulsive directions for songs and helped to foster the kind of happy accidents that Eno endorses. These would never have occurred if McCartney had hired, let's say, Elton John as his keyboardist and backing singer.

Based on their philosophies as laid out above, Pete Townshend, Brian Eno and Paul McCartney would all be in agreement with this notion: the ingénue will make choices that the maestro will never dream up.

This is why Linda McCartney matters.

## Great Balls of Fire

When she was asked about the off-key Knebworth recording that those chortling male DJs were spinning on their shows, Linda said she didn't care what people thought about her and joked that if she ever met the culprits she would stick her fingers in their eyes.[62] Years before that tape had emerged, she said she'd like to find those people who'd accused her of singing out of tune and 'go kick them in the teeth'.[63]

One phrase that crops up in interviews with her husband as well their children is that Linda had 'balls'. She had no musical training, and unlike her spouse, who she once said 'needs that dose he gets from the audience', she would have preferred to stay at home, 'feeding horses and taking pictures'.[64] She embraced her Wings role nonetheless. In Paul's view this made her 'the ballsiest member' of the group.[65] He added that, in general, she was 'Quite a ballsy person, really.'[66] When remembering her mum in a joint interview with sister Stella in 2017, Mary McCartney was still astonished by 'The balls she had'.[67] It's a curious way to remember a wife and mother, but then Linda was always a bit of a no-nonsense tomboy. She would fiercely defend her husband against his critics, for example by talking up his guitar playing or often overlooked skill behind the drums.[68] 'She's so pro-me it's incredible,' Paul once remarked.[69] 'Like Jimi Hendrix was a great musician, Paul is a great musician,' Linda would insist.[70] She'd point out Paul's vast range as a composer and rebuke those who wrote off his material as sentimental, corny or kitsch. 'I mean "Yesterday", you could say that's schmaltzy, but it's a nice piece of music,' Linda said about one of his most popular songs. 'You could say '[All I Have to Do Is] Dream' by The Everly Brothers is schmaltzy, but it gets *me* every time.'[71]

Linda had a point. In his book-length rumination on the problems with 'bad' taste versus 'good' music, confronted via the author's own contempt – at first – for the music of Celine Dion, Carl Wilson explored the notion of 'schmaltz'. As is touched on throughout *Let's Talk about Love* (first published in 2007), 'schmaltz' has often been patronizingly applied by those in the West to the music made or enjoyed by ethnic minority groups, foreigners, the lower classes (for example 'white trash') and women, in the latter case especially those who are deemed either too young (teenage girls) or too old ('granny music') to know any better. The term itself was introduced to the English language by Yiddish immigrants in the early twentieth century and has therefore always had ties to Otherness.[72] Among the sources cited by Wilson is Deborah Knight's paper 'Why We Enjoy Condemning Sentimentality: A Meta-Aesthetic Perspective' (1999). One of the explanations she provides is the macho, post-Enlightenment pursuit and veneration of rationalism. Knight notes the association of sentimentality with 'soft' (read: feminine) emotions such as tenderness and vulnerability, alongside other examples of heavily gendered vocabulary. To be moved by something sentimental is to allow one's inner feelings to be too easily manipulated, seduced or even 'violated' by an external force, such as the supposedly kitschy piece of art.[73] 'Sentimentality is a womanish – and, at the end of the day, a sluttish – attitude: indulgent, cheap, shallow, self-absorbed, excessive,' Knight explains. 'Sentimentality is a *femme fatale*, only she wields a contagion rather than a gun. Masquerading as an innocent, and working on the inside, it is the undoing of the rational self.'[74]

This leads me to, of all people, Andrew Falkous from the shouty alt-rock bands Mclusky and Future of the Left. He is quite the fan of conversational digression. Digressions-within-digressions, even. It is a passion we share. (Don't know if you'll have noticed that by now.) During an interview for a broadsheet newspaper supplement that was supposed to focus on a Mclusky tour, Falkous told me he had once been asked to leave his job at a British Gas call centre because he'd been caught conducting a survey that aimed to determine whether there was a correlation between people's favourite Beatle and the size of their feet. 'My boss wasn't very happy when she found that I'd been spending company time doing that,' he remembered. 'Typical George Harrison fan! She found out because I asked her. That was an oversight on my part. "Who's your favourite Beatle?" is a largely innocuous question but when it's accompanied by ". . . and what's your shoe size?" Hang on!'[75] So that was the end of his contract. It would still be interesting to know whether there really was a correlation. 'In the end there was,' Falkous told me. 'But sometimes you've got to go back through the data and work out why that's the case. And that is generally because more *women* preferred Paul McCartney. So really what I should have done was to run a few different surveys.'[76]

For our purposes, that's pretty helpful. (Thanks, Falco!) Based on what Wilson and Knight tell us, it's no wonder Paul McCartney has received so much hostility from the traditionally male-dominated profession of rock criticism. He was 'the cute one' in The Beatles. If Falco's survey is to be believed, he's the most popular one among women. Rightly or wrongly, he's the one that's accused of being most prone to sentimentality. 'But what's wrong with sentimental?' an exasperated McCartney once asked in an interview with *Smash Hits*. Its core audience made up of those teenage girls whose tastes were condemned by male, rationalist rockist types, even this magazine was suspicious of McCartney's schmaltzy tendencies. 'Sentimental means you *love*, you *care*, you *like stuff*,' he continued. 'The thing is, we're *frightened* to be sentimental.'[77]

In *Let's Talk about Love*, Wilson does not deny that some 'sentimental' art can be 'lousy'.[78] To paraphrase a saying that's often been attributed, appropriately enough given their earlier appearance in this chapter, to both Louis Armstrong and Duke Ellington,[79] there are two kinds of schmaltzy music: the good kind and the bad. McCartney, more often than not, plays the good kind(s). The kind that will still be applauded for decades after his death ('Yesterday'). The kind that regularly soundtracks weddings and first dances ('Maybe I'm Amazed'). The kind that's as gentle and soothing as a lullaby ('Junk'). The kind with dark subtexts ('The Lovers That Never Were'). The kind that can inspire great R&B hits for the likes of TLC ('Waterfalls'). The smooth kind ('Bluebird', 'Heaven on a Sunday'). The folkish, hippie-pacifist kind ('Calico Skies'). The unapologetically and infectiously optimistic kind ('Pipes of Peace'). The saucy kind ('Fuh You'). The kind that has killer bass lines ('Silly Love Songs') or sublime orchestration ('Somedays'). The kind that reflects on loss and resilience ('Here Today', 'Little Willow'). The kind that really means something to people and which touches them deeply, however irrationally, and will continue to do so.

What's more, sentimentality is by no means the only thing McCartney trades in, as Linda was prone to remind people. 'What else are you going to say about Paul?' she once asked. 'That he's cute? Or . . . It's all bullshit. It's *really* bullshit. But then there's a lot of bullshit in the world, if you'll excuse me.'[80]

Linda's ballsiness – if that's what we're calling it – was encapsulated not only in her ability to resist what she had to endure as the Othered member of her husband's band(s) and her determination to champion Paul's position as a truly great artist. It had increasing presence in her animal rights work and promotion of vegetarianism.

## Wild Life

It happens less frequently these days, the more that Morrissey pledges his support for far-right political parties and writes off entire nationalities as 'a subspecies'.[81] However, there was a time – a very long time, in fact – when it was common to bump into people who credited their own vegetarianism to his beliefs and lyrics, and specifically The Smiths' second LP, *Meat Is Murder* (1985). That's what plenty of folk claimed, anyway. You'd hardly meet anyone who said they'd stopped consuming the flesh of fellow creatures because they wanted to follow in the footsteps of the McCartneys, two of the most famous vegetarians on the planet. This anecdotal evidence must give a false impression, though. Statistically speaking, won't more people have been exposed to and affected by the McCartneys' celebrity campaigning than that of The Smiths, at their indie-er level of operations? Did fewer people heed the McCartneys' lifestyle advice in comparison to that of The Smiths because of the different passions involved in the fandom of each party? Did the cult of The Smiths have greater cultural sway in the 1980s because they were at their hippest back then and Paul McCartney, as we've seen, wasn't? Would most people have preferred to give the impression that their decision was based on *Meat Is Murder* because, for much longer than The Smiths were even active, this looked significantly cooler than admitting you'd been swayed by 'Fab Macca Wacky Thumbs Aloft' and his American-born wife in a telly interview conducted by Terry Wogan? Cultural capital influences the way everybody conducts their life, as the French thinker Pierre Bourdieu told us. Who in their right mind was going to damage their own social reputation so carelessly in a discussion of which pop star had lured them towards the plant-based hamburgers? Back in the 1980s and '90s, it was bad enough to announce conversion to a meat-free diet in the first place, viewed as it was with suspicion, bafflement and condemnation. Better to take the edge off by citing the recent serial winner of *NME* awards and not the writer of 'Once Upon a Long Ago'.

Vegetarians are still subject to social mockery. A good proportion of this has been shunted onto the more hardcore vegan cohort. Now that most English cafés offer avocado dishes galore, it's easy to forget how abnormal vegetarianism was seen to be throughout the latter decades of the twentieth century. Remember how few meal, menu and recipe options were available to those who signed up to the cause? Anyone who was a vegetarian at that time will recall being asked on a regular basis, 'But . . . do you eat chicken?' Even Delia Smith, the hugely popular TV cook, sometimes had a dig. Towards the end of Paul McCartney's interview on *TFI Friday* in 1997, Chris Evans asked a series of questions that had been sent to the show by other celebrities. Delia's read thus: 'To Paul: Although you are a strict veggie, do you still get the urge to eat meat? A nice juicy bit of pork with crackling perhaps?' McCartney took this slight in good humour: 'No, Delia. I see this nice juicy piece of pork as a little piggy with a life. And I don't want to kill it. I love it. I stroke it.' A sign of shifting attitudes, five years later Smith caved in with the cookbook *Delia's Vegetarian Collection*. She'd always had *some* veggie recipes in her previous books, its introduction asserted. It made sense to have them all in one place, for the benefit of vegetarians themselves and also 'the growing number of people who are not vegetarians but who find themselves entertaining vegetarians'.[82] The tone almost sounded resentful. Reading between the lines, Smith had realized how profitable vegetarianism had become in recent years. This was down in no small part to Linda McCartney.

It was Linda who had persuaded Paul to become vegetarian in the first place. The couple often repeated their epiphanic story about sitting down to enjoy a leg of lamb, looking out the window on to their Scottish farm to see the same animals prancing around outside, and never touching any meat from that moment forth.[83] In another telling, one of their lambs actually wanders through the door into the kitchen as they are tucking into their roast.[84] For Paul, the decision was also tied to the compassionate values of the hippie era and having survived to tell the tale of that radical time: 'That was it. Now we don't eat anything that has to be killed for us. We've been through a lot, coming through the Sixties with all those drugs and friends dropping like flies, and we've reached the stage where we really value life.'[85] Mistreatment of animals, he suggested, stoked unkindness in other areas of society, and if people really wanted to save the planet then one of the best ways to do it would be to stop eating meat.[86]

In his biography of Linda McCartney, Danny Fields writes that the McCartneys' conversion to a meat-free diet was more gradual than the supposed lamb-related immediate cessation, thought to have occurred in 1975. Members of Wings, he says, recall everybody tucking into a turkey at Thanksgiving.[87] Photographer Henry Diltz noted in his diary a dinner of 'steak and kidney pie with lots of wine' at the *London Town* sessions in May 1977.[88] When Paul and Linda visited Yoko Ono in 1981, the couple were still eating caviar.[89] They hadn't quite realized where it came from. 'Fish was the last to go,' Paul explained later.

'We continued eating caviar for a while because we thought it was luxurious, and told ourselves it was only eggs. Then we found out the mother sturgeon gets slit from top to bottom and the eggs fall out. That stopped caviar.'[90]

Paul says his own culinary talents lay in chopping the garlic.[91] Beyond that, Linda was responsible for preparing most of the family's meals. As such, she was always searching for appetizing alternatives to the then commonplace blandness of vegetarian meals, as well as new ways to fill that gap on the plate where would usually rest part of a dead animal.[92] At Christmas she concocted a makeshift 'turkey' from congealed macaroni cheese that could be sliced and served with the roast veg. Thus Paul could still fulfil 'the traditional male role of the carver'.[93]

Peter Cox, author of the bestselling *Why You Don't Need Meat* (1986), was impressed by Linda's alternative recipes and felt there would be the appetite for a cookbook based on them. They worked together on 1989's *Linda McCartney's Home Cooking*. Even with the celebrity name attached, Cox had trouble selling the book to publishers, who would suggest changes such as throwing in a few chicken recipes to help it sell.[94] It was acquired, finally, by the still fledgling Bloomsbury. Cox suspected the imprint didn't believe the book would do much business, and they likely saw it as stepping stone for signing a juicier Paul-authored memoir later down the line.[95] Within the MPL company itself, said Cox, the cookbook was first considered a quirky little hobby of Linda's.[96] That changed as the book soon sold over 400,000 copies, rocketing to the top of the publishing charts.

Its success was followed by the Linda McCartney range of vegetarian food products, launched in 1991 with the help of the entrepreneur Tim Treharne. It didn't take off in the United States, but it did prove an enormous success in the UK, where Linda McCartney Foods soon started earning more money for MPL than its music.[97] There was the occasional scandal, such as the accusation that the products were not as healthy as advertised (high salt content, for instance) and the infamous batch of veggie shepherd's pies that had to be recalled because they contained lamb.[98] Even so, the empire went from strength to strength. By 1995, the British vegetarian frozen-food industry was worth £100 million, with Linda's brand accounting for a third of the market.[99]

Chrissie Hynde of The Pretenders compared her own 'hardline' approach to that of her friend Linda. When women asked for advice on how to convert their husbands and families to vegetarianism, Hynde's advice was to abandon them. Linda, on the other hand, would suggest serving people veggie burgers without warning and, when they realized they were tasty, telling them how healthy they were as well.[100] This was reflected in a television commercial that showed a muscly cartoon farmer, blindfolded, who thoroughly enjoys a platter of 'beefy burgers' and lasagne until he is informed by his scarecrow friend that these dishes do not contain any meat. 'No meat?! Ooh, no. Not for me,' he decides. Over the fields strides the live-action Linda. 'You won't be wanting this tasty country pie, then?' she teases. Another member of Hynde and Linda's circle, the sitcom writer Carla Lane, was sceptical of veggie products that aimed to imitate meat dishes. Why reject meat and then consume its replica?[101] That was exactly what people wanted, the market said. Since Linda's death, there have been breakthroughs in the science of lab-grown meat. This just goes to show the lengths to which people will go to obtain such a product without the uncomfortable killing part.

Outside the pages of her cosily presented family cookbooks, beyond her wholesome advertisement persona, Linda showed greater militancy, and this could sometimes be provocative. 'It's like what Hitler did to people is what we're doing to animals,' she reasoned: 'We're gassing them, we're factory-farming them and we're murdering them.'[102] By her family she was nicknamed 'little Mrs Pankhurst'.[103] As an American, she was less reverent

The McCartneys tuck into Linda's meat-free burgers, 1991.

to monarchy than a bootlicking Briton might have been raised to be, so when she met Prince Philip, Duke of Edinburgh, Linda wasn't afraid to take him to task for the hypocrisy of being a president of the World Wildlife Fund who enjoyed shooting animals. 'Linda was the ballsiest woman,' Paul said (again) when recalling the incident, 'a very strong lady'.[104]

Paul and Linda have each been credited with coining the phrase 'If slaughterhouses had glass walls, we'd all be vegetarian.'[105] They may have come up with it together or borrowed it from conversations among animal rights campaigners. Perhaps they adapted it. A similar statement was uttered much earlier by congresswoman Martha W. Griffiths. 'Of course, if slaughterhouses had glass walls we would have had humane slaughter a long time ago,' she told the House of Representatives in 1957.[106] The Humane Methods of Slaughter Act was approved the following year and signed into law by President Dwight D. Eisenhower, who noted its popularity: 'If I went by mail, I'd think no one was interested in anything but humane slaughter.'[107] The act stipulated that meat companies had to render animals completely insensible to pain (that is, stunned or sedated) when they were killed in order to minimize the creatures' suffering. The UK had made similar laws in 1933 and 1954. These had not gone far enough, according to the McCartneys' later views.

If they could not compel slaughterhouses to install glass walls or force everybody to take traumatic tourist trips to the knacker's yard, then the McCartneys would bring the abattoir to them. In the build-up to the band taking the stage on the 1993 New World Tour, a short film was screened that combined archive footage of Paul's career with graphic scenes of animals being harmed or killed for commercial or research purposes, as well as for grotesque entertainment, as in the case of the Edison studio's film of the fatal electrocution of Topsy the elephant at Luna Park in 1903. This took 'balls' on the part of both Paul and Linda. Bear in mind that Paul's reputation was only just starting to recover from its 1980s nadir. While some people still mocked Linda's singing and keyboard playing, the public had grown used to her being around by now. Paul's admirers were a little less resentful towards Linda's presence than they had been in earlier years. Linda would less often receive unpleasant letters or actual faeces in the post. (The latter had been observed by one-time Wings member Laurence Juber.)[108] So just as the McCartneys were being treated with greater warmth, they began accusing their fans of murder.

The footage of animal cruelty was 'kind of a depressing way to open a rock show', one attendee remembers.[109] Some of the clips were so upsetting that audience members were seen gasping in shock and turning away, unable to stomach the horror.[110] This wasn't a Butthole Surfers concert, after all.[111] Live reviewers either didn't mention the screening at all, skirted over it in a single line,[112] or reported it as both disturbing and annoying, especially after being 'assailed' in the lobby, as David Sinclair of *The Times* put it, by campaigners for Greenpeace and Friends of the Earth.[113] Journalists who dwelled longer on the footage dug out the old John Lennon comparisons. The lyrics to the animal rights protest song 'Looking for Changes' and the 'tone' of the pre-concert film were 'closer to the aggressive, anti-war stance of Lennon in the late '60s and early '70s than traditional McCartney', wrote *Los Angeles Times* critic Robert Hilburn.[114] Speaking to Hilburn backstage, McCartney expressed concern that such heavy-handed activism could risk alienating certain people. He spoke of trying to get the balance right in his pursuit of 'gentle activism', as both musician and interviewer called it. Had these actions, whether they were gentle or otherwise, been carried out by John Lennon, they would have been taken more seriously and viewed with greater reverence by those who subscribed, as Hilburn does, to the questionable stereotypes of Paul as the eager-to-please one with the 'melodic flair' and John as the ex-Beatle with 'intensity, wit, and unfailing honesty as a writer'.[115]

More recently, Paul's views and his association with the likes of People for the Ethical Treatment of Animals (PETA) have come under fire from those who see such activists as proselytizing to the poor from their ivory towers. (The idea of an actual building made from elephant tusks would obviously disgust such campaigners.) Among those still unimpressed by celebrity animal rights crusaders is the award-winning Canadian Inuk throat singer Tanya Tagaq. She grew up Nunavut, where seal hunting is commonplace. She sees it as 'irrational and patronising' for pampered people who have no idea what life is like up there to chastise anyone for their diet. 'It's a mini version of gross colonialism and it makes me so angry,' she informed *The Quietus* in 2015. 'I wish I could talk to someone like Paul McCartney and tell him to fuck right off because there are children who are starving. Why is he talking about the seal ban? Is his family hungry?'[116]

Linda's business empire has also been accused of complicity in the broader 'McDonaldization' of food manufacture and consumption. Despite claiming the ethical superiority of not having to kill anything (besides plants), it was said to be the equivalent of industrial-level meat production in the way it prioritized profit and efficiency over quality of products and the impacts on agriculture, the environment and health of consumers. Critics of the enterprise said there was barely anything 'natural' about its production processes, which managed to churn out a million meat-free meals per week from a factory in Norfolk.[117] United Biscuits, which owned the frozen-food company Ross Young's, through which Linda's range was launched, was obviously more profit-oriented than animal-minded, as illustrated by their other products, which contained meat and fish. Its ties to the McCartneys provided the conglomerate with some sought-after 'green' credentials.[118] Linda was well aware that compromise would be necessary for her veggie range to succeed. She knew that she had to 'sleep with the devil', as she put it herself.[119] Her motto had always been, 'If I could save one animal then I'll be happy.'[120] In her husband's mind there is no doubt at all that she saved the lives of millions.[121]

## Glass Walls

Long accustomed to taking insults on the chin, Linda was a woman of principle who was on a mission to forge a revolution in vegetarianism, and in the way human beings treated their fellow creatures, through virtually any means necessary: via bookshops and libraries, pre-concert screenings, advertisements, the press, supermarkets and appearances on the most popular television shows of the time. A 1995 episode of *The Simpsons* depicted Lisa's conversion to vegetarianism, her difficulty in doing so and the ridicule it attracted. In it, both vegetarians and carnivores become targets of the cartoon's satire. Its strongest critique of meat-eating, notes Carrie Packwood Freeman, is in the spoof propaganda film *Meat and You: Partners in Freedom*, presented by the has-been actor Troy McClure and screened to children by Principal Skinner in the hope of stopping Lisa's campaign for meat-free alternatives in the school cafeteria. When McClure takes a curious child on a tour of an abattoir's killing floor, the boy emerges pale and shaken (glass walls, indeed), but he is still won over by McClure's absurd arguments about the food chain and the fact that 'If a cow ever got the chance, he'd eat you and everyone you care about.' Here at least, writes Freeman, the show 'made a clear statement that the ethical controversy over meat is warranted yet silenced by those in power'.[122] Paul and Linda agreed to voice themselves in the episode, in which they help to lift Lisa's spirits and make her feel less lonely. 'Linda and I both feel strongly about animal rights,' says Paul. 'In fact, if you play "Maybe I'm Amazed" backwards, you'll hear a recipe for a really ripping lentil soup.' The couple had a condition for appearing on the show. Lisa had to forswear meat-eating permanently, for as long as *The Simpsons* ran.[123] She became the longest-lasting and most famous vegetarian character in the history of American television.[124]

In Paul's view, 'Linda made vegetarianism mainstream.'[125] Hers was a crusade and a legacy that many would argue was far more important than that of recording a few silly love songs. There has always been speculation that Paul was never as committed to the cause as his wife. There were even rumours that, when no one was looking, he still enjoyed a steak or two.[126] Linda did devote more time to it than he. That doesn't mean Paul wasn't on board. After Linda's death, he made a special effort to engage with the animal rights press, discussing her life and legacy in interviews with publications such as *The Animals' Agenda* and *Viva! Life*. Here he showed how informed and passionate he continued to be on the same issues that had concerned his wife.[127] Others have speculated that Linda's vegetarian pursuits caused tension in the marriage. That's what Philip Norman was told by Peter Cox, who, having been bought out of his share after co-authoring that first cookbook, may have his own agenda for painting a dramatic picture of 'psychological war' between the couple.[128] Even if there was friction at first, it can't have lasted long because Paul was demonstrably supportive of Linda's causes for the rest of her lifetime and beyond. Soon after the launch of Linda McCartney Foods he would be heard hooting things like 'Imagine seeing your wife's face looking out from the freezer department at you.'[129]

It is doubtless that Linda's passions influenced the more outspoken material from the *Off the Ground* era, which was raised in this book's introduction. Linda's posthumous album, *Wide Prairie*, includes two songs, recorded towards the end of the 1980s, that dealt directly with animal rights. Co-written with Carla Lane (and Paul, naturally), 'Cow' narrates the titular creature's sentence to the slaughterhouse. 'The White Coated Man', meanwhile, acts as a companion piece to Paul's own later anti-vivisection song, 'Looking for Changes'.

According to *The Guardian*'s pop critic Alexis Petridis, the paradox of Paul McCartney's latter-day career is thus: 'The one thing he really needs is the one thing that he can't have, because it doesn't exist: an equal.'[130] While it is true that few of his later musical partners have had the traits that Lennon brought to the table, McCartney often excels in the face of competition. The sudden absence of his equal – and key rival – can help to explain McCartney's wavering in the 1980s. In the following decade, it was feasible that the spotlight would be snatched by a member of McCartney's own immediate family, despite their working in different fields. Alongside Linda's food empire, there was daughter Stella's success as a fashion designer. (Fur- and leather-free, of course.) McCartney was always supportive as a husband and father. He would surely be loath to admit it, but did this element of competition spur him to flex his musical muscles harder than in the decade prior?

As we have already seen, McCartney had long been typecast as the 'the cute one' from a partly girl-group-influenced pop band who sported androgynously floppy hair and had a large female following. His penchant for writing about love, romance, marriage and family was viewed as trading in sentimentalism, a supposedly feminine trait. He seemed to want a wife who played the traditional role in the family. He was also delighted by how 'ballsy' she turned out to be. Together they gave up meat, carnivorism having its traditional associations with masculinity, heterosexuality and the supposedly manly act of hunting. Mr McCartney had still wanted to be the big man carving away at the head of the table, even if the 'meat' itself was made from macaroni, and his 'tough cookie' wife had ended up winning more bread than him.[131] It must have been a humbling experience. Another emasculating one, even. But it was another phenomenon of this era that helped to free him, to liberate him from the pressures of being Paul McCartney, and to rouse his mojo once more.

Shortly after the release of 1984's maligned movie *Give My Regards to Broad Street*, Joan Goodman had conducted a joint interview with Paul and Linda for *Playboy* magazine. The topic arose of how success, fortune and domesticity can risk diminishing the 'hunger' of the artist. At first Paul agreed. He reflected on his and Lennon's early ambitions and noted that a lean greyhound will most likely run fastest. It took his staunchest supporter to challenge the theory. 'But Picasso wasn't hungry,' interjected Linda. At the time, it will have seemed to readers that McCartney was neither hungry nor on a par with Picasso. In the 1990s the appetite returned for popular music's own Pablo.

# 7
# The Experimental Ones

The only Britpop-era band that managed to persuade Paul McCartney to guest on one of their original songs was Cardiff's Super Furry Animals. While they too drew on pop's rich history, these psychedelic Welshmen did so in a far more diverse, progressive, arty and sonically chaotic way than the majority of their contemporaries. Super Furry Animals were originally signed to Creation Records, the same label as Oasis. The two bands could barely have been more different in their outlook and agendas. It's true that Super Furry Animals were fiercely ambitious, much like Oasis. As singer Gruff Rhys put it, 'We want to be like the KLF – having number one hits, and still completely doing people's heads in.'[1] Besides the shared appetite for successful singles, messing with audiences' minds was never part of Noel Gallagher's mission statement. On 'Receptacle for the Respectable' from Super Furry Animals' fifth album, *Rings Around the World* (2001), Paul McCartney was credited with 'celery and carrot' accompaniment. This could be seen as a nostalgic activity itself, albeit an unusual one, for it was a reference to The Beach Boys' 1967 song 'Vegetables', on which McCartney was rumoured to have contributed some percussive noises by chomping on celery and/or carrots.[2] The events connect two eras when McCartney was at his most experimental. Just picture McCartney recording his, shall we say, *fresh* vegetable parts for Super Furry Animals, on whichever day he did this in the early half of the year 2000. It's easy to imagine him crunching away while looking back over the decade that had just finished and marvelling at what an adventurous ten years it had been.

## Hardback Debunker

As we have already seen, in the 1990s Paul McCartney reasserted himself in various ways. One of these was to take back control, as best he could, of the narrative that had long cast him as the writer of insubstantial, melodic pop music, as opposed to Lennon, who was thought to be, among other laudable things, the bold and uncompromising experimentalist. This had bothered McCartney for some time. His frustration had usually been expressed in private. McCartney had presumed it was off the record when he spoke to Hunter Davies, author of 1968's *The Beatles: The Authorised Biography*, in May 1981. McCartney had telephoned Davies and, according to the writer, had spoken for over an hour about how hurt he was by misrepresentations in accounts such as Philip Norman's *Shout!* These were being printed and accepted as legitimate history, and echoed so often as to cumulatively transform into 'fact'. In this version of events, McCartney was cruel, calculating and cautious. 'John is now the nice guy and I'm the bastard. It gets repeated all the time.'[3] The reality was never that simple. 'He could be a maneuvring swine, which no one ever realized,' Davies recalled McCartney saying. 'Now since the death he's become Martin Luther Lennon. But that really wasn't him either. He wasn't some sort of holy saint. He was still really a debunker.'[4] McCartney was shocked when Davies included this conversation in an updated edition of his Beatles biography, published in 1982. Given Philip Norman's liberal approach to the truth (discussed in Chapter One), it's understandable that McCartney was upset. Appearing so soon after Lennon's death, the unusually candid 'interview', which McCartney had never intended for public consumption, made him look bitter and Lennon-obsessed, further marring his reputation at the time. Compounding the betrayal of trust (though McCartney should have been more careful when confiding in a professional journalist, of all people), Davies defended Norman as 'a fine writer and formerly a colleague of mine on the *Sunday Times*', thus implying that McCartney had overreacted.[5] Back when Davies was researching and writing his Beatles biography, he spent time with the band, their inner circle and their families. His technique was to either jot things down in his notebook at the time or to not even do that, instead typing up the whole day's events from memory when he got back home.[6] Seeing as nothing was recorded on Dictaphone, can Davies's quotations be trusted as verbatim? Presumably McCartney's 1981 telephone conversation was not recorded either. If the gist of the account is correct, however, it does help to show how the ideas of historical record, personal reputation and enduring misinformation have been important factors in McCartney's motives since.[7] 'They're ready should I die,' McCartney told an interviewer in 1982. 'They got me summed up already. That happened with John.'[8] He was referring to his own obituary that he knew had been commissioned, for when it would be needed, by *The Times* newspaper. It had been penned by Hunter Davies.

In the following decade, McCartney threw caution to the wind by putting greater effort into challenging the accepted storyline of The Beatles and the stereotypes they had been assigned. By then, John Lennon had been gone for ten years. McCartney felt less inclined to bite his tongue out of respect for his dead friend. In the souvenir programme for his comeback tour of 1989–90, McCartney reaffirmed his credentials as the experimental Beatle (or one of them, at least).[9] This theme continued through Barry Miles's official biography *Many Years from Now*, which drew on extensive interview sessions with McCartney. While some critics see this as a savvy rewriting of history on the part of McCartney, the evidence is apparent. Lennon had an art-school background and during his Beatles days had published two books of stories, drawings and poems, heavily influenced by surreal radio comedy *The Goon Show*. For a long time, however, he remained extremely sceptical of the avant-garde. He saw the term as 'French for bullshit' and the scene itself as populated by pompous 'intellectuals and university students'.[10] Into this movement McCartney had immersed himself while Lennon was living in the suburbs, unhappily married to his first wife and watching too much television. You could say that McCartney introduced Lennon to the avant-garde, where he found Yoko Ono, who curbed his cynicism towards the scene and pushed him further down that road. Many people remained convinced that Lennon had found it before McCartney, thanks to songs such as The Beatles' divisive sound collage 'Revolution 9' (1968) and Lennon's late-1960s collaborations with Ono. As recounted in *Many Years from Now*, McCartney had been closely involved with the Indica bookshop and gallery, the *International Times* underground newspaper and its associated club, UFO.[11] McCartney's relationship with Jane Asher had got him interested in modern theatre, and he mingled with the likes of Harold Pinter and Kenneth Tynan.[12] In Swinging London he was also exposed to boundary-pushing composers such as Karlheinz Stockhausen, John Cage, Luciano Berio, Morton Subotnick, Terry Riley and Steve Reich.[13] He discovered free jazz, too, and Surrealist visual art.[14] He once took part in a musical performance by the free improvisation group AMM in which there was no separation between the act and their audience, who were encouraged to participate. Using a penny from his pocket, McCartney decided to 'play' the room's radiator.[15]

At home, using two Brenell reel-to-reel tape recorders, McCartney made mock radio shows and created his first sound loops.[16] Around this time he hung out with William Burroughs and Ian Sommerville, who'd also been experimenting with cut-up tape collages. It's possible that McCartney would have made – and released – more of this kind of full-bore avant-garde music had the less open-minded people he played it to, Bob Dylan among them, not walked out of the room as soon as they heard the distorted racket.[17] The technique made its way into The Beatles' music when they recorded the milestone track 'Tomorrow Never Knows' in 1966. A longer and more abstract 'song' was created during the sessions for *Sgt. Pepper's Lonely Hearts Club Band*. A heavily reverbed, fourteen-minute noise sculpture, 'Carnival of Light' was recorded at McCartney's request and aired at London's Roundhouse in January 1967. This pre-dated Lennon's embrace of the avant-garde, as McCartney has been at pains to reiterate. 'John could only do "Revolution 9" because I put a couple of tape recorders together and showed him how to do it,' he said when promoting *Many Years from Now*. 'That's how he came to make *Two Virgins* [1968]. John could never have done it otherwise. He was hopelessly untechnical.'[18] To create 'Carnival of Light', unlike seasoned improvisers such as AMM, The Beatles had simply made a random racket, overdubbed it casually and made everything sound very echoey. Barry Miles compared it to The Mothers of Invention's superior piece 'The Return of the Son of Monster Magnet' (1966).[19] Daevid Allen of the Soft Machine, who heard 'Carnival of Light' at the Roundhouse, said it was 'not particularly memorable'.[20] The consensus is that McCartney was better at subversively weaving unconventional sounds and outside references into shorter pop songs than making overtly abstract music himself. The recording of 'Carnival of Light' was sandwiched between the studio album landmarks of *Revolver* and *Sgt. Pepper's Lonely Hearts Club Band*. McCartney had hoped the piece would be included on *Anthology 2*, but it was vetoed by the other parties involved.[21] McCartney is proud of the piece and remains hopeful for its release, not least because it counters his reputation as the conservative and cuddly moptop.

In fact, and this really is the genius of Paul McCartney, he *was* the safe, cuddly, saccharine and cute one at the same time as being the bold, daring and experimental one. Some people can't seem to get their heads around this. There is no contradiction or cognitive dissonance here. The same polymath who wrote 'The Long and Winding Road' and the self-deprecating but still soppy 'Silly Love Songs' was also behind the heavy metal precursor 'Helter Skelter', the satirical Beach Boys parody 'Back in the USSR', bittersweet songs like 'Eleanor Rigby' and 'Yesterday', and the effervescent electro-pop of 1980's 'Temporary Secretary/ Secret Friend' single.

Review-writing musos can be prone to insert the word 'experimental' into their copy as an intrinsically positive term, in explicit or implied comparison to more formulaic, clichéd, hackneyed or standardized material. (I've definitely been guilty of doing this myself.) The scientific idea of experimentation is to formulate hypotheses, design and conduct experiments to test out those hypotheses, make observations, evaluate the results, accept or reject the outcome and, if necessary, repeat or tweak the processes. It can get things wrong.

One of Paul McCartney's missteps in the 1990s, according to some, was to branch out into the world of classical music.

## Hi, Hi, Highbrow

Perhaps it was inevitable that sooner or later the Picasso of Pop would want to explore the classical realm. It's a route that was predicted in Howard Elson's book *McCartney: Songwriter* (1986). The author advised it, even, as a possible restorative for the 'hard edge' and 'hunger' that he felt had been absent from McCartney's recent studio output.[22]

Towards the end of Elson's book, a number of interviewees discuss whether McCartney's work will stand up to older music's greatest composers. Echoing critics in the 1960s who were convinced that The Beatles' music would lack longevity, the jazz musician Chris Barber thought that, for all his talent in the field of pop music ('a minor art form with very little lasting quality'), McCartney could never be compared to the likes of Beethoven.[23] Glam rocker Alvin Stardust disagreed. He saw McCartney as the modern equivalent of a classical composer whose work, like theirs, would loom large and survive down the ages for hundreds of years to come.[24] Status Quo's Francis Rossi put McCartney up there with George Gershwin and proposed that his finest work was still ahead of him.[25] As for the fantasy of shifting into classical composition, the award-winning songwriter Barry Mason considered McCartney capable of making pieces that would 'floor the whole world, if he wanted to'.[26] The American singer-songwriter Gene Pitney speculated that McCartney 'could be very good at it if he put his mind to it'.[27] The virtuoso flautist Elena Durán (who had played on 'We All Stand Together') noted that McCartney wasn't a particularly gifted composer, much more 'naïve' and 'simplistic' than the likes of Gershwin, but these shortcomings wouldn't necessarily prevent him from coming up with 'terrific ideas'.[28]

Before diving into pure classical, McCartney had some prior relationship with it. George Martin had suggested the string part to 'Yesterday', promising the songwriter a subtler treatment than 'You'll Never Walk Alone' by Gerry and the Pacemakers.[29] The producer helped McCartney with orchestral arrangements, on and off, from that moment on. The Asher family, with whom McCartney was living in the mid-1960s, were well versed in classical music. As with theatre, they eased McCartney into it.[30] The Beatles' manager, Brian Epstein, preferred classical to pop, his favourite composer being Jean Sibelius until he discovered Lennon and McCartney (or so he said).[31] The Beatles drew ideas from the classical canon on several occasions. For the piccolo trumpet part on 'Penny Lane', McCartney hired David Mason after seeing him perform Johann Sebastian Bach's Brandenburg Concerto No. 2 in F major with the English Chamber Orchestra on late-night BBC Two.[32] Another Bach piece, Bourrée in E minor, was adapted into the fingerpicking basis of 'Blackbird'.[33] For the orchestral arrangement on 'Eleanor Rigby', McCartney had requested something along the lines of Vivaldi.[34] Then, of course, there was the orchestral 'orgasm' that ends 'A Day in the Life'. There have also been classical elements identified in McCartney's approach to his colourful basslines.[35] Between *Revolver* and *Sgt. Pepper*, McCartney had composed the score for the Roy Boulting film *The Family Way*. Later, McCartney enjoyed making the incidental music for *Give My Regards to Broad Street*.[36] In both those instances George Martin was on hand again.

It wasn't until the early 1990s that McCartney the Classical Composer fully emerged. This side career began with *Paul McCartney's Liverpool Oratorio* (1991), written with Carl Davis to commemorate 150 years of the Royal Liverpool Philharmonic Orchestra. That was followed by *Standing Stone* in 1997, commissioned to celebrate EMI's centenary. *Working Classical* in 1999 featured orchestral renditions of older McCartney songs alongside new compositions. *Ecce Cor Meum* and *Ocean's Kingdom* arrived in the next millennium.

Such releases tend to hit respectable positions on the classical music charts. Beyond that, they have not been held in particularly high esteem. That said, nor have they been greeted with quite the same levels of horror and mockery as *Give My Regards to Broad Street*, a fate that McCartney risked repeating with such a move. Sure, the reviewer at *Newsday* considered *Liverpool Oratorio* to be a 'sprawling, mawkish, and excruciatingly embarrassing 90-minute exercise of the ego', but that was in 1991 when McCartney's reputation was in recovery and people were still getting used to this middle-aged pop upstart's incursion into music generally considered to be higher art.[37] McCartney had been victim to others' snobbery ever since his Beatles days, so it ought to be noted how loaded is that later title *Working Classical*. The Oratorio, as it happens, was performed at Liverpool Cathedral. This was the same building where, as a schoolboy, McCartney had failed an audition for a place in its choir. To put on such a grand piece in that particular location was, if not an act of revenge, then something that provided a sense of vindication.

I would argue that, like his wife's skills at the keyboards and tambourine, McCartney got better at it too. *Standing Stone* and *Working Classical* are more satisfying experiences than *Liverpool Oratorio* with its exhaustive length and semi-autobiographical libretto. But then I'm a rock person at heart, so what do I know? Classical McCartney's audience has been identified as mainly consisting of Beatles fans who are open to a novel listening experience, rather than those who know their Haydn from their Handel.[38] The pieces have received standing ovations in prestigious venues. Because McCartney is a celebrity, that doesn't tell us much about the actual aesthetic merits. His patrons, performers and collaborators from the classical world, and those insiders who have nominated his works for awards like the Classical Brits, could be opportunistically minded rather than artistically motivated, turning his 'celebrity capital into economic capital' and hoping for his presence to help classical music reach a bigger audience.[39] On the other hand, negative reviews in classical music magazines and broadsheet newspapers could be driven by their own agenda, be this unconscious bias or otherwise. Classical music, as it developed, became the cultural property of the educated elite. Taste is tied to social hierarchy and plays a role in reinforcing it, especially when equated to other art forms that are considered 'lower', less legitimate or vulgar, even.[40] By transgressing the boundaries between the supposedly crude and commercial world of pop music and

Issued Via
Marshall Arts Ltd
ROYAL ALBERT HALL
An EMI, Marshall Arts Ltd. and MPL
presentation in aid of The Music Sound Foundation
The World Premiere of
Paul McCartney's
Standing Stone
Tuesday, 14 October 1997
at 7:30 PM
Doors open at 6:30 PM
Door 8
Circle X
Row 6
Seat 224
Restricted View
£ 10.00


Ticket stub from the premiere of Paul McCartney's *Standing Stone* (1997). 'It was boring,' remembers the attendee, but they did have a restricted view.

that perceived to be higher-brow and more legitimate, McCartney did pose a threat to the status quo. In negative reviews of his classical efforts, the message could well have been for pop musicians to know their place, to stay in that lower position and to keep their noses away from areas they don't belong.[41] Or is that reading too much into it? Radiohead guitarist Johnny Greenwood's recent shift into classical composition has been accepted more favourably than McCartney's.[42] Then again, Greenwood can read and score music himself (unlike McCartney), and most of Greenwood's projects have been soundtracks for movies, a category that may have its own special position and implications within the cultural sphere. Furthermore, Greenwood was privately educated so he is already part of the upper group and therefore less of a menace.

A quick trawl through a few Internet discussion forums suggests that while limited knowledge of music theory, lack of formal training and the inability to read music do not matter, or can even have their advantages, where rock and pop music are concerned, the same does not apply to the classical field.[43] McCartney's activities compare poorly, it is argued, to those of another rocker-turned-orchestra-leader, Frank Zappa, whose grasp of classical composition was nourished from an early age.[44]

Another difference lies in the two men's nationalities, argues forum member Rob Hughes, with the 'norms' of the British classical establishment tending to be duller than those of other places. It is typically more conservative and smitten with the likes of Edward Elgar. Hughes proposes that McCartney either panders to this milieu or is compelled to pursue that cautious style by those with whom he has to collaborate as someone who can't make music like this on his own. The slight problem with this theory is that Carl Davis came from America, as did Lawrence Foster, who conducted *Standing Stone*. Even so, and notwithstanding McCartney's aforementioned admiration for Stockhausen and other sonic radicals, Zappa's works do seem to have drawn on wilder influences, such as Edgard Varèse and Dmitri Shostakovich, and they share a similar spirit with the American modern masters (Steve Reich, Terry Riley, John Adams and others).[45]

As mentioned earlier, in the practice of science, experiments don't always have to go well or produce the anticipated results. If McCartney's side gig as a classical composer has not proved too fruitful (critically, that is; commercially it's done all right), then his dalliances with ambient electronica could be viewed as more artistically successful and more readily accepted by the press and other gatekeepers. A Bourdieusian reading could be applied to this too. If it is not deemed to be acceptable when McCartney transgresses upwards, as it were, penetrating the fence of the classical hierarchy, it appears to be more tolerable (partly because it is less threatening) when he moves in the opposite direction, delving downwards instead into dance music, a genre that the elite might consider even more unfathomably vulgar than traditional rock 'n' roll.

## I Wanna Be Your Fireman

*Mojo* magazine runs a regular feature called 'All Back to My Place'. The page contains short interviews with celebrities, most often musicians, about their current listening habits. They are asked their favourite record of all time. The record best suited for a lazy Sunday morning. What they sing in the shower. That kind of thing. The interviewees might use the opportunity to show off their immaculate tastes, spotlight some music that has changed their lives, honour an obscurity deemed worthy of greater attention, or not even think about it that hard and just blurt out the first records that pop into their heads. Rarely do they choose their own music. For the January 1998 edition, when he was asked, 'What music are you currently grooving to?' Paul McCartney said it was *Strawberries Oceans Ships Forest* by The Fireman: 'my ambient dance record released in 1993'.[46]

It might come as a surprise that this electronic project was another thing that had its roots in the organic and live-sounding studio album *Off the Ground*. Martin Glover (aka Youth), who had been the original bassist in the misanthropic post-punk band Killing Joke before branching out into dub and techno alongside producing all sorts of other acts, was originally hired to remix some songs from *Off the Ground*, to be released on 12-inch singles. With his older 'Carnival of Light' material in mind, McCartney stipulated that the new sound collages should not include samples of other artists lest it end up sounding like another person's record. He didn't like the idea, for example, of there being 'a James Brown snare sound' (many a remixer's go-to sample).[47] Youth wove his sonic tapestry from parts of *Off the Ground*, the older song 'Cosmically Conscious',[48] and samples from Wings' final album, *Back to the Egg*. Engineer Chris Potter and programmer Matt Austin helped out too. McCartney then returned to the studio to add some banjo, bass, flute and whispering.[49] 'It was great fun,' Paul said of the session, 'because normally these are the bits that producers try to get me to shut up about – they usually say, "Stop messing around, Paul, sing the song properly" – but Youth wanted all the messing around. It was an interesting release for me.'[50] As with the foray into classical music, it was a risky one, too.

Back in 1987, Beatles expert Mark Lewisohn had already complained that the number of 12-inch remixes of singles from *Press to Play*, an album that wasn't received that well in the first place, was ripping off completists with an unnecessary glut that would alienate McCartney's remaining devotees.[51] To his credit, McCartney ignored such warnings and provocatively leaned further into it with The Fireman. Youth's efforts, which had escalated into an album's length of material, were deemed worthy of release in one whole set and marked the beginning of a long partnership. Youth remembers Paul worrying about whether Linda would like what they were making, 'as if Linda was the boss'.[52] When she heard it, the 'mother-hippie', as Youth found her to be, was delighted with it.[53] This should have been expected given her love of reggae, which is essentially where dub and remix culture came from.

The sleeve for *Strawberries Oceans Ships Forest*, released in November 1993, contained no mention of the musicians who'd made it. Philip Norman suggests this was because McCartney had promised not to market anything under his own name during the *Anthology* campaign.[54] This is likely to be nonsense, given it appeared two years beforehand and in the same month as *Paul Is Live* and the 'Biker Like an Icon' single. Rather, The Fireman was a joint project with a second musician, which merited a separate name in its own right. McCartney had hoped that no one would find out who was behind this music, like his erstwhile alias 'Percy Thrillington', who'd (re)recorded the *Ram* album in full as big-band instrumentals in 1971.[55] The nom de plume also recalls the way McCartney had once roused The Beatles out of possible complacency and taken the pressure off themselves when recording under the pretence of 'Sgt. Pepper's Lonely Hearts Club Band'. Shortly before *Strawberries*' release, the identity of The Fireman was leaked to the press, so it drew more mainstream attention than an album of this nature would otherwise have received. It's feasible the leak came from someone within Parlophone who was looking to boost its sales. At least one publication reported that the album was being released pseudonymously because the record company were hoping to sell it to the dance market and were concerned that the presence of McCartney's name would put off such listeners.[56] Given that major labels tend to value high sales figures over making inroads into narrower subcultures, this seems doubtful. Besides, Macca was hardly persona non grata on the dance floor anyway. For all that the grunge and Britpop scenes had done to salvage McCartney's street cred, the sample-heavy genres of dance music and hip-hop had also been rife with Beatles references. In the late 1980s, rap groups including Beastie Boys and Boogie Down Productions used Beatles samples in their backing tracks. Formed in 1992, Staten Island's Wu-Tang Clan trumpeted themselves as 'The Beatles of hip-hop'. Other oft-named contenders for that coveted title are acts who were around earlier, such as Run-DMC and De La Soul. In dance music, prior to becoming The KLF, Bill Drummond and Jimmy Cauty's 'All You Need Is Love', released in 1987 under the name The Justified Ancients of Mu Mu (or the JAMS), opened with a sample of The Beatles song from which its name was taken. As the three books that have had the greatest impact on his life, Drummond lists the Bible, *On the Road* by Jack Kerouac and Hunter Davies's Beatles biography.[57] As for the wider subculture, 'Revolution 9' from the 'White Album' had been a regular presence in rave's chillout rooms.[58] By 1990, McCartney had noticed people coming up to him and saying 'Man, *Sgt. Pepper*, it's like Acid House isn't it?'[59] That decade's superstar DJs, The Chemical Brothers, would fuse tracks like 'Tomorrow Never Knows' and 'Sgt. Pepper's Lonely Hearts Club Band' into their live sets. The influence was all over the duo's original music too, most obviously on the Noel Gallagher-assisted single 'Setting Sun' (1996). So apparent were their homages that by 1998 The Chemical Brothers had amassed a whole file of intimidating communications from The Beatles' lawyers. 'Considering we love them so much it's a bit of a shame it's come to this,' said the duo's Ed Simons, 'but it's always nice to get a letter "cc-ed" to George Harrison, Ringo Starr and Paul McCartney.'[60] At the time, The Chemical Brothers' electronic brand of psychedelia could stake a claim as the true heir to the adventurous musical experiments of the 1960s, and it threatened to leave other genres in the dust.[61]

The attempted anonymity of Thrillington and The Fireman invites the question of whether McCartney has ever been successful in producing art under aliases that have not yet been detected by the wider world. Maybe Richard 'Aphex Twin' James wasn't really the man behind 'Caustic Window' after all. Philip Norman also believed The Fireman's band name to be a call-back to the engine-driving professional mentioned in the third verse of 'Penny Lane'.[62] More importantly, however, this was the job that McCartney's father, Jim, had volunteered to do during the Second World War. Furthermore, it was when sheltering during an air raid that Jim and Mary, Paul's mother (née Mohin), had first hit it off.[63]

Even though The Fireman's identities had been rumbled, the project still allowed McCartney to have fun making much stranger music than usual, without any pesky label or sales pressures. Youth felt McCartney saw it as something of an 'antidote' to that side of his career.[64] It allowed McCartney to experiment with working 'outside of that box' and 'escape his legacy a bit', if only momentarily.[65] For somebody on whose shoulders chief responsibility often weighs, McCartney found it both liberating and invigorating to have somebody else play a major part in the decision-making, as he expressed in a later interview with *Mojo*: 'I go into the studio and make all the noises, and then he [Youth]'ll say, "Go and have a cup of tea." When I come back he'll have a drum track and some ideas I can play on top of.' McCartney agreed that this had a similarly laid-back spirit to his now more widely appreciated solo albums *McCartney* and *McCartney II*: 'go into the studio but don't feel like you are going to do any work. And we did some funny things, I must say.'[66]

If the funny things on *Strawberries Oceans Ships Forest* had been a promising start to McCartney's unexpected sideline in ambient techno, even better was The Fireman's second album, *Rushes*, released in September 1998. Unlike the debut, which had spiralled out of a few proposed remixes, this time the duo knew they were working on an album together from the outset. It was recorded quickly. McCartney values spontaneity, as we've seen. In the previous decade he'd felt that some of his mainstream output had been bogged down with too many producers, overdubs and computers spoiling the audio broth. His rejection of this impacted powerfully on his 1990s mainstream work, but also the way he and Youth's 'electronic' music was created.

Ian Peel suggests *Rushes*' sound was influenced by the likes of Pink Floyd and Mike Oldfield.[67] Given its two creators' catholic tastes, they will have been drawing on a far broader and less orthodox range than that. Youth played live bass on one song. McCartney plate-span with multiple instruments. On the thirteen-minute 'Auraveda', he performs electric guitar, synthesizer, keyboards, sitar, percussion, shaker, tabla, harmonium, flute, tambourine, bells and vocals (according to Luca Perasi).[68]

Linda McCartney had been seriously ill when *Rushes* was being recorded. Youth wasn't aware of this at first because it wasn't spoken about in the studio. The album was completed shortly after Linda's death, and Youth sees it as a direct tribute to her. Of all the records he's worked on, he remains proudest of this one. 'It was a heartbreaking experience,' he said later, 'but a huge privilege for me in my small way to be part of their journey.'[69] Linda's presence is there on the record, heavily yet ethereally. Lines from her haikus drift in the music. Among the field recordings worked into the mix was the sound of Linda's beloved horses. It is both an abstract and a deeply personal album. It was one way for Paul to express his feelings in a manner that his more conventional recordings wouldn't necessarily allow. 'Palo Verde' includes abstracted elements of a McCartney song, recorded in 1995, that to this day remains unreleased in its full form. It is called 'Let Me Love You Always'.

In spite of the bereavement that informed its creation, *Rushes* is not an album that wallows in sadness or loss. This is Paul McCartney we're talking about. The eternal optimist. The plucky survivor. The man with a Picasso's palette of sound. An artist whose motto is to 'play' music rather than 'work' it.[70] Among the playful elements of *Rushes*' content are samples the duo recorded by ringing up telephone sex lines, as well as their astrological equivalents. Presumably this meant the phone bill was tax-deductible.

*Rushes* feels like a journey. At times reminiscent of The Orb, with whom Youth had worked before, it is quite New Age-y in places, but the joy is in the way the sound is always changing and shifting, often slowly and seamlessly, from one place to another. Somewhat astutely, the groove is taken up a notch in the second half of the LP when McCartney starts bashing away on the drum kit, in a style not dissimilar to Ringo Starr's, on 'Appletree Cinnabar Amber'. Threatening to morph into rock (or perhaps post-rock) territory, it will rouse anyone who's slipped too deeply into meditation by that point in the proceedings. After reprising the previous song's classical-sounding piano motif during the fade-out, it's followed by 'Bison', which opens with a jazzy intro before giving way to Youth's chunky bass riff. This is complemented by swirling space-rock textures, disembodied chanting and an almost jaunty, childlike keyboard part. It's a comparatively short track, but it makes its presence felt firmly and could easily have exploded into industrial noise-rock if the reins hadn't been held. Instead, the next song segues smoothly back into a more placid sound to bring the voyage full circle. Here, McCartney's voice pops out from the mix more clearly than before. It's an excerpt from a second unreleased song, called 'Hey Now (What Are You Looking at Me For?)', and another listener-stirring moment, presented as if to suddenly remind you that the absorbing hour-long experience you've just been given was made by old-school rock royalty, not some hotshot act peddling audio haze from the Warp Records roster or else, erm, Brian Eno in disguise.

Knowledge of the McCartneys' ordeal gives extra poignancy to the listening experience. The fact that it was made by McCartney (and Youth) rather than a mysterious techno producer in a yellow helmet may skew people's subjective judgement of it one way or the other. Not everybody was happy with 'Rock codgers wasting our time trying to cash in on the new craze the kids call "ambient music"', as *Muzik* magazine complained. 'Würzel, guitarist with Motörhead, has just released *Chill Out or Die*, while Macca is passing himself off as the anonymous Fireman. Leave it!'[71] That said, both those rockers' ambient projects outshone, for instance, the cringeworthy efforts of Eric Clapton. He's more often spotted wearing the cap of the cultural Luddite, but under the 'x-sample' alias he co-created the *Retail Therapy* (1997) album with TDF (Totally Dysfunctional Family). It made David Bowie's drum-and-bassy *Earthling* and U2's disco-minded *Pop* (released the same year) look like 'works of genius', according to the *Westword* critic Michael Roberts, and it compared poorly to the 'surprisingly good' work of The Fireman. Roberts deemed Clapton's 'jarringly tepid' attempt to be 'dominated by somnolent, quasi-new-age picking decorated with undeniably slack dance beats . . . Keeping his name off the liner was the smartest move he could have made.'[72]

The Fireman's Martin 'Youth' Glover performing with Killing Joke, 2009.

## Any Time At All

Look beyond the official studio albums and Beatles archive projects, and the 1990s reveal themselves to be McCartney's most experimental period since the second half of the 1960s. In some ways they even surpass those days in terms of the radical and varied nature of the content, if not quite in terms of having the same public impact. During this extraordinarily prolific stage of his career, McCartney had composed several works of classical music and made two ambient dance albums with The Fireman. A third, *Electric Arguments*, would follow in 2008. Still sonically adventurous, it featured material that was much more 'song-based' than the project's prior albums, and this time the sleeve listed the two men's real names (well, if you count 'Youth' as such a thing). Made when his second marriage had come to an end for reasons most unlike the first, it saw McCartney venting different feelings. It is interesting, though, that again he used The Fireman to do this. The cover was one of McCartney's abstract paintings. As yet another form of artistic expression, McCartney had taken this up in 1983, and once he'd overcome his inferiority complex from having never been to art school, the first exhibition of his paintings took place in 1999.[73]

For a time it had felt as though McCartney was deliberately keeping his experimental and more conventional personas separate. 'Sometimes I am Sir Paul McCartney who got the Mega

McCartney shows his first exhibition of abstract paintings in the town of Siegen, Germany, 1999.

Lifetime Icon Award from Bono at the MTV Awards and was knighted by Her Maj. And I like that role,' he said when promoting *Electric Arguments*. 'But I am also James Paul McCartney a school kid from Liverpool who got sort of . . . elevated. Sometimes I have to let go of Sir Paul just to achieve creative freedom. That's when I become The Fireman.'[74] That said, the material on *Electric Arguments* shows him trying to reconcile his separate personas, or at least bring them closer together. The adventurous sound and production of albums that McCartney made in his seventies – *New* (2013), *Egypt Station* (2018), *McCartney III* (2020) – suggests that the mischievous Fireman has also been infiltrating, if subtly, the loftier character of 'Sir Paul'.

While there is not the space to delve into them all here, other out-there activities McCartney got up to in the 1990s included collaborating on a musical adaptation of the poem 'Ballad of the Skeletons' (1996) with Beat poet Allan Ginsberg, resuming his role as a DIY DJ with the creation of a 'wide-screen radio' show called *Oobu Joobu* (1995), making the *Liverpool Sound Collage* (recorded in 1999–2000) with Super Furry Animals, which led to his later vegetable-chewing appearance, and even helping out on 'Hiroshima Sky Is Always Blue' (1995) by Yoko Ono.[75]

This was hardly a person who was resting on his laurels or running out of ideas. For someone who has spent an awful lot of his life being asked to revisit and reflect on all the groundbreaking things he'd achieved by the end of his twenties, McCartney was always moving forwards. But perhaps that's too linear a way to observe his actions.

On the *Rushes* track 'Fluid', a voice can be heard repeating the question 'What does the concept of time mean to you?' What would McCartney's answer be to that question? With every ounce of superheroic strength in his body, time is something he has always tried to defy.

# 8

# Run, McCartney, Run!

Given the frantic pace at which McCartney had moved during the 1990s, it seemed only fitting that he should end the decade by titling an album with a reference to running. As with much of what we have already seen, this record was an attempt to reconcile with the past while still summoning the vigour to move ever onward. Far from mirroring the usual cash-in covers album, such as those Rod Stewart puts out most Christmases, 1999's *Run Devil Run* was a deeply personal and emotionally direct affair. McCartney had been stopped in his tracks, at least temporarily, by the death of Linda and had spent the following year in mourning. When he returned to the studio, the sessions saw him seek solace in the same songs that had eased the pain after his mother Mary's death way back when.

The album evoked, too, another dearly missed loved one: John Lennon, and especially his 1975 solo album *Rock 'n' Roll*, which had been full of songs originally performed by the likes of Gene Vincent and Chuck Berry. As Simon Reynolds sees it, Lennon's post-Beatles output saw the musician trying to bring himself back to earth by re-embracing his rock 'n' roll roots after stratospheric fame and herculean drug-taking had left him feeling mentally adrift.[1] If we want to get all Freudian about it, Lennon was also yearning for an impossible return to a stabler time when his mother (as well as Paul's) was still alive. A time before everything had gone askew.

*Run Devil Run* (1999).

Similarly, *Run Devil Run* saw McCartney ground himself again, not only after the passing of his wife but following the most remarkable and active decade he'd had since the 1960s. Although it was given a wider and more conventional release, and with three Macca originals sneaked into its tracklist, *Run Devil Run* was recorded in a similar spirit to 1988's *CHOBA B CCCP*. It even shared something with The Fireman's *Rushes* in that, as producer Chris Thomas recalled, 'He wasn't thinking it was going to be his next big record. He was just free to enjoy himself.'[2] For his backing band, McCartney assembled a supergroup of friends including Pink Floyd's Dave Gilmour, Mick Green (a connection dating back to The Quarrymen days who'd also played on

CHOBA B CCCP) and Ian Paice from Deep Purple. They recorded quickly, without any preciousness. McCartney wanted no polish, as few takes as possible, and no post-production.[3] In fact, he even imposed a ban on 'thinking'.[4] It also seems to be the case that Dave Gilmour, thankfully, wasn't allowed to sound like Dave Gilmour. 'Mick's like the rough diamond and Dave would be the smooth diamond,' McCartney explained; 'they're great guys and they complement each other.'[5] The result was certainly at the rougher end of the spectrum, and all the better for it. Cathartic is the right word for it. The record is largely raw and raucous, with some real goose-pimpling moments, such as when the band brings the energy down a notch with 'No Other Baby', originally by Dickie Bishop and the Sidekicks, or when McCartney wears his heart even more openly on his sleeve for the self-penned 'Try Not to Cry'. As for those who always said Lennon was the dabber hand (or throat, rather) at the primal emotional howl, McCartney really gives his ex-bandmate a run for his money on this collection.

Reviewing the album for the *Chicago Sun-Times*, Jim DeRogatis wrote that while *Run Devil Run* was 'McCartney in his Lennon mode' – unfair given both had the same roots – it was ultimately a far more thrilling experience than *Rock 'n' Roll*. A hot take such as this might have been considered heresy back in the 1980s. DeRegatis even struggled to think of any (mostly) covers album from any era that could top it (Yo La Tengo's *Fakebook* came close).[6]

McCartney had blasted out the cobwebs and, unlike Lennon, would not remain stuck in that old rock 'n' roll rut.[7] The new millennium would see McCartney return to world touring with a mostly newly recruited set of musicians. He'd record further studio albums, often using younger and not necessarily reverential producers. He would continue to write classical music (including some for ballet), and release yet more music with Youth as The Fireman, plus an album of mashed-up remixes with the DJ

Freelance Hellraiser. He also collaborated, finally, with the surviving members of his and James's cherished Nirvana. McCartney's first volume of poetry would be published, as well as books written for children. There would be further controversies, too. His ill-fated marriage to Heather Mills, for example, and the latest episode in the long-running dispute with Yoko Ono over 'Lennon–McCartney' songwriting credits. One thing is for certain, though. Thanks in no small part to the events of the 1990s, and the momentum established therein, this was a man who would remain on the run.

Back when the 1980s were drawing to a close, at least one of his biographers wondered whether McCartney's career would ever enjoy another comeback. He'd pulled it off a few times before, admitted Chet Flippo, but by this point it seemed much less likely.[8] Around the same time as those words were printed, there was even a manager who advocated McCartney's retirement. 'Perhaps he was right,' McCartney has quipped, 'but hopefully not.'[9] Needless to say, the biographer was way off the mark and the manager was soon given his marching orders.

Decades later, McCartney is now in his eighties, far from reliant on past glories and only written off by the dreariest critics. As a testament to his reputation as someone who is still widely considered to be vibrantly productive, with the ability to delight and surprise in equal measure, commentators continue to offer tantalizing speculation on which direction his career might – or perhaps should – head next. Their opinions may differ, but the level of anticipation is unequalled for any popular musician of the same age or generation, most of whom have become as predictable as the tides. Reviewing *McCartney III*, a friskily spirit-lifting album that was made during the COVID-19 pandemic lockdown of 2020, *Record Collector*'s Jamie Atkins wrote that McCartney's voice has matured unignorably, although not necessarily for the worse. Atkins singled out the striking performance on 'Women

McCartney in 2018 performing with the live band who have backed him since 2002.

and Wives' as a case in point, with McCartney's vocals being 'all treacle and trembles as he offers advice as if delivering an obscure sermon'.[10] As Atkins continues,

> That voice has come in for criticism in recent years, especially at gigs, but you can't help but feel that the problem could be that his material hasn't been adapted to suit his voice as he ages in the same way that, say, Dylan has always tried to do. Why attempt to belt out 'Helter Skelter' and struggle when material like this works so well? It's musically simple – rolling, rich piano chords; brushed drums; mournful double bass on a smouldering waltz – and feels like new territory for him, which is remarkable at this point.[11]

Could it be time for Paul to strip back again? Others have pulled this off nicely, yet it is hard to imagine McCartney resigning himself to a succession of Johnny Cash-style dark country records overseen by Rick Rubin. Atkins also highlights a rather different-sounding song. A 'humid rifforama' is how he describes 'Slidin''.[12] It appears to reference the hefty desert rock of Queens of the Stone Age, a sound that might not have developed as it did without the pioneering heft of The Beatles' McCartney-led 'Helter Skelter'. 'It's a more credible heavy sound than McCartney's long-standing and somewhat showbizzy live band have ever really cooked up, suggesting that, should he hit the road again, it might be wise to rethink the hired help,' argues Atkins.[13] Ought Sir Paul call up the surviving members of Nirvana once more and tour with them instead? Even that might be too obvious a move.

The idea that McCartney might run out of brilliant ideas, or be lured into winding things down, is even less conceivable now than it was some thirty years ago. At this stage, the thought of his retirement – or, god forbid, anything worse, even though we all know that heartbreaking day will eventually arrive – is too awful to fathom. As I write this, Willie Nelson (born 1933) has tour dates booked into the horizon, Tony Bennett only recently announced he was retiring from live shows at the age of 95 (shortly before his death in 2023), Tom Jones (two years McCartney's senior) has received some of the best reviews of his career, Yoko Ono is still going strong and The Rolling Stones, if now missing a vital part, are The Rolling Stones.

It almost seems daft that Paul McCartney, who still enjoys horse riding and does an unsupported headstand for five minutes every morning,[14] should have reflected on his own mortality as long ago as on 'The End of the End', released on 2007's *Memory Almost Full* and demoed even earlier in 2003. On the day that he dies, McCartney explains in its lyric, he doesn't want anyone to weep or be sad. He'd rather people crack jokes and wheel out old songs and stories. Hopefully that day is still a long time coming. With a little less humility in the song's second verse, he does put in a request for bells to be rung. McCartney, my dear, that will hardly be the half of it.

# REFERENCES


## Introduction: Looking for Changes

1 'Jerry Seinfeld Ended "Seinfeld" Because of the Beatles', www.youtube.com, accessed 6 October 2022.

2 Brian Logan, 'Jerry Seinfeld Review – Multimillionaire with a Masterly Common Touch', *The Guardian*, www.guardian.co.uk, 14 July 2019.

3 Charles Hutchinson, 'James Acaster Confronts Yoko Ono Hate and His M&S Wardrobe', *York Press*, www.yorkpress.co.uk, 22 October 2013.

4 Paul Du Noyer, *Conversations with McCartney* (London, 2015), p. 224.

5 *Room 101*, series 7, episode 4 (BBC One, aired 9 February 2018).

6 Playing devil's advocate, as is necessary on the show, *Room 101*'s host, Frank Skinner, asked Widdicombe if he ever listens to McCartney's more recent albums. The comedian replied with a candid 'No, of course not,' prompting laughter from the studio audience. If he was telling the truth, Widdicombe has missed out on many post-Beatles corkers.

7 Chris Ingham, 'Paul McCartney: *Flaming Pie*', *Mojo* (June 1997); David Sinclair, 'Jagger Still Fab, Macca Just Drab', *The Times* (6 February 1993).

8 Caroline Sullivan, 'I Believe in Yesterday: A Brave Effort, but Paul McCartney Can't Live Up to His Past', *The Guardian* (13 September 1993) ('tarnish-mark'); David Sinclair, 'No Mistaking an Original Master', *The Times* (13 September 1993).

9 Iman Lababedi, 'Paul McCartney's *Off the Ground* Reviewed', http://rocknyc.live, 17 October 2017; Greg Kot, 'McCartney Back on Top of His Pop Material', *Chicago Tribune* (5 February 1993).

10 Paul's son, James McCartney, is the family member who did work with Steve Albini. The engineer was hired to record James's 2016 solo album *The Blackberry Train*. James is a fan of Nirvana, and their final album, *In Utero* (1993), is one of Albini's most famous credits. It would have been very interesting to hear an Albini-recorded album by McCartney Sr.

11 Kot, 'McCartney Back on Top'.

12 Laura Gross, 'And It All Happened Like This', *Club Sandwich*, 65 (Spring 1993).

13 Tom Hibbert, 'Fab Macca Wacky Thumbs Aloft . . . At Your Service!!', *Smash Hits* (13–26 August 1986).
14 Ibid.
15 Gross, 'And It All Happened'.
16 Ibid.
17 Ibid.
18 Ibid.
19 'Paul McCartney-Banned Song- Big Boys Bickering', www.youtube.com, accessed 6 October 2022.
20 Ibid.
21 Ibid.
22 Quoted in 'Big Boys Bickering', www.the-paulmccartney-project.com, accessed 9 February 2024.
23 'Smoking Past the Band', *Comedians in Cars Getting Coffee*, season 5, episode 3 (Netflix, 2014).
24 Paul McCartney, 'Here Are Some Organisations to Support in the Fight for Racial Justice', Facebook (5 June 2020).
25 An early version of 'Get Back', recorded in 1969, satirized the anti-immigration rhetoric that The Beatles kept seeing in the national press.
26 Du Noyer, *Conversations*, pp. 204–5.
27 Des Burkinshaw, 'Paul McCartney', *Record Collector* (June 1997).
28 The Beatles, *The Beatles Anthology* (San Francisco, CA, 2000), p. 19.
29 George Martin with William Pearson, *Summer of Love: The Making of 'Sgt. Pepper'* (London, 1994), p. 165.

### 1 The Backstory: McCartney before the 1990s

1 'NASA Beams Beatles' "Across the Universe" into Space', www.nasa.gov, 31 January 2008.
2 *Penguin Podcast*, 'Paul McCartney with Nihal Arthanayake', www.youtube.com, 21 December 2019.
3 'Carpool Karaoke', *The Late Late Show with James Corden* (CBS, aired 21 June 2018).
4 It is a bit of a shame that so many viewers were exposed to this footage when taken out of its proper context, via social media. It's a key moment in Episode 1, rewarding the patience of the audience who have made it through The Beatles ordering cups of tea, having ciggy breaks, struggling for inspiration and lacking organization. When the magic finally arrives, it is spine-tingling.
5 Ian Leslie, '64 Reasons to Celebrate Paul McCartney', https://ianleslie.substack.com, 8 December 2020.
6 Rob Chapman, *Psychedelia and Other Colours* (London, 2015), p. 263.
7 Bob Stanley, *Yeah Yeah Yeah: The Story of Modern Pop* (London, 2014), p. 293n.

8 Highly recommended (by me) is the fifteen-minute hard-psych-jam-band rendition of Wings' animal rights anthem 'Wild Life' by California's Howlin Rain, released in 2008 on Three Lobed Recordings.

9 Valerie Siebert, 'The Demon Advocates: Gene Simmons' Favourite Albums', *The Quietus*, www.thequietus.com, 3 March 2015.

10 Michael Matts, 'Ringo', *Melody Maker* (31 July 1971).

11 'Billboard's Top Album Picks', *Billboard* (31 May 1980).

12 Luke Turner, '*McCartney II*: Paul McCartney Interviewed by Other Artists', *The Quietus*, www.thequietus.com, 15 June 2011.

13 Leslie, '64 Reasons'.

14 Erin Torkelson Weber, *The Beatles and the Historians: An Analysis of Writings about the Fab Four* (Jefferson, NC, 2016), p. 30.

15 Unlike the other three Beatles, McCartney did not have his own solo sequence in *A Hard Day's Night*. An intended scene was filmed, in which Paul flirts with a young actress played by Isla Blair. It was cut from the final edit by director Richard Lester, who considered it lacking in pace. 'Filming: Paul McCartney's Unused Scene in *A Hard Day's Night*', www.beatlesbible.com, accessed 23 March 2023.

16 This blurring was encouraged by manager Brian Epstein, who was homosexual at a time when this was still illegal. His vision 'dandied up' The Beatles by, among other tactics, swapping the rockier look of their formative days for dapper suits and ties, which complemented the subversive unkemptness of their moptop hairdos. The musicians' own interests fed into this 'queering'. They were very fond of girl groups, whose hit singles helped shape Lennon and McCartney's own songwriting habits. When performing their version of The Shirelles' 'Boys', sung by Ringo, The Beatles tweaked the words slightly but were so unconcerned about any gay connotations that its horny, male-celebrating chorus remained intact. The mid-song, high-pitched 'woo!', borrowed by The Beatles from the transgressive and make-up-wearing musician Little Richard, has maintained its presence throughout McCartney's career. Subtle gender-bending helped to fuel Beatlemania. The band's sexuality was 'more approachable than Elvis's alpha-male heat', as Dorian Lynskey observed, and this is seen as blueprint for the manufactured boy bands that came later. They were desirable but not threatening or overtly dangerous, runs the theory. Observing the novelty of The Beatles' screaming followers, some (usually male) writers in the early 1960s put the hysteria down to young fans' natural maternal instincts: their desire to 'mother' the members of the band, presumably before such girls were able to recognize or understand fully the less wholesome matter of their own sexual lust (equally natural, in reality). A less patronizing approach would suggest that the majority of the group's audience knew exactly what they desired – and why. For more on this, see Sasha Geffen, *Glitter Up the Dark: How Pop Music Broke the Binary* (Austin, TX, 2020), pp. 13–26.

The actress Maureen Lipman, incidentally, has written about the time she saw The Beatles play in Hull in 1963. She found John Lennon's performance particularly appealing. She describes this, and her own screaming response to it, as tantamount to an orgasmic loss of virginity. Maureen Lipman, 'Forty Pairs of Abandoned Knickers: Maureen Lipman on the Fab Four in Hull', *New Statesman*, www.newstatesman.com, 28 August 2014.

17 Weber, *The Beatles*, pp. 30–31.

18 Ray Coleman, 'The Story of a Hard Day's Night in the Life of a Beatle (and His Wife)', *Melody Maker* (10 April 1965). The two-dimensional personalities also featured in the children's cartoon series *The Beatles*, not that British viewers had the pleasure. Originally broadcast between 1965 and 1967 on the American ABC network, and sold to other countries as well, the series was blocked from broadcast in the UK by Brian Epstein, who feared the domestic audience would not take kindly to the voice actors' inaccurate accents and other ropey aspects of the show. 'It prototyped us into these terrible stereotypes. We should have stopped it right there,' McCartney said of the cartoon. 'I got that image of "Oh, don't do that, Ringo." The very sensible one. John was laconic, a satirical wit. Ringo was a right dummy and George was hardly in it.' While still not interested enough to provide their own voices, The Beatles were happier with the 1968 animated film *Yellow Submarine*, which British viewers did get to enjoy. Paul Du Noyer, *Conversations with McCartney* (London, 2015), pp. 296–7.

19 Weber, *The Beatles*, pp. 63, 68.

20 Barry Miles, *Paul McCartney: Many Years from Now* (London, 1997), pp. 569–70.

21 The Beatles, *The Beatles Anthology* (San Francisco, CA, 2000), p. 348.

22 John Lennon, *Skywriting by Word of Mouth* (London, 1986), p. 18.

23 *If These Walls Could Sing*, dir. Mary McCartney (Disney+, 2022).

24 Simon Reynolds, 'Myths and Depths: Greil Marcus Talks to Simon Reynolds', *Los Angles Review of Books* (27 April 2012).

25 Langdon Winner, 'McCartney', *Rolling Stone* (14 May 1970).

26 Jann Wenner, 'The Rolling Stone Interview: John Lennon, Part One: The Working Class Hero', *Rolling Stone* (21 January 1971).

27 Weber, *The Beatles*, pp. 28–9.

28 David Marchese, 'Jann Wenner Defends His Legacy, and His Generation's', *New York Times*, www.nytimes.com, 15 September 2023.

29 Wenner, 'John Lennon, Part One'.

30 Weber, *The Beatles*, p. 87.

31 Peter Doggett, *You Never Give Me Your Money: The Battle for the Soul of the Beatles* (London, 2010), p. 118.

32 Ibid., p. 124.

33 Weber, *The Beatles*, p. 72.

34 Doggett, *You Never Give Me Your Money*, p. 122.
35 Quoted in Weber, *The Beatles*, p. 75.
36 David Sheff, *All We Are Saying: The Last Major Interview with John Lennon and Yoko Ono* (New York, 2000), p. 137.
37 Weber, *The Beatles*, pp. 30, 34, 225n.
38 Ibid., p. 226n.
39 Ibid., p. 72.
40 Ibid., p. 71.
41 Sheff, *All We Are Saying*, p. 82.
42 John Lennon, *The John Lennon Letters: Edited with an Introduction by Hunter Davies*, ebook (London, 2012).
43 Weber, *The Beatles*, p. 95.
44 Sheff, *All We Are Saying*, pp. 194–5.
45 Miles, *Many Years from Now*, p. 162.
46 It had been proposed that the Lennon-sung numbers should appear on one side of the LP, with Ono's on the other. Ono disagreed with this sequencing, while Lennon feared that nobody would listen to his wife's side, which was not what he wanted. Geoff Edgers, 'Double Fantasy at 40: John Lennon's Last Album Was His Most Revealing', *The Independent*, www.independent.co.uk, 19 November 2020.
47 'I wish that Lennon had kept his big happy trap shut until he has something to say that was even vaguely relevant to those of us not married to Yoko Ono,' wrote Charles Shaar Murray. 'John Lennon and Yoko Ono: *Double Fantasy*', *NME* (22 November 1980).
48 Alan Smith, 'Close Up on Ringo Starr, a Beatle', *NME* (23 August 1963).
49 Tony Bacon, 'Paul McCartney: Meet the Beatle', *Bass Player* (July–August 1995).
50 Quoted in Rob Sheffield, *Dreaming The Beatles: The Love Story of One Band and the Whole World* (New York, 2018) p. 316.
51 Doggett, *You Never Give Me Your Money*, p. 187.
52 'Give Ireland Back to the Irish' was a number-one hit in the Irish singles chart. It also sold well in Spain, presumably having an appeal to the Basque independence market.
53 Tom Doyle, *Man on the Run: Paul McCartney in the 1970s* (Edinburgh, 2014), p. 87.
54 Peter Brown and Steven Gaines, *The Love You Make: An Insider's Story of The Beatles* (New York, 1983), p. 372.
55 Pattie Boyd with Penny Junor, *Wonderful Tonight: George Harrison, Eric Clapton, and Me*, ebook (New York, 2007).
56 Ibid.
57 Ibid.
58 Sheffield, *Dreaming The Beatles*, p. 268.
59 'Silly Love Songs' is not a love song. Rather, it is a rebuttal to the people in McCartney's personal life (that is, John Lennon) and those

in the media who'd had the gall to dismiss his hits as sentimental slush. He does this in a self-parodic and politely rendered way, but part of its message is a big 'fuck you'. The lyrics refute love's silliness and the supposedly frivolous business of writing about it. Love songs, McCartney insists, are important to people. It only takes the briefest glance at the history of popular music to realize they must have such value. It is also quite long for a silly love song at six minutes (although it doesn't feel like it), and is built around an absolutely killer bassline.

60 Andrew Ferguson, 'Love Me Do: Was Paul McCartney the Real John Lennon?', *Weekly Standard* (25 July 2016).
61 Simon Reynolds, 'Serious Mayhem', *London Review of Books* (10 March 2022).
62 Chas de Whalley, 'The Ramones: Gabba Gabba Hey in the UK', *Sounds* (28 May 1977).
63 Roy Lichtenstein, Claes Oldenburg and Andy Warhol with Bruce Glasser, 'A Discussion' [aired June 1964], *Artforum* (February 1966), archived at www.artforum.com, accessed 2 September 2021.
64 John Ingham, 'The Sex Pistols are Four Months Old . . .', *Sounds* (24 April 1976).
65 Kris Needs, 'Sex Pistols: Silver Jubilation', *ZigZag* (June 1977).
66 Peter Silverton, 'The Rich Kids: Back with a Bullet', *Sounds* (10 September 1977).
67 *Joe Strummer: The Future Is Unwritten*, dir. Julien Temple, DVD (Channel 4, 2007).
68 'John Lydon: The Dirty Rotten Scoundrel!', *Q Magazine: Q Awards* (November 2001), archived at www.johnlydon.com, accessed 8 September 2001.
69 Duncan Seaman, 'Interview: John Lydon', *Yorkshire Post*, www.yorkshirepost.co.uk, 4 October 2013.
70 Caroline Coon, *1988: The New Wave Punk Rock Explosion* (London, 1982), p. 3.
71 Ibid., p. 12.
72 Quoted in Victor Brockris, *Keith Richards: The Biography* (New York, 1992), p. 199.
73 Doggett, *You Never Give Me Your Money*, p. 178.
74 Miles, *Many Years from Now*, pp. 29, 142.
75 Blair Sabol, 'The McCartney Burial: "His Ego Was His Amigo"', *Village Voice* (2 September 1971).
76 Doggett, *You Never Give Me Your Money*, pp. 198–90.
77 Soon enough, quite a few of these iconoclastic punks would draw accusations of selling out to the Establishment themselves. As John Lydon once complained, 'The pathetic conclusion of that movement was one load of arseholes were replaced by another load. Nothing was

achieved.' 'Public Image Ltd. – Countdown Interview 1979', www.youtube.com, accessed 18 March 2022.
78 Coon, *1988*, p. 12.
79 Paul Morley, 'The Lurkers: Strange Daze in Sheffield (or Maybe Halifax)', *NME* (28 October 1978).
80 When I used to work in the Borders book and music store, I once played *All Over the World: The Very Best of Electric Light Orchestra* over the shop's stereo system. I did this out of curiosity, after hearing The Delgados' excellent Peel Session version of the greatest ELO song, 'Mr Blue Sky' (1977). On being unwillingly exposed to the music on this CD, the chap with the ponytail who oversaw the history department literally roared out loud in disapproval.
81 Mark Plummer, 'Steely Dan's Smart Rock', *Melody Maker* (21 July 1973).
82 Chris Charlesworth, 'Steely Dan: Steely Logic', *Melody Maker* (13 April 1973).
83 Andy Gill, 'Steely Dan: The Return of Steely Dan', *Mojo* (October 1995).
84 The crowd, in Minneapolis, booed Strummer. Country and western wasn't considered a cool enough alternative. Peter Silverton, 'The Clash Turn Pro (Sort Of)', *Sounds* (29 September 1979).
85 John Rockwell, 'The Bee Gees Are Getting as Big as The Beatles', *New York Times* (19 March 1978).
86 Gary Graff, 'Peter Frampton on *Sgt. Pepper* 50th Anniversary: "It's Still My Favorite Album"', www.billboard.com, 1 June 2017.
87 George Martin with Jeremy Hornsby, *All You Need Is Ears* (New York, 1979), pp. 215–16.
88 Mitchell Glazer, 'The Rise and Fall and Rise of the Brothers Gibb', *Playboy* (August 1978).
89 Janet Maslin, 'Screen: Son of *Sgt. Pepper*', *New York Times* (21 July 1978).
90 Tom Fordy, 'The Beatles, the Bee Gees and the Terrible Sgt. Pepper's Movie They'd All Rather Forget', *The Telegraph*, www.telegraph.co.uk, 25 November 2021.
91 James M. Decker, '"Baby You're a Rich Man": The Beatles, Ideology and the Cultural Moment', in *Reading The Beatles: Cultural Studies, Literary Criticism, and the Fab Four*, ed. Kenneth Womack and Todd F. Davis (Albany, NY, 2006), p. 193.
92 Fordy, 'The Beatles'.
93 Doyle, *Man on the Run*, p. 220.
94 Jimmy McDonough, *Shakey: Neil Young's Biography* (London, 2002), p. 543.
95 David Quantick, 'The Art of Cool Maintenance', *Record Collector* (March 2022).
96 Luke Haines, 'The Drugs Do Work – Very Well Indeed', *Record Collector* (March 2022).
97 Lennon, Starr and Harrison all battled with hard-drug problems as well. In the 1960s McCartney had dabbled in virtually everything on offer during

his semi-bachelor-about-London days, when he associated with users including William Burroughs. He was always warier of hard drugs than the other three Beatles, however, a stance he attributes to his mother's career as a nurse. His preference was for marijuana, which he and Linda publicly insisted was safer than mainstream recreationals such as alcohol. Judging from the anecdotes contained in his official biography, McCartney also drank an awful lot of tea. There are at least 33 pages that mention having a cup of tea, wanting a cup of tea, taking a tea break or someone offering somebody else a cup of tea. At one point, McCartney recalls being mocked by Burroughs's adventurous associates Ian Sommerville and Alan Watson for being a total 'tea-head'. Miles, *Many Years from Now*, p. 241.

98 Chapman, *Psychedelia*, p. 173.

99 Peter Ross, 'Wise Guy', *Sunday Herald* (9 January 2005).

100 McDonough, *Shakey*, p. 506.

101 Andy Dougan, *Robin Williams* (New York, 1998), p. 168.

102 Simon Hattenstone, 'David Crosby on Love, Music and Rancour: "Neil Young Is Probably the Most Selfish Person I Know"', *The Guardian*, www.guardian.co.uk, 2 September 2021.

103 Tony Bramwell with Rosemary Kingsland, *Magical Mystery Tours: My Life with The Beatles* (New York, 2005), pp. 260–61.

104 Callum G. Brown, *The Death of Christian Britain: Understanding Secularisation, 1800–2000* (London, 2001). Brown evokes the lines from Philip Larkin's 1967 poem 'Annus Mirabilis' about sexual intercourse beginning that same year, between the lifting of the ban on D. H. Lawrence's *Lady Chatterley's Lover* and the release of the first Beatles album, *Please Please Me*. By March 1966, John Lennon could claim, albeit to a backlash (particularly in America), that The Beatles were more popular than Jesus Christ. He was speaking at a time of declining church attendance and didn't necessarily believe that the public's change in favours was a good thing. Christianity's decline was also on Paul McCartney's mind when he wrote 'Eleanor Rigby', released by The Beatles in August 1966, with the Father McKenzie character who delivers sermons that nobody hears, either because they are not listening properly or they have simply ceased attending at all.

105 Dave Marsh, 'Ghoulish Beatlemania: Thoughts on the Death of John Lennon', *Rolling Stone* (22 January 1981).

106 David Hepworth, *Uncommon People: The Rise and Fall of the Rock Stars* (London, 2017), p. 258.

107 Nick Schager, 'Review: Chapter 27', www.slantmagazine.com, 20 March 2008.

108 Hepworth, *Uncommon People*, p. 258.

109 George Melly, 'John Lennon', *Punch* (17 December 1980).

110 The progressive idealism of the 1960s has also been identified as anticipating and fuelling the individualism, rampant consumerism and

reduction in civic-mindedness of subsequent decades. Citing Adam Curtis's 2002 documentary *The Century of the Self*, the playwright David Farr says that the liberally minded 1960s generation 'ironically . . . created the most selfish, individualistic age that there has ever been'. It can be traced further back, though. Curtis's documentary opens with the ideas of Sigmund Freud. Set in the 1980s, Chapter Nineteen of David Foster Wallace's unfinished novel *The Pale King* also riffs on the idea that the 1960s marked the beginning of America's 'decline into decadence and selfish individualism'. One character believes the 1920s were more decadent, however, while other mooted starting points are the Magna Carta (1215) and the French Revolution (1789): 'This emphasis on man as the individual and on the rights and entitlements of the individual instead of the responsibilities of the individual.' Claire Armitstead, 'David Farr: "The 60s Generation Created the Most Selfish Age There Has Ever Been"', *The Guardian*, www.theguardian.com, 21 October 2022; David Foster Wallace, *The Pale King* (London, 2012), pp. 134, 146.

111 Hepworth, *Uncommon People*, p. 259.

112 Philip Larkin, 'Fighting the Fab', *The Observer* (9 October 1983).

113 Hepworth, *Uncommon People*, p. 260.

114 Martin Amis, 'Lennon: From Beatle to Househusband', *The Observer* (14 December 1980).

115 Doubly discourteous, Christgau attributed this question to his partner ('As my wife said despondently an hour after the event . . .'), but he's the one who typed it out and elaborated on the theme. Robert Christgau, 'John Lennon, 1940–1980', *Village Voice* (22 December 1980).

116 'Paul McCartney on Lennon's Death', www.dailymotion.com, accessed 25 July 2022.

117 Robert Christgau, 'Double Fantasy: Portrait of a Relationship', in *The Ballad of John and Yoko*, ed. Jonathan Cott and Christine Doudna (Garden City, NY, 1982), pp. 295, 296, 301.

118 Robert Christgau and John Piccarella, 'Portrait of the Artist as a Rock 'n' Roll Star', in *The Ballad of John and Yoko*, ed. Cott and Doudna, p. 240.

119 Ibid., p. 241.

120 Ibid., p. 242.

121 Dan Raviv, 'John or Paul? Data Resolves the Age Old "Who Was the #1 Beatle" Question', https://towardsdatascience.com, 12 November 2019. More subjectively, the author contends that McCartney had the edge in terms of consistency.

122 Simon Reynolds, *Retromania: Pop Culture's Addiction to Its Own Past* (London, 2011), p. 280.

123 Ibid., p. 288.

124 Hepworth, *Uncommon People*, pp. 281–6.

125 Jem Roberts, *Fab Fools: The Beatles, The Rutles and Rock 'n' Roll Comedy!* (Cardiff, 2021), p. 278.

126 Ibid., pp. 260, 263.
127 Quoted ibid., p. 277.
128 Ibid., p. 275.
129 Ibid.
130 'Martin Rowson – The Power of the Political Cartoon', www.youtube.com, accessed 10 March 2022.
131 In December 2021, the revived *Spitting Image* poked fun at McCartney's insistence at his own ordinariness with the parody song 'Regular Christmastime'.
132 Doyle, *Man on the Run*, pp. xvii–xviii.
133 Published in some editions with the alternative subtitle *The Beatles in Their Generation*.
134 Stephen Thomas Erlewine, 'These Are the Best Beatles Books', *Pitchfork*, www.pitchfork.com, 23 May 2018.
135 Colin Fleming, '10 Best Beatles Books', *Rolling Stone*, www.rollingstone.com, 10 April 2020.
136 'The Beatles: The Best Films, Reissues and Books to Check Out', *The Times*, www.thetimes.co.uk, 26 August 2021.
137 Weber, *The Beatles*, p. 116.
138 Ibid., p. 117.
139 Ibid.
140 Ibid., p. 123.
141 Ray Bonici, 'Paul McCartney Flying on Clipped Wings', *Music Express* (April–May 1982).
142 Ibid.
143 Howard Sounes, *Fab: An Intimate Life of Paul McCartney* (London, 2010), p. 376. In 1990 Angie would auction Paul's birth certificate to a collector for $18,000. Her 2013 autobiography was subtitled *My Long and Winding Road* (foreword by Cynthia Lennon). She is also the entrepreneur behind the 'Mrs McCartney' brands of wine and tea. Cup of 'Abbey Road Apple', vicar? I could brew a pot of 'Maharishi Peach', if you prefer? Fancy something stronger? 'Strawberry Fields' is quite the vintage . . .
144 Joan Goodman, 'The *Playboy* Interview', *Playboy* (December 1984).
145 Sounes, *Fab*, pp. 388, 391.
146 Ibid., pp. 388, 393.
147 Stephen Holden, '*Tug of War*', *Rolling Stone* (27 May 1982).
148 'Ebony and Ivory Voted Worst Duet', *BBC News*, http://news.bbc.co.uk, 6 October 2007.
149 Katie Kapurch and Jon Marc Smith, 'Blackbird Singing: Paul McCartney's Romance of Racial Harmony and Post-Racial America', in *New Critical Perspectives on The Beatles: Things We Said Today*, ed. Kenneth Womack and Katie Kapurch (London, 2016), pp. 54–5.
150 Ibid., p. 52.

151 Parke Puterbaugh, '*Pipes of Peace*', *Rolling Stone* (19 January 1984).
152 Penny Reel, 'Paul McCartney: *Pipes of Peace*', *NME* (5 November 1983).
153 J. D. Considine, 'Paul McCartney: *Pipes of Peace*', *Musician* (January 1984).
154 This was the first time one of their original recordings had featured in an advertisement. Previous owners of Northern Songs had licensed rerecordings of Beatles compositions to the likes of Schweppes and Hewlett-Packard, which was bad enough already as far as the band were concerned. Doggett, *You Never Give Me Your Money*, p. 289.
155 Terry Atkinson, 'Paul: Signs of Hope before the Letdown', *Los Angeles Times* (31 August 1986).
156 Sounes, *Fab*, p. 406.
157 Ibid., pp. 400–401, 404.
158 Ibid., 400.
159 Miles, *Many Years from Now*, pp. 191–3, 196–8.
160 Ibid., p. 363.
161 Ibid., pp. 360, 366.
162 Ibid., p. 350.
163 Ibid., p. 368.
164 Sounes, *Fab*, p. 384.
165 Ibid., pp. 347, 384–6.
166 Chris Ingham, 'Paul McCartney: *Flaming Pie*', *Mojo* (June 1997); Mick Houghton, 'Seal of Approval', *Mojo* (June 2001); Robert Hilburn, 'McCartney Reclaims His Legacy', *Los Angeles Times* (19 November 1989); Geoffrey Giuliano, *Blackbird: The Life and Times of Paul McCartney* (New York, 1991), p. 247.
167 Roger Ebert, '*Give My Regards to Broad Street*', *Chicago Sun-Times* (1 January 1984), available at www.rogerebert.com.
168 Paul Grein, 'Broad Street Is McCartney's Folly', *Variety* (3 November 1984).
169 Paul Attanasio, 'Paul McCartney's Wrong Way "Broad Street"', *Washington Post* (26 October 1984).
170 Sounes, *Fab*, p. 396.
171 'McCartney and Peter Sissons Channel 4 News 1984', www.youtube.com, accessed 25 July 2022.
172 'Paul McCartney – 1984 Russell Harty interview', www.youtube.com, accessed 4 July 2022.
173 Ibid.
174 Henry W. Sullivan, 'Paul, John and *Broad Street*', *Popular Music*, VI/3 (October 1987), p. 334.
175 Ibid.
176 Ibid., p. 328.
177 Ibid., p. 332.
178 Ibid., p. 333.

179 Ibid., p. 333.
180 As a fan of Jimi Hendrix, McCartney must surely have also heard about Hendrix leaving some master tapes for *Axis: Bold as Love* in a London taxi, back in 1967.
181 Doyle, *Man on the Run*, p. 78–9.
182 Du Noyer, *Conversations*, p. 165.
183 Sounes, *Fab*, p. 274.
184 'Arrests Made in Plot to Kidnap Paul McCartney's Wife', *UPI* (11 November 1984), archived at www.upi.com, accessed 19 July 2022.
185 In clips from *The Ed Sullivan Show*, its host appears noticeably grumpier when having to introduce videos for the likes of 'Paperback Writer' than he did when The Beatles had appeared in person on his programme.
186 '*Give My Regards to Broad Street* Press Conference (Chicago) October 1984', www.the-paulmccartney-project.com, accessed 25 July 2022.
187 As my father observed during some anniversary rerun of the event, 'Freddie Mercury's performance was all about the crowd, whereas Bono's was all about . . . Bono.' Mercury might have been one of the biggest show-offs in the history of popular music but compare the footage and you'll see how the empathetic Mercury gives, gives, gives, striving to make everybody in the stadium – and at home – feel included in this incredible global community. Bono suggests the opposite. He feeds his ego by taking from the crowd – literally in the case of the young women who are beckoned out of the audience to dance with him, the idea itself likely pilfered from Bruce Springsteen's 'Dancing in the Dark' video, filmed a year earlier. Bono sucks, sucks, sucks like a disastrously mulleted vampire.
188 '*Give My Regards to Broad Street* Press Conference'.
189 'McCartney and Peter Sissons'.
190 'Paul McCartney – 1984 Russell Harty'.
191 Ibid.
192 *TV Times* interview (1988), quoted in Alan Clayson, *Ringo Starr* (London, 2003), p. 332.
193 Paul Attanasio, 'Movies', *Washington Post* (9 December 1985).
194 Nick de Semlyen, *Wild and Crazy Guys: How the Comedy Mavericks of the '80s Changed Hollywood Forever* (New York, 2020), p. 160.
195 Mitchell Cohen, 'Julian Lennon, *Valotte*', *Creem* (March 1985).
196 Robert Christgau, 'Christgau's Consumer Guide', *Village Voice* (2 April 1985), archived at www.robertchristgau.com, accessed 19 July 2022.
197 When I was a student in Newcastle upon Tyne in the early 2000s, one of the city's sacred record shops had a Post-it note attached to a second-hand Julian Lennon LP that read, 'This is one of the worst albums ever recorded. DO NOT BUY IT!' (Or words to that effect.) With admirably honest promotional tactics such as that, *Steel Wheels* did not survive the ensuing CD and vinyl sales slump. The building has since been turned into a pub owned by the mass-market, low-budget, Brexit-promoting,

pandemic-lockdown-resisting, staff-exploiting, binge-encouraging, hope-draining and dismally cynical booze chain Wetherspoons. It can't get much worse, as John Lennon once sang.
198 Chet Flippo, *Yesterday: The Unauthorized Biography of Paul McCartney* (New York, 1988), p. 377.
199 Chris Salewicz, *McCartney* (New York, 1986), p. 244.
200 Flippo, *Yesterday*, p. 377.

### 2 Off the Ground and Back on the Road

1 James Henke, 'Can Paul McCartney Get Back?', *Rolling Stone* (15 June 1989).
2 Quoted in 'Once Upon a Long Ago', www.the-paulmccartney-project.com, accessed 22 August 2022.
3 Ibid.
4 David Hutcheon, 'You Can't Do That . . .', *Mojo* (August 2011).
5 Henke, 'Can Paul McCartney Get Back?' It has also been suggested that HandMade Films' earlier and more successful period was partly what drove McCartney to compete with *Give My Regards to Broad Street*. Peter Doggett, *You Never Give Me Your Money: The Battle for the Soul of The Beatles* (London, 2010), p. 281.
6 Laura Gross, 'And It All Happened Like This', *Club Sandwich*, 65 (Spring 1993).
7 Michael Wilmington, '"Imagine" Lennon on a Pedestal', *Los Angeles Times* (6 October 1988).
8 Erin Torkelson Weber, *The Beatles and the Historians: An Analysis of Writings about the Fab Four* (Jefferson, NC, 2016), p. 138.
9 Ibid., pp. 139–40.
10 Ibid., p. 137.
11 Albert Goldman, *The Lives of John Lennon* (London, 1988), pp. 140, 466, 478.
12 David Fricke and Jeffrey Ressner, 'Imaginary Lennon: The True Story behind Albert Goldman's Character Assassination of John Lennon', *Rolling Stone* (20 October 1988).
13 Ibid.
14 Weber, *The Beatles*, p. 140.
15 Ibid., p. 142.
16 Jeff Kaye, 'Help! Lennon Tribute Goes Slightly Awry', *Los Angeles Times* (7 May 1990).
17 Ibid.
18 Michael Gray, 'Dead Aid/Instant Bad Karma by the Mersey: The John Lennon Memorial Concert, Pier Head, Liverpool', *The Times* (7 May 1990).
19 To be fair to John Oates, he went on to say that he and Darryl Hall did delve into The Beatles after discovering *Sgt. Pepper's Lonely Hearts Club*

*Band*. 'John Lennon Tribute Concert Liverpool May 1990', www.youtube.com, accessed 6 September 2022.
20 Ibid.
21 'Top Pop Mop-Top Pot Shot Plot Flops!', *Viz*, 44 (October–November 1990).
22 Jon Pareles, 'More Nostalgia than Rock in Paul McCartney's Return', *New York Times* (13 December 1989).
23 Robert Hilburn, 'Paul McCartney: Back in the USA', *Los Angeles Times* (25 November 1989).
24 Quoted in Doggett, *You Never Give Me Your Money*, p. 293.
25 McCartney said that 'The Fool on the Hill' was written with 'someone like Maharishi [Mahesh Yogi]' in mind: 'His detractors called him a fool. Because of his giggle he wasn't taken too seriously.' Barry Miles, *Paul McCartney: Many Years from Now* (London, 1997), p. 365.
26 Steve Turner, 'McCartney at Peace with Past', *The Times* (3 January 1990).
27 'EP.144 – Paul McCartney', *The Adam Buxton Podcast*, 11 December 2020, www.adam-buxton.co.uk.
28 Ted Montgomery, *The Paul McCartney Catalog: A Complete Annotated Discography of Solo Works, 1967–2019* (Jefferson, NC, 2020), p. 82.
29 The full version was included on the 'Off the Ground' single.
30 McCartney would essentially recycle the verse's melody for his theme tune to 2002's *Vanilla Sky*, a film with an ending that received similar mockery to that of *Give My Regards to Broad Street*.
31 Quoted in 'Unplugged (The Official Bootleg)', www.the-paulmccartney-project.com, accessed 30 August 2022.
32 Howard Sounes, *Fab: An Intimate Life of Paul McCartney* (London, 2010), pp. 429–30.
33 The band had to restart 'We Can Work It Out' when McCartney forgot the first few lines. Peter Doggett thinks this mistake was actually 'carefully planned'. Doggett, *You Never Give Me Your Money*, p. 305.
34 Gross, 'And It All Happened'.
35 Ibid.
36 Ibid.
37 Paul McCartney and Adrian Mitchell, *Blackbird Singing: Poems and Lyrics, 1965–1999* (London, 2001), p. 15.
38 Ibid., p. 18.
39 Philip Norman, *Paul McCartney: The Biography* (London, 2016), p. 653; Sounes, *Fab*, pp. 439–40.
40 Sounes, *Fab*, p. 441.
41 Ibid.
42 Andrew Ferguson, 'Love Me Do: Was Paul McCartney the Real John Lennon?', *Weekly Standard* (25 July 2016).
43 Chris Campling, 'Not Half the Man He Used to Be', *The Times* (3 September 1993).

44 Jon Young, 'Paul McCartney: Docklands Arena, London', *Musician* (April 1993).

### 3 Britpop and Beyond

1 Luke Haines, *Bad Vibes: Britpop and My Part in Its Downfall* (London, 2010), pp. 160–61.
2 Stuart Maconie, 'Who Do You Think You Are Kidding, Mr Cobain?', *Select* (April 1993).
3 By Irish, I mean, sadly, U2.
4 '*Rock Family Trees*: The Birth of Cool Britannia' (BBC Two, aired 9 April 2022).
5 The Smiths/Morrissey. The Stone Roses. Happy Mondays. The Fall. The Cure. Billy Bragg. The Proclaimers. Madness. Inspiral Carpets. The Housemartins. The Beautiful South. Squeeze. The Wedding Present. And so on.
6 Ed Power, 'Insatiable Healing', *Hot Press* (10 October 2018).
7 Martin Aston, 'Cocker Gets Cocky', *Attitude* (November 1995).
8 David Stubbs, 'Upper Class', *Melody Maker* (23–30 December 1995).
9 Blur's chart-topping third album, *Parklife* (1994), was originally going to be titled *London* and likely would have sold fewer copies had that been the case. When the album was released, the cover of *The Face* magazine featured an image of Damon Albarn superimposed onto the Union Jack (like Brett Anderson before him on the front of *Select*), with the caption 'Blur: Brit Up Your Ears'. 'I was singing out my slightly dystopian vision of the future, of the country, and everyone was going, "This is brilliant! It's great!"' recalled Albarn. 'I suffered profound anxiety for years after as a result. And then Oasis came along, and went, "Huh! We're going to go with this pure, euphoric optimism. We're going to lift the people up." And that's exactly what happened next.' Daniel Rachel, *Don't Look Back in Anger: The Rise and Fall of Cool Britannia, Told by Those Who Were There* (London, 2020), pp. 75–6.
10 Even if fellow Greater Mancunians The Fall, Happy Mondays and The Stone Roses had paved the way with their own mouthy chutzpah, this marked the music press's shift away from the more modest and unstarry shoegaze scene.
11 'Oasis – 1996-02-19 – Brit Awards Uncut, Earls Court, London, England', www.youtube.com, accessed 16 September 2022. Noel then slagged off Michael Hutchence, who had presented the award, as a 'has-been'.
12 Tom Doyle, 'Interview: Paul McCartney', *Q: 30th Birthday Special Issue* (2016).
13 Daniel Dylan Wray, 'Lads, Gak and Union Jacks: The Oral History of "Cool Britannia"', *Vice*, www.vice.com, 1 November 2021.
14 Chris Hutton and Richard Kurt, *Don't Look Back in Anger: Growing Up with Oasis* (London, 1997), p. 102.

15 Ibid.
16 Ibid. p. 103.
17 John Doran, *Jolly Lad* (London, 2015), pp. 46–7.
18 Hutton and Kurt, *Don't Look Back in Anger*, p. 103.
19 John Harris, 'Oasis: The Bruise Brothers', *NME* (23 April 1994).
20 Rich Pelley, 'Liam Gallagher: "Would I Give Noel a Kidney? Without a Doubt"', *The Guardian*, www.theguardian.com, 26 May 2022.
21 Hutton and Kurt, *Don't Look Back in Anger*, pp. 102–3.
22 Ibid., pp. 103–4.
23 Ibid., p. 104. There was a five-year gap between the first and second albums by The Stone Roses, partly owing to a contract dispute played out in court but also a drying up of the collective's mojo.
24 Cliff Jones, 'Oasis: Never Mind the Bollocks, Here's the Sex Beatles . . .', *The Face* (August 1994).
25 'Oasis – What's the Story? MTV Special (1996)', www.youtube.com, accessed 16 September 2022.
26 Alex Niven, *Definitely Maybe* (London, 2014), pp. 24–6.
27 Taylor Parkes, 'A British Disaster: Blur's Parklife, Britpop, Princess Di and the 1990s', *The Quietus*, www.thequietus.com, 28 April 2014.
28 'A better game plan, in my experience, is to nick off something no one would ever suspect,' says The Fall's ex-bassist Steve Hanley. 'I've got a couple like this knocking around at the moment: one's a perverted Wham riff, the other's from a Dolly Parton song. The perfect crime. Who'd ever suspect? It was me, in the library, with the Country and Western tape.' Steve Hanley and Olivia Piekarski, *The Big Midweek: Life Inside The Fall* (London, 2016), p. 250.
29 'From now on, it was alright to rip something off as long as I was not the first person to do it. The first person is the originator. The second person is the rip-off. The third person is just taking an established style. If George Harrison copies "He's So Fine" for "My Sweet Lord", which writer's gonna sue me when I write "She's My Lord" with the same melody over the same chord sequence?' Julian Cope, *Repossessed* (London, 2005), pp. 40–41.
30 Jones, 'Oasis'.
31 Parkes, 'A British Disaster'.
32 Jones, 'Oasis'.
33 Paolo Hewitt, *Forever the People: Six Months On the Road with Oasis* (London, 2000), pp. 115–16.
34 Rachel, *Don't Look Back*, p. 49.
35 'The cover of *GQ*? It was horrible, that,' remembered Cocker. 'I really wasn't very well at that time. They did a billboard of it as well and I remember thinking, "There's nothing going on behind the eyes." It's a kind of vacant, nobody-at-home kind of look basically. That was probably the point at which I realised I had to sort myself out.' Andrew Perry, 'Last Orders', *Mojo* (April 2003).

36 Rachel, *Don't Look Back*, p. 253.
37 McCartney himself was curiously absent from all of the Brit Awards hosted between 1990 and 2008. 'I try to avoid those 'cause it feels like you're gonna die the next second,' he said before (finally?) accepting the 2008 award for Outstanding Contribution to Music, a title he preferred to the more terminal-sounding 'Lifetime Achievement'. 'Paul McCartney Says He Thought about Rejecting Brit Award', *NME*, www.nme.com, 20 February 2008.
38 For example, Richard Power Sayeed, 'How Cool Britannia Helped Fuel Brexit', *Vice*, www.vice.com, 24 October 2017. 'If you're going to put a Union Jack on the cover of a magazine under the headline Yanks Go Home, then you are a fucking cretin,' reflected the still angry Luke Haines in 2021. 'Maybe all that had a subliminal effect. All those teenagers who bought *Select* became middle aged in 2016 and voted for Brexit. Was *Select* magazine responsible for Brexit? Probably.' Wray, 'Lads, Gak and Union Jacks'.
39 Rachel, *Don't Look Back*, p. 237.
40 Euan Ferguson, 'He's Behind You . . .', *The Observer* (3 November 2002). At the time of writing, the 1990s really do look like a foreign country. Remember when politicians used to resign – or be forced to resign – when they'd been caught doing something that they knew they shouldn't have, be it personally or politically dubious? The best the current lot offer is a mere (non-)apology for any 'offence' that may have been caused by their actions, while still clinging to their post like an oligarch-backed limpet.
41 Prime minister Boris Johnson demonstrated this when he hid in a fridge to avoid a media interview in 2019.
42 'Noel Gallagher Backs Tony Blair during the Brit Awards', www.youtube.com, accessed 7 October 2022.
43 Quoted in Alwyn Turner, *All in It Together: England in the Early 21st Century* (London, 2022), p. 61.
44 Rachel, *Don't Look Back*, p. 257.
45 John Redwood, 'There's Always England', *The Guardian* (20 March 1996).
46 '*Rock Family Trees*: The Birth of Cool Britannia'.
47 Luke Haines, 'How Bastard Thatcher's Pocket Money Made Her the Mother of Indie Music', *Record Collector* (January 2018).
48 'Late Review – Sensation Exhibition (BBC Two, 1997)', www.youtube.com, accessed 16 November 1997.
49 By 2015 Tony Parsons himself was writing things like 'I will vote Tory for the rest of my life.' Tony Parsons, 'Why I've Become Tory Scum', *GQ*, www.gq-magazine.co.uk, 15 September 2015.
50 Considered by many to be one of the more sophisticated and forward-thinking bands of their era, and not one that's suffered under the curse

of 'Britpop' pigeonholing, Radiohead sang about wishing it was the 1960s on 'The Bends' (1995). Frontman Thom Yorke later claimed he was being sarcastic. Three months after the album's release, he told Caitlin Moran of *Melody Maker* that 'it's become the bane of my life. Hundreds of journalists asking – every single f***ing interview asking – "Do you wish it was the Sixties?" NO! I DON'T wish it was the f***ing Sixties – LEVI'S JEANS WISH IT WAS THE SIXTIES – I certainly f***ing don't.' The Yorkey doth protest too much, methinks. Would such a serious band use something they considered to be a 'joke song' as the title track to their second album? Caitlin Moran, 'Radiohead: Head Cases', *Melody Maker* (10 June 1995).

51 Rachel, *Don't Look Back*, pp. 120–22.

52 Keith Harris, 'How Tiffany Saved the Beatles from Their Worst Boomer Fans', https://racketmn.com, 19 May 2022.

53 Gary Hall, *Living Life without Loving The Beatles: A Survivor's Guide*, revd edn (London, 2006), p. 11. Hall's book is Richard Dawkins's *The God Delusion* for people who think they're being clever, controversial and somehow original when they say The Beatles are overrated. It is an amusing stab at a sacred cow, nevertheless.

54 Rachel, *Don't Look Back*, pp. 120–21.

55 Dan Stubbs, 'Giles Martin on the Mammoth Tasking of Mixing "The White Album": "My Job Is to Be a Bit of a Bastard"', *NME*, www.nme.com, 23 November 2018.

56 Ironically, it was John Major's government that arranged Paul McCartney's knighthood in its final New Year Honours list before being voted out. To some extent, Blair's triumph rode the coat-tails of the earlier election of the sax-playing baby boomer President Bill Clinton in the USA. Each leader's reputation would eventually be tarnished by actions including military attacks on the Middle East and the neoliberal policies of deregulation that arguably led to the financial crisis of 2007. It's hard to imagine it being the case in either later or earlier times, but Clinton's extramarital sex life was viewed in extraordinarily light-hearted terms in that superficially feel-good era. See Chuck Klosterman, *The Nineties* (New York, 2022), Chapter 11.

57 Noel said that meeting McCartney 'didn't mean a great deal at the time, to be honest'. This could strengthen Hutton's thesis, which questions whether Noel had ever been such an obsessive Beatles fan in the first place. Rachel, *Don't Look Back*, p. 122.

58 Paul Du Noyer, *Conversations with McCartney* (London, 2015), p. 175.

59 Chris Ingham, 'Paul McCartney: *Flaming Pie*', *Mojo* (June 1997).

60 Steve Richards, 'Paul McCartney – Meet the Beatle', *New Statesman* (26 September 1997).

61 Just as they became more and more Beatles-fixated, Oasis grew increasingly anti-grunge, egged on again by the media and also rival

band Blur's determination to obliterate American rock. As Alex Niven notes, Noel Gallagher does not share Kurt Cobain's outlook on life but the heavy sound of *Definitely Maybe* is actually pretty grungy. Niven, *Definitely Maybe*, pp. 42–4.

62 'Paul McCartney on TFI Friday !', www.youtube.com, accessed 20 September 2022.

63 Neil Kulkarni, 'The Ten Most Overrated Albums in Pop History', www.medium.com, 19 May 2021 ('dickheads'); Neil Kulkarni, 'On Oasis and the Gallaghers', https://neilk.substack.com, 10 June 2021.

64 Ibid.

65 Neil Kulkarni, 'Kula Shaker – *K*', *Melody Maker* (14 September 1996). Kula Shaker's niche was to tap into the Indian elements of The Beatles' catalogue, which bands like Oasis hadn't really bothered with.

66 Hewitt, *Forever the People*, p. 118.

67 Sean O'Hagan, 'Foreword: Is the New Lad a Fitting Role Model for the Nineties?', *Arena* (May–June 1991).

68 Cassandra Jardine, '"I Knew It Was Time to Clean Up My Act"', *The Telegraph*, www.telegraph.co.uk, 26 July 2004.

69 Laura K. Williams, 'What Do I Do Now', *Classic Pop* (August 2017).

70 Richards, 'Paul McCartney'.

71 Alex Bilmes, 'Martin Amis: "Women Have Got Too Much Power for Their Own Good"', *Daily Telegraph* (2 February 2010).

72 As for football, The Beatles never showed much interest in the sport. Not wishing to alienate, McCartney claims to support both Liverpool FC and their rival club, Everton. It's more likely that he has little emotional investment in either side's league table position. On 'Somedays', from 1997's *Flaming Pie*, there is a lyric about his lack of concern for which football team won that day's match or who scored the winning goal.

73 Juliet Gellatley, 'The Fight Goes On', *Viva! Life* (*c.* 1998), available at https://web.archive.org, accessed 20 February 2023.

74 Parkes, 'A British Disaster'.

75 Ibid.

76 Roger Lewis, 'Classless Society – or Just a Society with No Class?', *MailOnline*, www.dailymail.co.uk, 22 August 2013.

77 Ibid.

78 Ibid.

79 Pete Townshend, 'Why He Died before He Got Old', *The Observer* (3 November 2002).

80 Spin Staff, 'Nirvana's *Nevermind* Turns 25', *Spin*, www.spin.com, 24 September 2016.

81 Dave Simpson, 'Ray Davies: "I'm Not the Godfather of Britpop . . . More a Concerned Uncle"', *The Guardian* (17 July 2015).

82 Jim Berkenstadt, 'The Vig Issue', *Vox* (March 1995).

83 Push, 'Soundgarden: Daylight Shrubbery', *Melody Maker* (5 October 1991); Jed Gottlieb, 'How Soundgarden's Fearlessness was Inspired by The Beatles', https://ultimateclassicrock.com, 13 July 2011.
84 Rachel, *Don't Look Back*, p. 122.
85 WiseJake237, 'Eddie Vedder's Favourite Records', www.discogs.com, accessed 23 September 2022.
86 'Backbeat', *Time Out*, www.timeout.com, 17 October 2011.
87 Larry Fitzmaurice, 'We've Got a File on You: Thurston Moore', www.stereogum.com, 24 September 2020.
88 My previous book heralded The Beatles' 'Helter Skelter', written by Paul McCartney, as the foundation for all heavy music. This assessment was deemed 'massively problematic' by Neil Kulkarni in an otherwise glowing review. Neil Kulkarni, 'Review: *Electric Wizards: A Tapestry of Heavy Music, 1968 to the Present*', *The Wire* (November 2021).
89 Quoted in Kenneth Womack, *The Beatles Encyclopedia* (Santa Barbara, CA, 2014), p. 68.
90 David Fricke, 'Kurt Cobain: Success Doesn't Suck', *Rolling Stone* (27 January 1994).
91 John Robb, 'Nirvana: Nirva Mind the Bollocks', *Siren* (August 1992).
92 Edwin Pouncey, 'Tad, Nirvana: Astoria, London', *NME* (16 December 1989).
93 Jann S. Wenner, 'Mick Jagger Remembers', *Rolling Stone* (14 December 1995).
94 Tori Amos's 1996 song 'Professional Widow' is believed to have been aimed at Cobain's wife, Courtney Love, from the band Hole. The same phrase has been used to condemn Yoko Ono. It overlooks the fact that Love and Ono are successful artists in their own right.
95 '*Rock Family Trees*: The Birth of Cool Britannia'.
96 Oasis PR Johnny Hopkins quoted in Rachel, *Don't Look Back*, p. 109.
97 Michael Azerrad, *Come as You Are: The Story of Nirvana* (London: 1996), pp. 318–19.
98 Even so, as Simon Reynolds notes, grunge '*felt* new because that sound had never had any presence in the mainstream'. Simon Reynolds, *Retromania: Pop Culture's Addiction to Its Own Past* (London, 2011), p. 200.
99 Kurt Cobain, liner notes to Nirvana, *Incesticide* (DGC, 1992), available at www.discogs.com, accessed 28 September 2022.
100 Ibid.
101 Phil Sutcliffe, 'Noel Gallagher: The Greatest Songwriter of the 90s?', *Q* (February 1996).
102 Perhaps most famously (though it's only the tip of the iceberg), Gallagher objected to Jay-Z headlining Glastonbury in 2008. Hip-hop's presence at the festival, he said, was 'wrong'. Colin Paterson, 'Hip-Hop "Wrong" for Glastonbury', *BBC News*, http://news.bbc.co.uk, 14 April 2008.

103 Luke Haines, 'Luke Haines Deems the Monkees' *Good Times!* the Album of the Year', www.thetalkhouse.com, 2 June 2016.
104 Dan Stubbs, 'Courtney Love talks about Nirvana "Reunion" – and Doubts Krist Novoselic's Bass-Playing', *NME*, www.nme.com, 13 December 2012.
105 Simon Vozick-Levinson, 'Paul McCartney: Playing with Nirvana's Surviving Members was "Powerful"', *Rolling Stone*, www.rollingstone.com, 22 July 2013.
106 Rob Sheffield, *Dreaming The Beatles: The Love Story of One Band and the Whole World* (New York, 2018), pp. 259–60.
107 David Hutcheon, 'You Can't Do That . . .', *Mojo* (August 2011).
108 Andy Greene and Kory Grow, 'Inside Taylor Hawkins' Final Days as a Foo Fighter', *Rolling Stone*, www.rollingstone.com, 16 May 2022.
109 Ibid.
110 Ashley King, '*Rolling Stone*'s Article about Taylor Hawkins Criticized as "Sensationalized and Misleading" – "I Am Truly Sorry to Have Taken Part in This Interview"', www.digitalmusicnews.com, 18 May 2022.

### 4 The Beatles Anthology

1 'Beatles Anthology Book', https://forums.stevehoffman.tv, accessed 5 October 2022.
2 Peter Doggett, *You Never Give Me Your Money: The Battle for the Soul of The Beatles* (London, 2010), p. 302.
3 Ibid., p. 308.
4 'I've listened to all the tapes: there are one or two interesting variations, but otherwise it's all junk. Couldn't possibly release it,' George Martin said in 1993, although it retrospect it sounds like he may have been cracking a sarcastic joke. Joseph Connolly, 'A Long Way from Abbey Road', *The Times* (5 March 1993).
5 Mark Cunningham, 'The Story of The Beatles' *Anthology* Project', www.soundonsound.com, December 1995.
6 Jamie Atkins, 'The *Anthology* Series', *Record Collector Presents The Beatles, vol. 3: Ascension (1968–2019)* (2019).
7 Jackson's film has been a revelation for some viewers' perceptions of McCartney, and even of themselves. Lias Saoudi, singer for the debauched squat-rockers Fat White Family, had this to say on the subject: 'Up until watching that film I'd always fancied myself more of a John type, but then came that scene where only Ringo bothers showing up to rehearsal and Macca nearly starts crying, and I knew in a heartbeat the dreadful truth, I am a Paul person. It seems fairly explicit that no one really gives a fuck anymore, John barely speaks for the first hour, George is done playing the third wheel and Ringo is, well, only the drummer, yet onwards Paul ploughs. He just wants the lads to "rock it one more time". Bless. At one point he bemoans the lack of order, of structure, what we

need is a schedule, he claims. When John does finally open his mouth, a quarter of the way into episode two, he's speaking in tongues. A tragi-comic disparity in the extreme. Every band, great or miniscule, needs someone pathologically uptight at its core.' Lias Saoudi, 'I Blame the Music: Lias Saoudi's Baker's Dozen', *The Quietus*, www.thequietus.com, 16 February 2022.

8 Jonathan Dean, 'Paul McCartney: The Film *Get Back* Changed How I See the Beatles' Break-Up', *The Times*, www.thetimes.co.uk, 13 November 2021.

9 Barbara Skelton, 'The Compilations: The 70s and 80s', *Record Collector Presents The Beatles*.

10 Paul Gambaccini, 'Ringo Remembers', *Rolling Stone* (18 November 1976).

11 Skelton, 'The Compilations'.

12 Vulnerable to scratches, fingerprints, temperature damage and 'laser rot', CDs were not indestructible, as most consumers had already realized, to their annoyance, by the time the *Wall Street Journal* reported, in 2001, that 'discs just aren't what they were cracked up to be.' Pooja Bhatia, 'Consumers Face Rising Piles of Damaged Compact Disc', *Wall Street Journal*, www.wsj.com, 2 February 2001. To their credit, CDs are lighter and take up less space than the superior-sounding vinyl format. And you don't have to heave yourself off the sofa to turn them over halfway through.

13 Robert Christgau, 'The Beatles', www.robertchristgau.com, accessed 4 November 2022.

14 Jon Savage, 'The Beatles: Live at the BBC', *Mojo* (January 1995).

15 Caroline Sullivan, 'CD of the Week: The Beatles Live at the BBC (EMI)', *The Guardian* (2 December 1994).

16 Quoted by '*The Beatles Anthology* sessions', www.the-paulmccartney-project.com, accessed 12 October 2022.

17 Ibid.

18 Mat Snow, 'Paul McCartney', *Mojo* (November 1995).

19 Paul Du Noyer, 'They Were the Most Brilliant, Powerful, Lovable, Popular Group on the Planet . . . But Now They're Really Important', *Q* (December 1995).

20 Ibid. Six years earlier Harrison had been quoted as saying, 'As far as I'm concerned, there won't be a Beatles reunion as long as John Lennon remains dead.' Associated Press, 'No 3-Beatle Reunion, George Harrison Says', *New York Times* (1 December 1989).

21 Jim Irvin and Paul Du Noyer, 'Anticipointment? *The Beatles Anthology*: The World Decides', *Mojo* (February 1996).

22 Nicholas Barber, 'The Old Kids on the Block', *The Independent* (19 November 1995).

23 It was impossible to know whether Lennon would have approved of the song, as George Martin explained at a press conference for *Anthology 1*:

'John changed his mind more often than he changed his socks and if you had him in the right mood he would've said "Great. Yeah. Fantastic. Fab." In another mood he'd have just slagged it off.' The fact that 'Free as a Bird' had the blessing of Yoko Ono, who was the closest person to Lennon, was good enough for Martin. 'The Beatles – Anthology 1 (Press conference 1995)', www.youtube.com, accessed 28 October 2022.

24 Irvin and Du Noyer, 'Anticipointment?'
25 Ibid.
26 Ibid.
27 Ibid.
28 Barber, 'The Old Kids'.
29 'British MP in Plea for Beatles', *Irish Times*, www.irishtimes.com, 9 March 1996.
30 A few Conservative politicians have appeared on Radio 4's *Desert Island Discs* over the years. The music they could not live without has included Aled Jones's rendition of the Christian hymn 'How Great Thou Art', a requiem by the musical theatre impresario Andrew Lloyd Webber and, in John Major's case, the cricket commentary of John Arlott. In the 2000s, no doubt inspired by New Labour's electoral success, Conservatives cottoned on to the idea of using cooler selections (or were being advised to do so). Sitting alongside the more traditional music from the classical canon, artists chosen by Iain Duncan Smith included Bruce Springsteen, Nina Simone and Jerry Lee Lewis. In 2005 the future law-breaking prime minister Boris Johnson plumped for The Beatles ('Here Comes the Sun'), Booker T & The MG's, The Rolling Stones, Van Morrison and (of all things) The Clash. The following year saw the most excruciating attempt to appear hip, courtesy of David Cameron, who proclaimed to love The Killers, REM, Pink Floyd, Radiohead and The Smiths. Johnny Marr, ex-guitarist for the latter band, tweeted in response to Cameron, 'stop saying that you like The Smiths, no you don't. I forbid you to like it.'
31 Paul Du Noyer, *Conversations with McCartney* (London, 2015), p. 178.
32 Irvin and Du Noyer, 'Anticipointment?'
33 Doggett, *You Never Give Me Your Money*, p. 312.
34 That being said, the first recording session of the reunited 'Threatles' had to be rescheduled because Ringo decided he'd rather go skiing. Ibid., p. 311.
35 Geoff Baker and Mark Lewisohn, 'The Beatles Story', *Club Sandwich*, 76 (Winter 1995). Harrison was never most original thinker to have been in The Beatles. He was accused, in court, of plagiarizing 'My Sweet Lord' from the Ronnie Mack song 'He's So Fine' (1963).
36 Chris Ingham, 'Paul McCartney: *Flaming Pie*', *Mojo* (June 1997).
37 Allan Kozinn, 'Telling Their Own Story: "Beatles Anthology" Promises to Be Most Complete Project Done so Far on the Legendary Band from Liverpool', www.spokesman.com, 12 November 1995.
38 Atkins, 'The *Anthology* Series'.

39 'Why Did Paul Delay the Release of *Anthology 2*?', https://forums.stevehoffman.tv, accessed 3 November 2022.
40 'Anthology 1 (Press conference 1995)'.
41 Chris Morris and Ed Christman, 'Sales of Beatles Set Give Retailers Hope', *Billboard* (2 December 1995).
42 'Fans in a Rush for Beatles Album', *The Independent* (22 November 1995).
43 Robert Goldberg, 'Television: The Fab Four 25 Years Later', *Wall Street Journal* (20 November 1995).
44 Joe Joseph, 'The Beatles: Pop Music's Latest Craze', *The Times* (11 November 1995).
45 Mark Tran, 'Beatlemania Back in U.S. Even Bigger than Before', *The Guardian* (1 December 1995).
46 Ibid.
47 Lynne Truss, 'Audience Involvement Not to Be Sniffed At', *The Times* (27 November 1995).
48 Weber, *The Beatles*, p. 173.
49 See *Mr Blue Sky: The Story of Jeff Lynne and ELO*, dir. Martyn Atkins (2012).
50 Ray Connolly, 'Ringo Revealed', *Daily Mail* (4 September 2000).
51 Jem Roberts, *Fab Fools: The Beatles, The Rutles and Rock 'n' Roll Comedy!* (Cardiff, 2021), p. 305.
52 Connolly, 'Ringo Revealed'. Along with the multiple takes of the song that Paul, in perfectionist mood, persuaded The Beatles to repeatedly record, Starr's memories of witnessing such horrendously violent attacks first-hand could be another reason he considered 'Maxwell's Silver Hammer' to be 'the worst track we ever had to record'. Austin Scaggs, 'Ringo Starr Q&A', *Rolling Stone* (24 January 2008).
53 Philip Norman, *Shout! The Beatles in Their Generation* (New York, 1981), p. 115.
54 Barry Miles, *Paul McCartney: Many Years from Now* (London, 1997), p. 74.
55 Tony Bacon, 'Paul McCartney – Meet the Beatle', *Bass Player* (July–August 1995).
56 Mindy LaBernz, 'In Defense of Paul McCartney: Milquetoast Balladeer or Songwriting Stud?', *Austin Chronicle*, www.austinchronicle.com, 15 December 1995.
57 *The Beatles Anthology* [1995], DVD (Apple, 2003).
58 Adam Curtis, 'From Massive Attack to Miley Cyrus: Adam Curtis's Favourite Cover Versions', *The Guardian* (6 February 2021).
59 Ibid.
60 This inspired the Dave Chapelle sketch in which a club DJ drops a Tupac song with vocals allegedly recorded in 1994 but packed with newer references to Blackberry pagers, *Grand Theft Auto: San Andreas*, Eminem and President George W. Bush's air strikes on Afghanistan.

Either Shakur was a prophet with greater powers than Nostradamus or, as conspiracy theorists would have it, his death had been faked.

61 Serge Simonart, 'Prince 1998 Guitar World Interview', available at https://sites.google.com/site/themusicinterviewarchive, accessed 8 November 2022.

62 Simon Cowell with Tony Cowell, *I Don't Mean to Be Rude, but...* (Reading, 2004), p. 96.

63 Chas Newkay-Burden, *Simon Cowell: The Unauthorized Biography* (London, 2009), p. 42.

64 *Spitting Image*, series 20, episode 1 (ITV, aired 14 January 1996).

65 Rob Sheffield, *Dreaming The Beatles: The Love Story of One Band and the Whole World* (New York, 2018), p. 296.

66 Anthony Elliott, *The Mourning of John Lennon* (London, 1999), pp. 176–7.

67 'Letters', *Mojo* (February 1996). The reader went on to bemoan Lynne's 'mush and sludge' job, which made the track sound like everything else he'd ever produced. 'But what a tune, eh?' he conceded. 'I can't get it out of my head.'

68 Elliott, *The Mourning*, pp. 176–7.

69 Greil Marcus, 'Days between Stations: (06/96)', https://greilmarcus.net, accessed 7 November 2022.

70 Du Noyer, 'They Were the Most'.

71 Doggett, *You Never Give Me Your Money*, pp. 319–20.

72 See www.thebeatles.com/announcement, accessed 12 February 2024.

73 Simon Reynolds, *Retromania: Pop Culture's Addiction to Its Own Past* (London, 2011), p. 161.

74 Theodore Sturgeon, 'On Hand: A Book', *Venture* (September 1957), p. 49.

75 The noise-rock genre is the exception that proves the rule. See JR Moores, *Electric Wizards: A Tapestry of Heavy Music, 1968 to the Present* (London, 2021), pp. 212–13.

76 David Bennun, 'White Heat Can't Melt Black Steel: Public Enemy's *Nation of Millions* Revisited', *The Quietus*, www.thequietus.com, 11 June 2018; JR Moores, 'The One with the Conservative Agenda: Why The Offspring Is Punk's Equivalent of *Friends*', *The Quietus*, www.thequietus.com, 20 November 2018; Dele Fadele, 'Nick Cave and the Bad Seeds' *Murder Ballads* as Gangsta Rap Album', *The Quietus*, www.thequietus.com, 1 March 2016.

77 Simon Reynolds, 'Acen: *Trip II The Moon 2092*', *The Wire* (February 2021).

78 Atkins, 'The *Anthology* Series'.

79 Charles Shaar Murray, 'The Numbers Racket', *Mojo* (December 2000).

80 Pam Mitchell, '1', *Record Collector Presents The Beatles*.

81 Wayne Friedman, 'Via 1, Beatles Reborn as Ultimate Boy Band', *Advertising Age*, 26 (March 2001).

82 Archived at www.the-paulmccartney-project.com, accessed 21 November 2022.

83 Neil Spencer, 'The Beatles, Love', *The Observer*, 12 November 2006.
84 Another immortal line sees Partridge pressed on his favourite Beatles album: 'Tough one. I think I'd have to say . . . *The Best of The Beatles*.'
85 Mick Houghton, 'Seal of Approval', *Mojo* (June 2001).
86 Ken Lieck, 'Rutle to the Core: Neil Innes Exposes His Nasty Side', *Austin Chronicle*, www.austinchronicle.com, 15 November 1996.
87 Bruce Eder, '*Archaeology* Review', www.allmusic.com, accessed 21 November 2022.
88 *Sgt. Pepper's Musical Revolution with Howard Goodall* (BBC Two, aired 3 June 2017).
89 Miles, *Many Years from Now*, p. 319.
90 Ian MacDonald, *Revolution in the Head: The Beatles' Records and the Sixties* (London, 2008), p. 221.
91 Pete Paphides, 'Learning to Love Stereo: Hearing The Beatles' *Sgt Pepper's* with New Ears', *The Quietus*, www.thequietus.com, 11 April 2017.
92 Ibid.
93 Du Noyer, *Conversations*, p. 178.
94 Ibid., p. 180.

### 5 *Flaming Pie*

1 Creation Records' Alan McGee did push for 'Wake Up Boo!' (1995) by The Boo Radleys. Other options that were discussed included George Michael's 'Faith' and M People's 'Moving On Up' (1993). Daniel Rachel, *Don't Look Back in Anger: The Rise and Fall of Cool Britannia, Told by Those Who Were There* (London, 2020), p. 273. The sight of Labour's Neil Kinnock, Robin Cook, John Prescott and Peter Mandelson awkwardly dancing to 'Things Can Only Get Better' is etched in the memory of all who saw it.
2 Dorian Lynskey, '"Flattened by the Cocaine Panzers" – The Toxic Legacy of Oasis's *Be Here Now*', *The Guardian*, www.theguardian.com, 6 October 2016.
3 Charles Shaar Murray, 'Oasis: *Be Here Now*', *Mojo* (September 1997).
4 Previously a guest on the show, Noel Gallagher never spoke to Chris Evans again.
5 Lynskey, '"Flattened"'.
6 Adrian Deevoy, 'Blur: Stop the Band, I Wanna Get Off!', *Q* (March 1996).
7 Tom Clayton, *When Quiet Was the New Loud: Celebrating the Acoustic Airwaves, 1998–2003* (Pontefract, 2001), p. 11.
8 Paul McCartney, liner notes to *Flaming Pie* (MPL/Parlophone, 1997).
9 Anthony DeCurtis, 'Paul McCartney: *Flaming Pie*', *Rolling Stone*, www.rollingstone.com, 6 June 1997.
10 Thom Duffy, 'McCartney Turns Back the Clock', *Billboard* (12 April 1997).
11 Chris Ingham, 'Paul McCartney: *Flaming Pie*', *Mojo* (June 1997).

12 Ibid. In the same interview, McCartney teases Lynne by saying, 'ELO were good, you know, pity about the haircut. *(Pause)* I'm only kidding about the haircut, you'd better put in brackets – he'd kill me. He's still got it.' This might sound a little rich coming from someone who still looks fairly mulletted in many of the *Anthology*'s interviews.
13 Ibid.
14 Ibid.
15 Roy Carr, 'Crust Almighty', *Vox* (June 1997).
16 The actual *McCartney III* would arrive in the distant future of 2020 because those self-titled solo efforts have to coincide with a round-numbered year, it seems. Also, the COVID-19 lockdown had imposed a DIY procedure.
17 McCartney, *Flaming Pie*.
18 Ibid.
19 Ibid.
20 Ingham, '*Flaming Pie*'.
21 DeCurtis, '*Flaming Pie*'.
22 Vincent P. Benitez, *The Words and Music of Paul McCartney: The Solo Years* (Santa Barbara, CA, 2010), p. 144.
23 Mark Lewisohn, 'The Songs', *Club Sandwich*, 82 (Summer 1997); McCartney, *Flaming Pie*.
24 Ibid.
25 DeCurtis, '*Flaming Pie*'.
26 'In fact, I still haven't done the guitar as much as she wanted,' Paul confessed. Quoted in 'The World Tonight', www.the-paulmccartney-project.com, accessed 17 December 2022.
27 Ibid.
28 Paul McCartney, *The Lyrics* (London, 2021), p. 818.
29 In-person event: 'The Lyrics: Paul McCartney in Conversation', Royal Festival Hall, London, 5 November 2021.
30 Ibid.
31 McCartney, *Flaming Pie*.
32 McCartney, *The Lyrics*, p. 818.
33 DeCurtis, '*Flaming Pie*'.
34 McCartney, *Flaming Pie*.
35 Ingham, '*Flaming Pie*'.
36 McCartney, *Flaming Pie*.
37 Benitez, *The Words and Music*, p. 146.
38 Carr, 'Crust Almighty'.
39 Quoted in 'Somedays', www.the-paulmccartney-project.com, accessed 21 December 2022.
40 Geoff Baker and Mark Lewisohn, 'Digging around the Back', *Club Sandwich*, 82 (Summer 1997). In his lyrics book, McCartney also seems a little emotionally distant from 'Somedays', highlighting its use of anadiplosis ('essentially, it's repetition') and comparing its composition

to completing a crossword. He does say the song is a 'very meaningful' one to him but is also very pleased with the lyric's 'wonderful ambiguity'. McCartney, *The Lyrics*, pp. 681–2.

41 Carr, 'Crust Almighty'; Benitez, *The Words and Music*, p. 146.
42 My exclamation mark. Benitez, *The Words and Music*, p. 147.
43 Baker and Lewisohn, 'Digging'.
44 Lewisohn, 'The Songs'.
45 McCartney, *The Lyrics*, pp. 59–60.
46 Ibid., p. 60.
47 Barry Miles, *Paul McCartney: Many Years from Now* (London, 1997), p. 11.
48 'Flaming Pie' is not one of the 154 songs discussed in McCartney's *Lyrics* book of 2021.
49 Baker and Lewisohn, 'Digging'.
50 Benitez, *The Words and Music*, p. 147.
51 Edna Gunderson, 'A Nostalgic Slice of "Pie"', *USA Today* (27 May 1997).
52 McCartney, *Flaming Pie*.
53 Ian Leslie, '64 Reasons to Celebrate Paul McCartney', https://ianleslie.substack.com, 8 December 2020.
54 Lewisohn, 'The Songs'.
55 Could this have been Harrison trying to return those missed calls?
56 Bob Spitz, 'He May Be Sir Paul, But He's Still a Beatle', *New York Times* (25 May 1997).
57 Ibid.
58 Laura Cross, 'More Angles on the Pie, *Club Sandwich*, 83 (Autumn 1997).
59 Benitez, *The Words and Music*, p. 149.
60 Lewisohn, 'The Songs'.
61 Quoted in Baker and Lewisohn, 'Digging'.
62 Lewisohn, 'The Songs'.
63 Stephen Thomas Erlewine, '*Flaming Pie* Review', www.allmusic.com, accessed 4 January 2022 ('most ambitious pieces'); Benitez, *The Words and Music*, p. 149 ('symphonic'); 'Singles Reviews', *Music Week* (6 December 1997) ('best ballad').
64 Ingham, '*Flaming Pie*'.
65 Carr, 'Crust Almighty'.
66 Carol Clerk, 'Paul McCartney: *Flaming Pie*', *Uncut* (June 1997).
67 Caroline Sullivan, 'Mac's Back', *The Guardian* (11 May 1997).
68 Caroline Sullivan, 'I Believe in Yesterday: A Brave Effort, but Paul McCartney Can't Live Up to His Past', *The Guardian*, 13 September 1993.
69 Sullivan, 'Mac's Back'.
70 Ibid.
71 Andy Gill, 'Paul McCartney, *Flaming Pie*', *The Independent* (9 May 1997).
72 Ibid.
73 Howard Sounes, *Fab: An Intimate Life of Paul McCartney* (London, 2010), p. 472.

74 Ibid.
75 For more on this, see Luke Turner, 'When Did Music Journalism Stop Wielding the Axe?', *Crack*, https://crackmagazine.net, 27 July 2017.
76 Kory Grow, 'Paul McCartney Delivers a Bounty of Rarities, Curiosities and Gems on "Flaming Pie" Box Set', *Rolling Stone*, www.rollingstone.com, 30 July 2020.
77 Graeme Ross, 'The Beatles: Their 10 Best Solo Albums Ranked, from *Flaming Pie* to *Imagine*', *The Independent*, www.independent.co.uk, 16 April 2020.
78 Sounes, *Fab*, p. 472.
79 Des Burkinshaw, 'Fab? If You Say So, Pop Pickers', *The Times* (25 April 1997).
80 On refusing a title: Alex Bilmes, 'Paul McCartney Talks Songs, Fame and the Beatles', *Esquire* (August 2015). Quotation from Gunderson, 'A Nostalgic Slice'. Personally, I prefer the attitude of The Cure's Robert Smith, who, as a member of the punk generation, objects to such honours on principle. Disappointed that Elizabeth II's Silver Jubilee and Sex Pistols' 'God Save the Queen' did not sound the death knell of the royal family, Smith believes that hereditary privilege is 'inherently wrong', and it upsets him whenever anyone he admires accepts a title from the royal establishment. Smith says he'd cut off his own hands before he'd accept one himself, 'because how dare they presume that they could give me an honour? I'm much better than them. They've never done anything. They're fucking idiots.' [Sticks tongue out and puts two fingers up at the camera.] 'Robert Smith (The Cure), interview by Télérama.fr (July 2012)', www.youtube.com, accessed 14 December 2022.
81 Bilmes, 'Paul McCartney'.
82 Gunderson, 'A Nostalgic Slice'.
83 Duffy, 'McCartney Turns Back the Clock'.
84 Ibid.
85 Gunderson, 'A Nostalgic Slice'.
86 The answer to whether he finds it easier to make good records in unhappier periods, McCartney said in 2013, was 'neither and both'. However, he did compare the songwriting process to visiting a therapist: 'Going away when you're really upset about something and putting it in your song – you come out of that cupboard, toilet or basement and go, "I really feel better." You've actually exorcised the demon. So it is one of the great joys of songwriting.' Pat Gilbert, 'Don't Look Back in Anger', *Mojo* (November 2013).
87 Kim Stallwood and Jill Howard, 'The Extraordinary Activist', *Animals' Agenda* (January 1999), available at https://maccarchives.livejournal.com, accessed 6 January 2023.

### 6 Behind Every Great Man

1 Shaun Brady, 'Yoko Ono Didn't Break Up the Beatles. But She Did Help Invent Alternative Music', https://tidal.com, 18 February 2022.
2 Ben Myers, 'Yoko Ono: The Coolest Beatle?', *The Guardian*, www.theguardian.com, 10 July 2009.
3 Howard Sounes, *Fab: An Intimate Life of Paul McCartney* (London, 2010), pp. 388, 393.
4 Dalma Hayn, 'The Alarmingly Normal McCartneys', *McCall's* (1 August 1984).
5 Ibid.
6 Diane de Dubovay, 'An Intimate Conversation with Pop's Preeminent Pair', *Playgirl* (February 1985).
7 Ibid.
8 Maureen Cleave, 'The Gospel According to Paul', *London Evening Standard* (26 August 1993).
9 Paula Yates, 'In Front of Every Great Man . . .', *Record Mirror* (21 June 1980).
10 Danny Fields, *Linda McCartney: The Biography* (London, 2000), p. 220.
11 John Blake, *All You Needed Was Love: The Beatles after The Beatles* (New York, 1981), p. 132; Cathy Booth, 'Paul at Fifty', *Time* (8 June 1992).
12 For example, Paul Du Noyer, 'Linda McCartney: *Wide Prairie*', *Mojo* (December 1998).
13 Sounes, *Fab*, pp. 264–5.
14 Ibid., p. 425.
15 Langdon Winner, 'McCartney', *Rolling Stone* (14 May 1970).
16 Mike Hennessey, 'The Heart of McCartney', *Record Mirror* (4 December 1971).
17 For example: Alan Smith, 'Paul and Linda McCartney: *Ram*', *NME* (22 May 1971); and Jon Landau, 'Paul McCartney: *Ram*', *Rolling Stone* (8 July 1971).
18 Ken Freedman, 'Audio Hoaxes and Urban Legends, Part One', https://blog.wfmu.org, 31 March 2006.
19 As late as 2017, Bill Burr used the recording for the same kind of hack material, filling the air in the newer podcast medium. 'Thursday Afternoon Monday Morning Podcast 11-2-17', www.youtube.com, accessed 6 February 2023.
20 Freedman, 'Audio Hoaxes'.
21 Dan Ozzi, 'Courtney Love's Isolated Vocal and Guitar Tracks Are Even Worse Than You'd Imagine', *Vice*, www.vice.com, 9 September 2014; Ben Kaye, 'Courtney Love's Isolated Vocals and Guitar Will Make You Cringe', https://consequence.net, 9 September 2014; Josh Kurp, 'You'll Cringe the Hole Way through Courtney Love's Isolated Vocals and Guitar', https://uproxx.com, 9 September 2014.
22 'Hole – Celebrity Skin Live (solo vocal & guitar mics)', www.youtube.com, accessed 6 February 2023.

23 Ozzi, 'Courtney Love's Isolated Vocal'.
24 As argued by Harriet Gibsone, 'Raw Power: Why Mocking the Isolated Vocals of Courtney Love Is Misogynistic', *The Guardian*, www.theguardian.com, 10 October 2014.
25 Judy Berman, 'Did You Hear the One about How Courtney Love Can't Sing or Play Guitar?', www.flavorwire.com, 12 September 2014.
26 Ibid.
27 Ibid.
28 Ibid.
29 Sounes, *Fab*, p. 264.
30 Geoffrey Giuliano, *Blackbird: The Life and Times of Paul McCartney* (New York, 1991), p. 268.
31 Andrew Smith, 'Elastica Limits', *The Observer* (10 March 2002).
32 Louise Wener, *Just for One Day: Adventures in Britpop* (London, 2011), pp. 121–2. In one interview, Wener, who was more of a Stones fan, claimed that she hated The Beatles because 'they had Paul McCartney in them, for a start.' Ian Fortnam, 'Material World: Sleeper', *Vox* (June 1996).
33 Joan Goodman, 'Paul and Linda McCartney's Whole Story', *Playboy* (December 1984).
34 Paul Du Noyer, *Conversations with McCartney* (London, 2015), p. 312.
35 Fields, *Linda McCartney*, p. 150.
36 Ibid.
37 'Letters', *Mojo* (June 1998).
38 Quoted in Tom Doyle, *Man on the Run: Paul McCartney in the 1970s* (Edinburgh, 2014), p. 162.
39 Linda McCartney pointed this out herself: 'He doesn't take it as seriously as everyone else does, meaning journalists.' Quoted in Du Noyer, *Conversations*, p. 315.
40 Maureen Cleave, 'The Gospel According to Paul', *London Evening Standard* (26 August 1993).
41 Ibid.
42 Fields, *Linda McCartney*, p. 83.
43 Kris Needs, *George Clinton and the Cosmic Odyssey of the P-Funk Empire* (London, 2014), p. 105.
44 Jimmy McDonough, *Shakey: Neil Young's Biography* (London, 2002), p. 270.
45 Quoted in 'The World Tonight', www.the-paulmccartney-project.com, accessed 17 December 2022.
46 Du Noyer, *Conversations*, pp. 79–80.
47 Geoff Baker and Mark Lewisohn, 'The Beatles Story', *Club Sandwich*, 76 (Winter 1995).
48 Tony Bacon, 'Paul McCartney – Meet the Beatle', *Bass Player* (July–August 1995).

49 Du Noyer, *Conversations*, p. 216. The moment to which McCartney is referring actually occurs later in the recording, during the song's third and fourth minutes.
50 Ibid., p. x.
51 Kim Stallwood and Jill Howard, 'The Extraordinary Activist', *Animals' Agenda* (January 1999), available at https://maccarchives.livejournal.com, accessed 17 February 2023.
52 Du Noyer, *Conversations*, p. 201.
53 The original quote was 'Honour thy error as a hidden intention.' See Martin Schneider, 'Brian Eno and Peter Schmidt's "Oblique Strategies", The Original Handwritten Cards', https://dangerousminds.net, 24 February 2014.
54 Du Noyer, *Conversations*, p. 201.
55 Harry Sword, *Monolithic Undertow: In Search of Sonic Oblivion* (London, 2021), pp. 152–4.
56 Danny Bowman, 'Interview: Sir Paul McCartney', *Reader's Digest UK*, www.readersdigest.co.uk, 2 November 2021.
57 Ibid.
58 Available at Matt Rickard, 'List of All Oblique Strategies', https://matt-rickard.com, 24 May 2022.
59 Pete Townshend, *Who I Am* (London, 2012), p. 205.
60 Jann Wenner, 'Pete Townshend Talks Mods, Recording, and Smashing Guitars', *Rolling Stone* (14 September 1968).
61 Chrissie Hynde, 'Tears and Laughter', *USA Weekend* (30 October 1998).
62 Peter Castro, 'Band on the Run', *People Weekly* (5 July 1993).
63 Du Noyer, *Conversations*, p. 312.
64 Fields, *Linda McCartney*, p. 213.
65 Ibid., p. 310.
66 Ibid.
67 Deborah Ross, 'My Date with the McCartneys', *The Times*, www.thetimes.co.uk, 6 May 2017.
68 Du Noyer, *Conversations*, p. 315.
69 Hayn, 'Alarmingly Normal'.
70 Du Noyer, *Conversations*, p. 315.
71 Ibid.
72 Carl Wilson, *Let's Talk about Love: Why Other People Have Such Bad Taste* (London, 2019), p. 55.
73 Deborah Knight, 'Why We Enjoy Condemning Sentimentality: A Meta-Aesthetic Perspective', *Journal of Aesthetics and Art Criticism*, LVII/4 (Autumn 1999), p. 416.
74 Ibid., p. 418.
75 Andrew Falkous, interview with the author, 2022.
76 Ibid.

77 Mark Ellen, 'Paul McCartney', *Smash Hits* (24 November–7 December 1983).
78 Wilson, *Let's Talk*, p. 132.
79 The phrase 'There are only two kinds of music, good and bad' has also been credited to Gioachino Rossini (1792–1868).
80 Du Noyer, *Conversations*, p. 315.
81 Simon Armitage, 'Morrissey Interview: Big Mouth Strikes Again', *The Guardian*, www.theguardian.com, 3 September 2010.
82 Delia Smith, *Delia's Vegetarian Collection* (London, 2002), p. 9.
83 Tom Hibbert, 'Fab Macca Wacky Thumbs Aloft . . . At Your Service!!', *Smash Hits* (13–26 August 1986).
84 Hayn, 'Alarmingly Normal'.
85 Ibid.
86 Dan Mathews, 'We'll Keep Linda's Torch Burning', *The Guardian* (24 September 1998).
87 Fields, *Linda McCartney*, p. 223.
88 Ibid., p. 186.
89 Ibid., p. 215.
90 Mathews, 'We'll Keep'. In 2017 the world's first no-kill caviar farm was opened in Leeds, Yorkshire.
91 Stallwood and Howard, 'The Extraordinary Activist'.
92 Linda McCartney, *Linda McCartney's Home Cooking* (London, 1989), p. 1.
93 Paul McCartney, 'Introduction', in Linda McCartney with Paul, Mary and Stella McCartney, *Linda McCartney's Family Kitchen* (London, 2021), p. 9.
94 Philip Norman, *Paul McCartney: The Biography* (London, 2016), p. 618.
95 Ibid.
96 Ibid.
97 Ibid., p. 646.
98 Philip Norman wonders whether the meat pies were put in Linda McCartney packages by a factory employee who still held a grudge against 'the Woman Who Married Paul'. Ibid.
99 Keith Tester, 'The Moral Malaise of McDonaldization: The Values of Vegetarianism', in *Resisting McDonaldization*, ed. Barry Smart (London, 1999), p. 219.
100 Fields, *Linda McCartney*, p. 225.
101 Norman, *Paul McCartney*, p. 617.
102 George Varga, 'Linda Lets Her Voice Be Heard', *San Diego Union* (29 November 1989).
103 Stallwood and Howard, 'The Extraordinary Activist'.
104 Juliet Gellatley, 'The Fight Goes On', *Viva! Life* (*c.* 1998), available at https://web.archive.org, accessed 20 February 2023.
105 Linda McCartney, *Linda's Kitchen: Simple and Inspiring Recipes for Meals without Meat* (London, 1995), p. 7; 'Paul McCartney: "If

Slaughterhouses Had Glass Walls . . ."', www.youtube.com, accessed 20 February 2023.

106 'Humane Slaughter: Hearings before the Subcommittee on Livestock and Feed Grains of the Committee on Agriculture, House of Representatives, Eighty-Fifth Congress' (Washington, DC, 1957), p. 8.

107 Quoted in Owen Walsh, 'Does the Humane Slaughter Act Really Protect Animals?', https://thehumaneleague.org, 17 January 2023.

108 Fields, *Linda McCartney*, p. 160.

109 'Paul McCartney – The 1993 New World Tour', https://forums.stevehoffman.tv, accessed 22 February 2023.

110 Robert Hilburn, 'McCartney Puts His Activism on Stag', *Tampa Bay Times* (7 May 1993).

111 Less moralistic than the McCartneys, during their gigs the Texan noise-rock provocateurs would project stomach-churning footage of horrendous traffic accidents and penis reconstruction surgery.

112 Caroline Sullivan, 'I Believe in Yesterday: A Brave Effort, but Paul McCartney Can't Live Up to His Past', *The Guardian* (13 September 1993): 'The show had begun thrillingly, with film footage of the Beatles (the Fabs boarding a plane, cackling with the Maharishi, etc.) set to the recorded strains of Help! This dissolved into a horrifying animal-rights video, after which McCartney, spouse and band took to the stage and kicked off with Baby, You Can Drive My Car.'

113 'Almost as sad' as the animals in the film, added Sinclair, 'were the songs from McCartney's most recent album, *Off the Ground*'. David Sinclair, 'No Mistaking an Original Master', *The Times* (13 September 1993).

114 Robert Hilburn, 'For McCartney, It's Not Easy Being Green', *Los Angeles Times* (16 April 1993). Hilburn later published a book called *Corn Flakes with John Lennon and Other Tales from a Rock 'n' Roll Life* (New York, 2009). It had an introduction by Bono and the sleeve blurb stated that Hilburn had 'met John Lennon during his lost weekend period in Los Angeles and they became friends'.

115 Hilburn, *Corn Flakes*, p. 68.

116 John Freeman, 'Breath of the Inuit: Tanya Tagaq Interviewed', *The Quietus*, www.thequietus.com, 28 January 2015.

117 Tester, 'The Moral Malaise', p. 219.

118 Ibid.

119 Fields, *Linda McCartney*, p. 327.

120 Hynde, 'Tears'.

121 Ibid.

122 Carrie Packwood Freeman, 'Chapter 11: Lisa and Phoebe, Lone Vegetarian Icons: At Odds with Television's Carnonormativity', in *How Television Shapes Our Worldview: Media Representations of Social Trends and Change*, ed. Deborah A. Macey, Kathleen M. Ryan and Noah J. Springer, ebook (Plymouth, 2014), p. 169.

123 Ibid., p. 162.
124 Ibid., p. 158.
125 Gellatley, 'The Fight Goes On'.
126 Mathews, 'We'll Keep'.
127 Gellatley, 'The Fight Goes On'; Stallwood and Howard, 'The Extraordinary Activist'.
128 Norman, *Paul McCartney*, pp. 624–5, 645.
129 Cathy Booth, 'Paul at Fifty', *Time* (8 June 1992).
130 Alexis Petridis, 'Paul McCartney: *New* – Review', *The Guardian* (11 October 2013).
131 Edna Gunderson, 'After Linda, McCartneys Still Making Sweet Music', *USA Today* (19 November, 1998), archived at www.the-paulmccartney-project.com, accessed 16 March 2022.

## 7 The Experimental Ones

1 Quoted in Jonathan Buckley, *The Rough Guide to Rock* (London, 2003), p. 1034.
2 McCartney has no recollection of this happening. Given the 'substances' indulged in at the time, he accepts it as a possibility. 'McCartney (Robin Bextor, 2001)', www.youtube.com, accessed 14 March 2023.
3 Hunter Davies, *The Beatles*, 2nd revd edn (New York, 1985), p. 372.
4 Ibid., p. 370.
5 Ibid., p. 368.
6 Hunter Davies, 'How It Feels to Be in the Studio with The Beatles Recording', *The Times*, www.thetimes.co.uk, 28 May 2017.
7 Erin Torkelson Weber, *The Beatles and the Historians: An Analysis of Writings about the Fab Four* (Jefferson, NC, 2016), p. 128.
8 Ray Bonici, 'Paul McCartney Flying on Clipped Wings', *Music Express* (April–May 1982), available at www.the-paulmccartney-project.com, accessed 15 March 2023.
9 'It Started to Be Art', *The Paul McCartney World Tour* programme (London, 1989), pp. 50–51.
10 'French for bullshit': quoted in Barry Miles, *Paul McCartney: Many Years from Now* (London, 1997), p. x; other sources cite Lennon as repeating the phrase often. 'Intellectuals and university students': ibid., p. 229.
11 Ibid., p. xiii.
12 Ibid., pp. 123–4.
13 Ibid., p. 233.
14 Ibid., pp. 230, 233.
15 Ibid., p. 237.
16 Ibid., pp. 218–20.
17 Marianne Faithfull with David Dalton, *Faithfull: An Autobiography* (Boston, MA, 1994), p. 55.

18 Steve Richards, 'Paul McCartney – Meet the Beatle', *New Statesman* (26 September 1997).
19 Miles, *Many Years from Now*, p. 309.
20 Ian Peel, *The Unknown Paul McCartney: McCartney and the Avant-Garde* (Richmond, 2002), p. 53.
21 Vanessa Thorpe, 'Forty Years On, McCartney Wants the World to Hear "Lost" Beatles Epic', *The Observer* (16 November 2008).
22 Howard Elson, *McCartney: Songwriter* (London, 1986), pp. ix–x.
23 Ibid., p. 171.
24 Ibid., p. 178. 'It's a pity I shan't be around to be proved right!!' added Stardust. He died in 2014.
25 Ibid., p. 182.
26 Ibid., p. 174.
27 Ibid., p. 176.
28 Ibid., pp. 179–80.
29 Ibid., p. 65.
30 Ibid., pp. 65–6.
31 Brian Epstein, *A Cellarful of Noise: The Man Who Made the Beatles* (London, 2021), p. 37.
32 Mark Lewisohn, *The Complete Beatles Recording Sessions: The Official Story of the Abbey Road Years, 1962–1970* (New York, 1989), p. 93.
33 'Paul McCartney: Parkinson Show December 2005', www.youtube.com, accessed 17 March 2023.
34 David Sheff, *All We Are Saying: The Last Major Interview with John Lennon and Yoko Ono* (New York, 2000), p. 140.
35 Phillip McIntyre and Paul Thompson, *Paul McCartney and His Creative Practice: The Beatles and Beyond* (Cham, 2021), p. 57.
36 Elson, *McCartney*, p. 164.
37 Tim Day, 'Paul McCartney's *Liverpool Oratorio*', *Newsday* (20 November 1991).
38 'Album Reviews – McCartney and Davis: Paul McCartney's *Liverpool Oratorio*', *Billboard* (9 November 1991).
39 David C. Giles, 'Field Migration, Cultural Mobility and Celebrity: The Case of Paul McCartney', *Celebrity Studies*, VI/4 (2015), p. 546.
40 See Pierre Bourdieu, *Distinction: A Social Critique of the Judgement of Taste*, trans. Richard Nice (Cambridge, MA, 1984).
41 Giles, 'Field Migration', p. 545.
42 Ibid., pp. 549–50.
43 'Paul McCartney's Remarkable Classical Works', https://forums.stevehoffman.tv, accessed 17 March 2023.
44 Ibid.
45 Ibid.
46 'All Back to My Place', *Mojo* (January 1998).
47 Mark Lewisohn, 'The Fireman Rushes In', *Club Sandwich*, 69 (Spring 1994).

48 The Beatles-era song that appeared as a snippet on *Off the Ground* and in fuller form as a B-side of the title track's single release.
49 Lewisohn, 'The Fireman'.
50 Ibid.
51 Cited in Peel, *Unknown*, p. 114.
52 Eoghan Lyng, 'Youth: The Fireman Interview', https://wearecult.rocks, 5 May 2018.
53 Ibid.
54 Philip Norman, *Paul McCartney: The Biography* (London, 2016), p. 662.
55 The press release for *Thrillington*, which wasn't released until 1977, provided an elaborate and enigmatic back story for the fictional conductor. It claimed he was a Coventry-born friend of McCartney, that the latter merely 'helped out on the album with encouragement' and they were not the same person. It wasn't until the world tour of 1989–90 that McCartney began admitting that Percy Thrillington was, in fact, 'me and Linda'. 'Thrillington', www.beatlesbible.com, accessed 25 March 2023.
56 Mick Green, 'UK', *Cash Box* (27 November 1993).
57 Bill Drummond, 'Corrugated Iron: Bill Drummond on David Keenan, John Higgs and the 1960s', *The Quietus*, www.thequietus.com, 22 August 2022.
58 Ian McCann, 'Call for an Ambience', *Vox* (November 1992).
59 His reply? 'What do you mean it's *like* Acid House – it *is* Acid House, it's the *start* of Acid House is Pepper, it's where it all came from.' 'The Long and Winding Down', *Club Sandwich*, 55–56 (Winter 1990–91).
60 Dorian Lynskey, 'Chemical Highs', *Mixmag* (August 1998).
61 'Non-linear, abstract, impressionistic, yet with enough of the required structure, cadences and, I'll be blowed, middle-eights to make it work for ears raised on trad forms of pop, the Chemicals' music has more in common with the spirit of the '60s than anything that purports to be influenced by the period, Oasis included.' Cliff Jones, 'Yesterday Never Knows', *Mojo* (April 1997).
62 Norman, *McCartney*, p. 662.
63 Mark Lewisohn, *The Beatles, All These Years*, vol. I: *Tune In* (London, 2013), p. 28.
64 Howard Sounes, *Fab: An Intimate Life of Paul McCartney* (London, 2010), p. 438.
65 Ibid.; Joe Muggs, '"I Treated Working with Paul McCartney as Art" – Youth on His Five Favourite Albums', *The Guardian*, www.theguardian.com, 18 February 2016.
66 David Hutcheon, 'You Can't Do That . . .', *Mojo* (August 2011).
67 Peel, *Unknown*, p. 162.
68 Luca Perasi, *Paul McCartney: Recording Sessions (1969–2013): A Journey through Paul McCartney's Songs after The Beatles* (Milan, 2014), p. 339.
69 Muggs, 'Youth'.

70 Hutcheon, 'You Can't Do That'.
71 'Warm Up: Saints and Sinners', *Muzik* (November 1998).
72 Michael Roberts, 'Future Shock', *Westword* (24 April 1997).
73 'Lifelines: Paul McCartney', *The Paul McCartney World Tour* programme, p. 9.
74 Michael Odell, 'Percy Thrillington, Magritte and Me', *The Guardian*, www.theguardian.com, 29 November 2008.
75 Presumably during a truce between both parties bickering over Lennon–McCartney songwriting credits and whatnot. Sean Lennon appears on the song too, as do Linda, Heather, Mary, Stella and James McCartney.

### 8 Run, McCartney, Run!

1 Simon Reynolds, *Retromania: Pop Culture's Addiction to Its Own Past* (London, 2011), pp. 280, 288.
2 Peter Ames Carlin, *Paul McCartney: A Life* (New York, 2009), p. 312.
3 Ibid.
4 Paul McCartney, *Run Devil Run: Interview Disc* (Parlophone, 1999).
5 Ibid.
6 Jim DeRogatis, 'Undercover McCartney', *Chicago Sun-Times* (17 October 1999).
7 To be fair, there is a chance Lennon wouldn't have either, if he had been blessed with more time on this planet.
8 Chet Flippo, *McCartney: The Biography* (London, 1989), pp. 377–8.
9 David Hutcheon, 'You Can't Do That . . .', *Mojo* (August 2011).
10 Jamie Atkins, 'Three Is the Magic Number', *Record Collector* (Christmas 2020).
11 Ibid.
12 Ibid.
13 Ibid.
14 Danny Scott, 'Paul and Mary McCartney on Meat-Free Life, Losing Linda and Craving Normality', *The Times*, www.thetimes.co.uk, 26 December 2021.

## SELECT DISCOGRAPHY

The Beatles, *Live at the BBC* (Apple, 1994)
—, *Anthology* 1 (Apple, 1995)
—, *Anthology 2* (Apple, 1996)
—, *Anthology 3* (Apple, 1996)

The Fireman, *Strawberries Oceans Ships Forest* (Parlophone, 1993)
—, *Rushes* (Hydra, 1998)
—, *Electric Arguments* (One Little Indian, 2008)

John Lennon and Yoko Ono, *Double Fantasy* (Geffen, 1980)

Linda McCartney, *Wide Prairie* (Parlophone, 1998)

Paul McCartney, *McCartney* (Apple, 1970)
—, *McCartney II* (Parlophone, 1980)
—, *Tug of War* (Parlophone, 1982)
—, *Pipes of Peace* (Parlophone, 1983)
—, *Give My Regards to Broad Street* (Parlophone, 1984)
—, *Press to Play* (Parlophone, 1986)
—, *CHOBA B CCCP* (Melodiya, 1988)
—, *Flowers in the Dirt* (Parlophone, 1989)
—, *Tripping the Live Fantastic* (Parlophone, 1990)
—, *Paul McCartney's Liverpool Oratorio* (EMI Classics, 1991)
—, *Unplugged (The Official Bootleg)* (Parlophone, 1991)
—, *Off the Ground* (Parlophone, 1993)
—, *Paul Is Live* (Parlophone, 1993)
—, *Flaming Pie* (Parlophone, 1997)
—, *Paul McCartney's Standing Stone* (EMI Classics, 1997)
—, *Run Devil Run* (Parlophone, 1999)
—, *Working Classical* (EMI Classics, 1999)
—, *McCartney III* (Capitol, 2020)

Paul and Linda McCartney, *Ram* (Apple, 1971)

Nirvana, *Nevermind* (DGC, 1991)
—, *Incesticide* (DGC, 1992)
—, *In Utero* (DGC, 1993)

Oasis, *Definitely Maybe* (Creation, 1994)
—, *(What's the Story) Morning Glory?* (Creation, 1995)
—, *Be Here Now* (Creation, 1997)

Pulp, *Different Class* (Island, 1995)
—, *This Is Hardcore* (Island, 1998)

The Rutles, *The Rutles* (Warner Bros., 1978)
—, *Archaeology* (EMI, 1996)

Super Furry Animals, *Rings Around the World* (Epic, 2001)

Percy 'Thrills' Thrillington, *Thrillington* (Regal Zonophone, 1977)

Various artists, *Sgt. Pepper's Lonely Hearts Club Band* (soundtrack) (A&M, 1978)

Wings, *Wild Life* (Apple, 1971)
—, *Band on the Run* (Apple, 1973)
—, *Red Rose Speedway* (Apple, 1973)
—, *Venus and Mars* (Capitol, 1975)
—, *Wings at the Speed of Sound* (Capitol, 1976)
—, *Wings over America* (Capitol, 1976)
—, *London Town* (Parlophone, 1978)
—, *Back to the Egg* (Parlophone, 1979)

# ACKNOWLEDGEMENTS

First of all, I would like to thank those who bought, borrowed, reviewed and read my last book, and to anybody who said anything nice about it on the Internet or perhaps spread the word in a more traditional manner, such as recommending it to a friend in the pub or to someone at a gig. This writing lark is largely about momentum and even the smallest-seeming gestures can have immeasurable impact.

*Off the Ground* is dedicated to my grandma, or 'Bubbles' as she was known to us, who passed away in early 2024. We spent a lot of time together when I was little, especially after my younger brother and sister arrived (as twins), and she was great at looking after me. Before I was old enough to pronounce her nickname properly, Bubbles took me on a train journey during which, in a crowded carriage, I kept referring to her loudly as 'Balls', something she liked to remind me about often. She loved classical music and sang in choirs for decades, and I remember her telling me that all popular music just sounded like awful noise to her. (Even The Beatles!?!) She was proud of me writing about this stuff, though. She lived a long and happy life and 'popped off', as she would have put it, without causing a fuss, just as she had always hoped to do.

The second dedication is in memory of Owen Pegg. We grew up drawing the same bands' logos and angsty lyrics on our pencil cases. We formed (terrible) bands at around the same time, something he took much more seriously than I ever did. He would often arrive at school with a hot take he'd been mulling over, which we would all enjoy debating for the rest of the day, when we should have been concentrating on our GCSE or A level curricula. 'John.' [A pause, with his hands on hips and perhaps a widened stance for full dramatic effect.] 'I have decided that Therapy? are better than Nirvana.' What?! Wait. Hang on . . . Well, when you give it a bit of thought . . . He would go on to write, perform and record various types of music, often heavy although not exclusively, whereas I would go on to write about it. No matter how long it was between seeing each other, whenever we reunited it felt as if no time had passed at all. I would not be who I am today, nor the kind of writer that I am, were it not for Owen's friendship and wisdom. We laughed so heartily, and so very often. He would almost certainly have chuckled at the preposterous idea of writing a whole book about Paul McCartney in the 1990s. I have done my best without the insight, contentions and unique angles on the subject that would have been offered by Owen.

On a lighter note, the passionate and remarkably accurate renditions of 'Sgt. Pepper's Lonely Hearts Club Band' performed with total gusto by my young nephew, Wren, have been a life-affirming joy to behold. This provides living proof that The Beatles' music will continue to pass down the generations. Thanks to Mum and Dad, who nurtured my own love of The Beatles, and much more than that besides. Those aforementioned twins, Chris and Kate, and their partners, Jane and Neil, have always shown great interest, encouragement and enthusiasm for my harebrained writing schemes. So, too, has my partner, Stephanie, to whom my previous book was dedicated. Anyone who knows her realizes that Stephanie's knowledge of (and devotion to!) Paul McCartney is even greater than my own. She provided endless love and support, and also helped to weed out some of my nonsense when scrutinizing the drafts.

We would both like to thank Stephanie's sister, Jenny Reid, for giving us access to *Get Back* and *McCartney 3,2,1* via the Disney+ platform. I am also grateful to Annie Lewis and her husband for donating to me a huge backlog of *Mojo* magazines a few years back, as these proved to be extremely useful in my research. Thank you to Sam and Lauren King for, among other great things, transporting all those back issues over from Leeds! My apologies to Amber King because I failed to include her requested in-depth historical analysis of Paul McCartney's mullet hairstyle which, as she correctly observes, existed well into the 1990s. That will have to be the subject of a future conference paper.

Dave Watkins's enthusiasm for my initial idea got the ball rolling (again). I am also grateful to David Hayden, Alex Ciobanu, Emma Devlin and everyone else at Reaktion Books who've helped to bring this title to print. A finished book is only as good as its copy-editor and proofreader, so special thanks to Aimee Selby and John Gaunt for their vital contributions.

I am forever indebted to *The Quietus*'s John Doran and Luke Turner, whose site must have published more of my words than any other platform by this point, as well as their extended family of contributors, readers and editors. Thanks also to the many writers whose work this book has drawn on. I would like to pay my respects to Neil Kulkarni, one of music journalism's all-time greats, who died in January 2024. I didn't know him personally but I am glad that I was able to thank him on social media for the piece he wrote about my last book in *The Wire* magazine, a review with which I could not have been more delighted. Because of my familiarity with Kulkarni's work and opinions, I feel there is a good chance that he would have been appalled by the subject and scope of this follow-up. Now we will never know. I hope I did him justice by including some of his riotous thoughts on Britpop. His words will not be forgotten.

I do wonder whether this book would exist were it not for Matthew Hutchinson's habit of spending significant chunks of his student loan on mid-price post-Beatles McCartney CDs, and sharing those discoveries with his fellow university flatmates, back in the early 2000s.

Finally Sir Paul is owed infinite credit, of course. Thank you for all of the music, from (not so) silly love songs to the abstract electronica. Here's hoping there is plenty more to come.

# PHOTO ACKNOWLEDGEMENTS

The author and publishers wish to express their thanks to the sources listed below for illustrative material and/or permission to reproduce it:

Alamy Stock Photo: pp. 6 (Associated Press/Chris Ecker), 103 (PA Images/Fiona Hanson), 128 (Associated Press/Ron Frehm), 207 (Associated Press/Nigel Marple), 234 (dpa Picture-Alliance); ETH-Bibliothek Zürich, Bildarchiv (CC BY-SA 4.0): p. 41 (photo Kurt Schollenberger); Flickr: pp. 95 (photo Steve Mathieson (badgreeb pictures), CC BY-SA 2.0), 125 (photo Raphael Pour-Hashemi (Raph_PH), CC BY 2.0), 224 (photo Steve Mathieson (badgreeb pictures), CC BY-SA 2.0), 240 (photo Raphael Pour-Hashemi (Raph_PH), CC BY 2.0); Library of Congress, Prints and Photographs Division, Washington, DC: p. 29 (photo Marion S. Trikosko); Nationaal Archief, The Hague: p. 34 (photo Eric Koch); courtesy PETA US: p. 17; Public Record Office of Northern Ireland, Belfast: p. 144 (photo Nick Newbery); Wikimedia Commons: p. 233 (photo Tuomas Vitikainen, CC BY-SA 3.0).

# INDEX

Page numbers in *italics* refer to illustrations